The New Enchanted Broccoli Forest

This book is dedicated
with love
to my parents,
Betty Heller Katzen and Leon Katzen;
and to their mothers,
Minnie Handleman Heller
(1892-1968)
and
Mollie Berman Katzen
(1883-1943).

The New Enchanted Broccoli Forest

RECIPES, DRAWINGS,
AND HAND-LETTERING
BY

Mollie Katzen

Handlettering, illustrations, and book design by Mollie Katzen
Layout and design support for 1995 edition by Sarah Levin
Book production supervised by Hal Hershey
Cover design: Fifth Street Design, Nancy Austin, and Mollie Katzen, with input from Donna Gray
Typesetting for revised edition: Star Type, Berkeley
Food photography: Richard Jung
Food styling: Andrea Lucich
Prop styling: Lorraine Battle
Author photo on back cover: Lisa Keating

10

Ten Speed Press
P. O. Box 7123
Berkeley, California 94707
www.tenspeed.com

Correspondence for the author can be sent to the above address, or visit Mollie's web site at www.molliekatzen.com.

Distributed in Australia by Simon & Schuster Australia, in Canada by Ten Speed Press Canada, in New Zealand by Southern Publishers Group, in South Africa by Real Books, and in the United Kingdom and Europe by Airlift Book Company.

Library of Congress Cataloging-in-Publication Data is on file with publisher.

First printing, 2000

Printed in the United States of America

5 6 7 8 9 10 — 08 07 06 05

ACKNOWLEDGEMENTS

I want to express my deepest appreciation for all the support and encouragement I receive, always, from the folks at Ten Speed Press. This includes Aaron Wehner, Nancy Austin, Hal Hershey, Lorena Jones, Phil Wood, Kirsty Melville, Dennis Hayes, Jo Ann Deck, Anna Erickson, Brook Barnum, Dave Pereira, Raúl Carrizales, and last but not least, George Young (who, although no longer at Ten Speed, is still one of my guardian angels). I am indebted, also, to Linda Davis, who organized the laying-out and pasting-up process for this new edition, and to Phil Gardner and Janet Fohner, who helped her.

Many thanks to Richard Jung, the very gifted photographer who shot the photos; to Andrea Lucich and her assitant, Elisabet der Nederlanden, who styled the food; to Lorraine Battle, who styled the props for both the photos and my T.V. show; and to Lissa Ivy and Diana Alexander, who assisted with the shoot. Props for the photos were generously loaned by Sur La Table, Sante Salvoni, and Cyclamen, among others.

I am grateful to Torri Randall for all her love and support over the years, and to the other producers of "Mollie Katzen's Cooking Show": Peggy Lee Scott, Tina Salter, and Kate Zilavy. I also want to acknowledge the show's food stylist, Heidi Gintner, as well as the wonderful crew. Vincent Nattress, the chef-supervisor of the back kitchen, was a great inspiration, as was Rich Hartwig and the other terrific folks at KTVU in Oakland, California, where the show is taped. Thanks, also, to everyone at Maryland Public Television, my partner station. I am deeply indebted to Boca Burger, Inc., not only for their delicious products, which often sustain me, but also for their generous underwriting of my show. I especially want to thank Katie Torres.

I couldn't do any of this without the rich love and encouragement I get from my husband, Carl, and my children, Sam and Eve. And last of all, thanks so much to all you readers out there for continuing to cook and enjoy the recipes. As always, this book is for you.

✳ TABLE OF CONVERSIONS ✳

✳ DRY INGREDIENTS ✳
Beans: 1 cup = 200 grams = 7 oz.
Cornmeal: 1 cup = 150 grams = 5¼ oz.
Flour, white unbleached: 1 cup = 140 grams = 5 oz.
Grains, dried (any kind): 1 cup = 200 grams = 7 oz.
Sugar, brown or granulated: 1 cup = 200 grams = 7 oz.

✳ BULK INGREDIENTS ✳
Cheese: 1 pound = 454 grams = 4 to 5 packed cups, grated
Nut butter: 1 cup = 250 grams = 8 ¾ oz.
Nuts, chopped: ⅓ to ½ cup = 50 grams = 1¾ oz.
Raisins: ⅓ cup = 50 grams = 1¾ oz.
Sesame or sunflower seeds: ¾ cup = 100 grams = 3½ oz.
[1 pound = 454 grams]

✳ LIQUIDS ✳
1 cup = 8 oz. = 250 ml.
1 Tbs. = ½ fluid oz. = 16 ml.
16 Tbs. = 1 cup = 8 oz.
1 quart = 4 cups = 32 oz. (approximately 1 litre)
1 gallon = 4 quarts = 128 oz.

✳ TEMPERATURES ✳
300°F = 148.8°C
325°F = 162.8°C
350°F = 177°C
375°F = 190.5°C
400°F = 204.4°C

✳ DIMENSIONS ✳
Inches to centimeters: multiply by 2.54
Centimeters to inches: multiply by .39

elcome to
The New Enchanted Broccoli Forest!

Here is a collection of recipes for soups, breads, sauces, dips, spreads, entrées, and desserts, influenced by many different ethnic cooking styles. The recipes are all vegetarian, utilizing a large variety of vegetables, fruits, nuts, legumes, grains, herbs, and spices. This cuisine is about celebrating the bounty of nature in general, and a garden- and orchard-based way of eating in particular. Yet this is not an exclusive message for vegetarians! What I find from traveling around the country, listening and talking to many people about food — as well as from the mail I receive — is that an ever-increasing number of people who don't identify themselves at all as vegetarian are interested in eating less meat. And most people prefer not to label their eating choices at all — they just want to enjoy good, wholesome food, whether it contains meat or not.

When <u>The Enchanted Broccoli Forest</u> was first published in 1982, vegetarian cookbooks were still few and far between. The times were quite different then, and the general knowledge about food, nutrition, and cooking — especially vegetarian cooking — was not nearly as sophisticated as it is today. For the most part, vegetarian cooking was widely assumed either to be heavy and bland, beige and boring, or all of the above. With my two cookbooks (<u>Moosewood</u> and <u>Enchanted Broccoli</u>) I was attempting to translate my own infatuation with fresh vegetables into useful recipes for others. My mission was (and still is) to spread the word that this kind of cooking can be beautiful, delicious, and accessible — and have universal appeal.

I've learned a good deal more about cooking in the years since I wrote the first editions of my cookbooks. I've also been very fortunate to have responsive readers who write to me and tell me of their needs, tastes, and circumstances. So I revised this book in 1995, and again with this new edition, to reflect what I've learned along the way. The preparations have all been simplified and stream-lined to address people's very real time constraints. I've also modified the oil and butter content of many of the recipes — without sacrificing flavor — to achieve a nutritional balance that is the essence of a healthy lifestyle. Dairy is largely optional. I have found that soy milk can substitute for cow's milk almost across the board, without compromising taste or texture. I've learned how to make food taste good through bold seasoning, rather than through the addition of rich ingredients. The simplification of good vegetarian cooking has been greatly helped by the increased availability of high-quality fresh produce around the country, giving us options we could only have dreamed of when these books were first published.

I am very pleased and excited to present in this new edition sixteen color photographs of some of the most popular recipes in the book. As an illustrator and painter, I have always had a very visual approach to my cookbooks, designing and decorating each page individually by hand. This marks the first time I have added color photos to the mix (both here and in the new edition of Moosewood Cookbook), and I have loved participating in the process. I'm thrilled with the photos, which were shot in a serene setting in natural daylight. I feel they deeply reflect my feelings about the food.

My most important goal in writing cookbooks is to make whole-some, delicious food accessible to as many people as possible. We care greatly about food — it's our most basic common language and activity, and cooking is a powerful way to reach out to others. Our relationship with food may be complex at times, but ultimately it is quite simple. We want to be nourished well with food that tastes great, and is appealing and interesting. We also want cooking and eating — and the sharing of food — to be an abundant source of pleasure and fun. I hope these recipes, drawings, and photos serve this purpose.

Mollie Katzen
Berkeley, California
1999

CONTENTS

INGREDIENT CHECKLIST

You can make just about every recipe in this book from the following inventory:

BAKING SUPPLIES: Baking soda, baking powder, salt, pure vanilla extract, unsweetened cocoa, semisweet chocolate chips.

BEANS & LEGUMES (DRIED AND/OR CANNED): Kidney beans, black beans, pinto beans, chick-peas, white beans, lentils. You can keep many other types of beans on hand as well (see p. 209-11). If you're using canned beans, the best brands are Eden and American Prairie. They're organically grown and packed without sugar or additives.

BUTTER: Use unsalted or lightly salted.

CANNED FOODS: Artichoke hearts or crowns, green chiles, pineapple (packed in juice), tomato products (the best brand is Muir Glen), water chestnuts, pumpkin.

CONDIMENTS: Prepared horseradish (white—not pink!), Dijon mustard, dill pickles, Worcestershire sauce. (NOTE: Worcestershire sauce normally contains anchovies. There does exist a very good vegetarian brand called "The Wizard's". Look for it at natural foods stores, or order it through Edward & Sons Trading Co., Box 1326, Carpinteria CA 93014. Phone: 805/684-8500. Fax: 684-8220.)

DAIRY: Cheddar, Swiss, mild white cheese, feta, parmesan, provolone, and other cheeses of your choice. Milk, buttermilk, yogurt, cottage cheese, cream cheese, sour cream — you can use lowfat versions of all of these. (NOTE: Soy milk can substitute for cow's milk in any of these recipes.)

EGGS: These recipes were tested with Grade A large eggs.

FLOURS: Unbleached white, whole wheat (plain or pastry), whole wheat bread flour, rye.

FRUIT (basic to cooking and baking): Lemons, limes, oranges, apples. Dried apricots, currants, raisins, dates.

GARLIC: Buy it frequently so it stays fresh.

GINGER: Fresh ginger root keeps well — either by itself, or in a jar of wine in the refrigerator.

GRAINS: Brown rice, basmati rice, bulgur, millet, cornmeal, rolled oats, wheat berries, barley. And there are many more! See pages 212-15.

HERBS & SPICES: <u>Fresh</u>- parsley, basil, dill, chives, and whatever else is available. (Also, consider planting an herb garden, indoor or out.) <u>Dried</u>- See the lists on pages 274-75.

MISO: This is a fermented paste made from soybeans and grains, and it is used as a base for sauces and soups. Look for it in Japanese groceries or natural foods stores.

NUTS, NUT BUTTERS, SEEDS: Almonds, cashews, hazelnuts, peanuts, pecans, pistachios, walnuts; peanut butter, almond butter, sesame butter and/or tahini; pumpkin, poppy, sunflower, and sesame seeds.

OILS: Extra-virgin olive oil (from the first pressing of the olives) is best for salads. For cooking you can use virgin or pure olive oil. Canola oil is good as an "all-purpose" oil for cooking or baking. Refined peanut oil works very well for stir-fries. Walnut and other nut oils have a strong, deep flavor. Use them in salads or to season other oils. Buy nut oils in the gourmet section of the supermarket, and store them in the refrigerator. Chinese sesame oil has an inimitable dark, toasty flavor. It is used primarily as a seasoning. Look for it in Asian groceries.

PASTA: Keep a variety of shapes and sizes of dried pasta in your cupboard at all times. Also, Japanese noodles (soba, saifun, and udon) should be part of your basic inventory. Look for them in Japanese groceries or in natural foods stores.

RICE MILK } These come in boxes, refrigerated or not, in
SOY MILK } natural foods stores and in some supermarkets. Use them to replace cow's milk in any recipe.

SOY SAUCE: Japanese soy sauces (tamari or shoyu) are stronger and slightly sweeter than Chinese soy sauces, which tend to be saltier. Use whichever type you like best.

SUGARS: Granulated sugar, light or dark brown sugar, honey, molasses, real maple syrup, confectioner's sugar.

TOFU: There are many different varieties from very soft to very firm; silken, savory baked, five-spiced, etc. See p. 180 for more details.

TORTILLAS: Corn and flour tortillas; tortilla chips.

VEGETABLES (basic to cooking): Onions, carrots, celery, potatoes, and cleaned, dried salad greens should be on hand at all times. Add to this list whatever else is in season.

VINEGARS: Red wine, cider, rice (from Asian groceries), fruit-flavored, balsamic.

WINES AND LIQUORS: Mirin (Japanese cooking sake, available in Asian groceries), dry sherry, dry red and white wines, brandy, rum.

YEAST: Active dry yeast comes in little triplet packages and keeps for a long time in the refrigerator. You can also buy yeast in bulk in some natural foods stores. Keep it on hand so you can bake bread when the spirit moves you.

A FEW NOTES ABOUT USING THIS BOOK:

I've tried to give precise measurements for most of the ingredients in these recipes. Occasionally, though, I'll say "a medium-sized tomato" or "a small bunch of spinach"—something along those imprecise lines. In these cases, it is perfectly fine to use your own judgment—these things are not rigid, and I want to encourage flexibility. Remember, cooking is not an exact science, it is more of an art. (Baking, on the other hand, _is_ a science, and must be taken more literally.)

Here are some tips for using the recipes in this book:

- Read through the recipes first, to get an overview of the procedures. Figure out what needs to be done ahead, what can be assembled while something else cooks, etc. This will help you to feel more on top of things, and you'll enjoy cooking more.

- There is an estimated preparation time and yield posted at the top of each recipe. When you are reading through the recipe, try to gauge your own pace. If you are a beginner, or if you like to work meditatively or dreamily, the recipes might take longer to prepare than estimated. Also, since appetites tend to vary, the yield is an approximation.

- "To taste" doesn't always mean that you literally have to taste something. Sometimes it means by sight or by feel.

⁘ MODIFICATIONS ⁛

The fat, dairy, and egg contents in these recipes have been reduced from what they were in the original edition to a very moderate level. You can modify to reduce these ingredients even further, if you'd like. Here are some pointers:

OIL SPRAYS: These enable you to spray a mist of oil onto the food or pan, instead of using oil by the tablespoon. Commercial oil sprays are available in many supermarkets and natural foods stores. Used in combination with high-quality nonstick cookware, oil sprays can greatly reduce the fat content of your cooking without sacrificing flavor or texture.

DAIRY SUBSTITUTION / REDUCTION:
   Milk can be substituted with soy or rice milk, both of which are nondairy (see p. XII).
   There are some lowfat cheeses ~ as well as nondairy soy cheeses available. Remember, you can always reduce the amount of cheese called for in a recipe, and in many cases, you can omit it altogether. Mashed tofu can sometimes substitute for cottage or ricotta cheese in a casserole.

EGGS:
   Of the approximately 95 entrées in this book, fewer than 25 contain eggs, and almost all of these (including all the soufflés!) are yolk-optional. There is also a selection of desserts made without eggs, or with egg whites only. If you need to modify further, experiment with egg substitutes.

FOR A LIST OF ALL THE VEGAN (NO DAIRY, NO EGGS), LOWFAT, AND NONFAT RECIPES IN THIS BOOK, SEE THE APPENDIX ON PAGE 282.

SOUPS
Table of Contents

Here is a chapterful of vegetarian soups, both hot and chilled, from basic and wholesome (Vegetable Soup, Potato-Leek Soup, Corn Chowder) to exotic and wholesome (Curried Peanut Soup, Arizona Pumpkin Soup, Green Gazpacho). Between the basic and the exotic is a range of tasty and personable combinations, suiting a variety of moods and seasons.

The average yield of these recipes is about 4 to 6 servings. These quantities are easily doubled, if you have a big enough pot.

These soups are highly seasoned, and work very well with water instead of stock. (NOTE: Almost all can be made vegan; soy milk can always substitute for dairy in a creamed soup.)

If you would prefer to make your own homemade stock and use this instead of water, here is a method:

HOMEMADE STOCK:
Collect skins (cleaned) from onions, garlic, potatoes, carrots, etc. Also collect limp-but-still-OK vegetables, like zucchini, mushrooms, etc. Avoid strongly flavored items, such as celery, cabbage, broccoli, or cauliflower (or at least go lightly with these). Absolutely avoid artichokes or anything downright bitter. Boil your collection in a large kettleful of water for anywhere from 30 minutes to 1 hour. Salt the water lightly during the cooking. Cool, strain, and taste. If you like the flavor, use the stock for soup. (If not, you can always toss it.)

ANOTHER KIND OF STOCK:
Leftover water from steaming vegetables, boiling potatoes, or cooking beans.

A broad soup repertoire can give one's menu-planning a tremendous boost. Many of these soups are substantial and interesting enough to make a complete meal with salad and bread. Chilled soups are a good solution to the problems called Lunch and Dinner in incapacitatingly hot weather. They can be prepared well in advance, so the preparer doesn't swelter through last-minute heating. Cold soups are also an elegant second course for dinner any time of the year.

Vegetable Soup...

Preparation time:
about 1 hour
(much of it
simmering time)

Yield:
4 to 6
servings

You can't get much more basic than this. Just chop the vegetables and let them simmer themselves into soup. The amounts are flexible, as are the vegetables themselves. So use whatever is available and in season.

1 large potato, scrubbed and diced
2 cups chopped onion
2 cups chopped cabbage
½ lb. mushrooms, sliced
1 large stalk celery, minced
1 large carrot, diced
6 cups water
2 tsp. salt
2 bay leaves

3 to 4 medium-sized ripe tomatoes
1½ cups tomato juice
6 medium cloves garlic, minced
1 medium-sized zucchini, diced
5 scallions, minced (greens and whites)
freshly ground black pepper
OPTIONAL: small amounts of minced
      fresh herbs (thyme, marjoram,
   basil, dill, parsley, etc.)

1) Combine the potato, onion, cabbage, mushrooms, celery, carrot, water, salt, and bay leaves in a soup pot or Dutch oven. Cover and bring to a boil. Lower the heat, and simmer, covered, for about 20 minutes.

2) Meanwhile, core the tomatoes, and gently drop them, whole, into the simmering soup. After about 20 seconds, fish them out with a fork. Pull off their skins, cut them open, and squeeze out and discard the seeds. Mince the remaining pulp, and add this to the soup, along with the tomato juice. Simmer another 20 minutes.

3) Add garlic, zucchini, and scallions, and simmer for about 10 more minutes. Season to taste with freshly ground black pepper, and check to adjust salt. Serve hot, topped with a light sprinkling of minced fresh herbs.

... & Its Many Variations

1) **Multi-Vegetable Soup:** Many other vegetables will blend in well. Add harder vegetables (broccoli, cauliflower) earlier, and softer vegetables (bell peppers, greens) closer to serving time. Leftover cooked beans and/or grains are also welcome; add them shortly before serving. You might want to adjust seasonings to accommodate these extras.

2) **Zuppa Alla Pavese:** The same soup, but with a different presentation. Serve the soup in ovenproof bowls, topped with croutons (see page 26) and a generous sprinkling of parmesan cheese. Broil briefly before serving. (Don't forget to caution your guests about the hot bowls.)

3) **Vegetable-Tofu:** Add about ½ pound diced tofu to the soup during the last 10 minutes of simmering.

4) **Vegetable-Eggdrop:** Beat 3 eggs (yolks are optional) together with 1 teaspoon soy sauce in a small bowl. Just before serving, stir the soup briskly as you slowly drizzle in the beaten eggs. Remove from heat and serve immediately.

5) **Alphabet Soup:** Cook 1 cup alphabet noodles in a small potful of boiling water until just tender. Drain, rinse with cold water, then drain again. Distribute the noodles among the serving bowls, ladle in the hot soup, and serve.

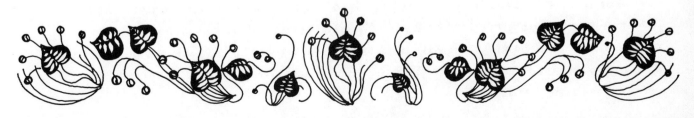

SESAME·EGGDROP SOUP

Preparation time:
30 minutes (after preliminary step,
which can be done well ahead).

Yield:
6 servings

1 oz. dried black mushrooms
3 cups boiling water
5 cups additional water
1 2-inch knob ginger, in thin slices
1 large carrot, in thin matchsticks
¼ lb. firm tofu, in small cubes
3 to 4 Tbs. soy sauce
2½ tsp. salt
1 Tbs. cider vinegar
1 Tbs. sugar or honey

5 large cloves garlic, minced
3 medium-sized ripe tomatoes
6 scallions, minced (keep
  whites and greens separate)
fresh black pepper to taste
2 eggs (OK to delete yolks)
1 cup peas, fresh or frozen
Chinese sesame oil   } for the
toasted sesame seeds   }   top

PRELIMINARY: Place the black mushrooms and 3 cups boiling water in a bowl and cover with a plate. Let stand at least 30 minutes (longer is fine). Drain the mushrooms in a colander or strainer over a bowl, squeezing out and saving all the water. Remove and discard the stems; slice the caps and set aside.

1) Pour the mushroom-soaking water (from "PRELIMINARY") into a soup pot. Add the additional 5 cups water, along with the ginger, carrot, tofu, soy sauce, and salt. Bring to a boil, lower the heat, and simmer, partially covered, for about 15 minutes.

2) Add the sliced black mushrooms, vinegar, sugar or honey, and garlic. Keep it simmering.

3) Core the tomatoes, and place them in the hot soup for about 20 seconds. Retrieve them with a fork or slotted spoon; pull off and discard the skins. Cut the tomatoes in half, and squeeze out the seeds. Chop the tomato pulp, and add this to the soup.

4) Stir in the scallion whites and black pepper to taste. Adjust seasonings, if necessary. At this point, the soup can rest for up to several hours before serving time.

5) About 10 minutes before serving, heat the soup to a gentle boil. Beat the eggs, and drizzle them in, stirring constantly. (This part is fun to watch— the eggs virtually blossom!) Stir in the peas. Serve hot, topped with minced scallion greens, a drizzle of sesame oil, and a sprinkling of sesame seeds.

DILLED VEGETABLE-BARLEY SOUP

This soup tastes best the day after it's made. However, as it sits around, the barley expands, so it usually needs a little additional water upon reheating. Adjust the seasonings, if necessary.

Preparation time: 40 minutes, after the barley is cooked. (It takes 30 to 40 minutes to cook the barley, and you can do this ahead.)

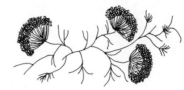

Yield:
6 servings

½ cup uncooked pearl barley
1½ cups water
2 to 3 Tbs. butter or canola oil
2 cups minced onion
1½ to 2 tsp. salt
1 bay leaf
2 medium carrots, diced
1 medium stalk celery, minced
1 lb. mushrooms, chopped
4 cups water
6 Tbs. dry white wine (optional)

1 Tbs. fresh lemon juice
3 Tbs. minced fresh dill (1 Tbs. dried)
½ cup minced fresh fennel (optional)
2 large cloves garlic, minced
fresh black pepper to taste

OPTIONAL TOPPINGS:
sour cream or yogurt
toasted sunflower seeds
minced fresh parsley
     and/or chives

1) Place the barley and 1½ cups water in a small saucepan. Bring to a boil, cover, and lower heat to a simmer. Cook about 30 to 40 minutes- until tender.

2) Melt the butter or heat the oil in a soup pot or Dutch oven. Add onion, salt, and bay leaf, and cook over medium heat until the onion begins to soften (5 to 8 minutes).

3) Add carrots, celery, and mushrooms, and cook over medium heat, stirring occasionally, for about 10 minutes. Add 4 cups water, the optional wine, lemon juice, and cooked barley. Lower the heat to a quiet simmer. Cover, and let it bubble peacefully for about 30 minutes. The soup will thicken, and you might want to add more water.

4) Shortly before serving, stir in the dill, fennel, garlic, and black pepper. Taste to adjust seasonings. Serve hot, with all, some, or none of the optional toppings.

Spicy Eggplant Purée

a little oil for the baking tray
1 1½-lb. eggplant
a little salt
2 to 3 Tbs. olive oil
3 to 4 medium cloves garlic, minced
2 cups chopped onion
1½ tsp. salt

fresh black pepper to taste
2 Tbs. lemon juice
2 to 3 cups water
¼ cup yogurt
2 Tbs. tahini
2 Tbs. honey
¼ tsp. cayenne (to taste)

minced fresh parsley and /or cilantro
extra yogurt
finely minced red bell pepper
} TOPPINGS

1) Preheat oven to 375°F. Lightly oil a baking tray.

2) Slice the eggplant in half lengthwise. Lightly salt each open side, and place them open side down on the tray. Bake for 30 minutes, or until very soft. Cool until handle-able, remove and discard the seeds and skin, and set the pulp aside.

3) Heat the olive oil in a small skillet. Add garlic, onion, salt, and pepper, and sauté over medium heat until the onion is soft (8 to 10 minutes). Stir in lemon juice; remove from heat.

4) Purée the eggplant, onion sauté, water, yogurt, tahini, and honey together in a food processor or blender. You might need to do this in several batches.

5) Transfer to a large, heavy saucepan and heat very gently. Add cayenne, and taste to adjust seasonings. Serve hot, with or without toppings.

Mediterranean Lemon Soup

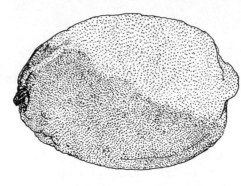

Preparation time:
    25 minutes
(Cook the rice while
preparing the soup.)

Yield:
6 servings

Good at any temperature, and in any season.

This soup is tart! Use more or less lemon juice, depending on your taste.

NOTE I: You can use leftover cooked rice (white or brown— or even barley) with equally good results. Use 1½ cups cooked grains.

NOTE II: The flavor of mint is important to the success of this soup. Use dried if you can't find fresh.

½ cup uncooked white rice
1 cup water
1 Tbs. butter or olive oil
3 cups finely minced onion
1½ tsp. salt
⅓ to ½ cup fresh lemon juice

4 cups water
2 beaten eggs (OK to delete yolks)
fresh black pepper to taste
3 Tbs. minced fresh mint
3 Tbs. minced fresh parsley
3 Tbs. minced fresh chives

1) Place the rice and 1 cup water in a small saucepan and bring to a boil. Lower the heat, cover, and let simmer undisturbed until the rice is tender (about 15 minutes).

2) Meanwhile, melt the butter or heat the oil in a soup pot or Dutch oven. Add the onion and salt, and sauté over medium-low heat for about 15 minutes, or until the onion is translucent and very soft.

3) Add the lemon juice and 4 cups of water. Heat to a quiet boil.

4) Stir the soup rapidly as you drizzle in the beaten egg. Add the cooked rice and black pepper, stirring until everything is well combined.

5) Serve hot, at room temperature, or cold, topped with minced fresh herbs.

Fresh Corn Chowder

Preparation time:
35 minutes

Yield:
6 servings

A delicately seasoned, soothing, light soup, this is equally delicious made with fresh or frozen corn, so you can enjoy it throughout the year.

1 medium-sized potato
2½ cups water
2 to 3 Tbs. butter
1½ cups chopped onion
1½ tsp. salt
1 medium stalk celery, minced
1 small red bell pepper, minced

about 5 cups corn (5 cobs or
   a 1-lb. bag frozen/defrosted)
fresh black pepper to taste
¼ tsp. dried thyme
½ tsp. dried basil (more, to taste)
1 cup milk (lowfat or soy OK),
   at room temperature

1) Scrub or peel the potato, and cut it into small dice. Place it in a small saucepan with the water. Bring to a boil, lower heat to a simmer, cover, and cook until tender but not mushy. Set aside.

2) Meanwhile, melt the butter in a soup pot or Dutch oven. Add the onion and salt, and cook over medium-low heat, stirring. After about 5 minutes, add celery and keep cooking. About 5 minutes later, add the cooked potatoes with all their liquid, the red bell pepper, corn, black pepper, and herbs. Stir well and cover. Reduce heat and let it cook about 5 minutes more.

3) Use a blender or food processor to purée about half the solids in some of the soup's own liquid. Return this to the pot, and let it rest until serving time.

4) Stir in the milk about 10 minutes before serving. Heat the soup gently – don't cook it any further. Serve as soon as it's hot.

Curried Apple Soup

Preparation time: 30 minutes

Yield: 4 to 6 servings

Ordinary ingredients yield extraordinary results in this tart, beautiful, bright yellow soup. This is a real winner: easy to make and lowfat, yet richly seasoned. Serve hot or cold, any time of the year.

2 to 3 Tbs. peanut oil
2 cups chopped onion
3 large cloves garlic, minced
2 Tbs. minced fresh ginger
2 tsp. salt
2 tsp. dry mustard
1 tsp. turmeric
1 tsp. ground cumin
1/2 tsp. ground cardamom
1/2 tsp. allspice
1/4 tsp. cayenne

5 cups peeled, chopped tart apple
4 cups water
2 cinnamon sticks
2 Tbs. fresh lemon juice
OPTIONAL: 3 to 4 Tbs. honey
    or brown sugar (to taste)

POSSIBLE TOPPINGS:
    lightly toasted shredded coconut
    lightly toasted slivered almonds
    a drizzle of yogurt
    a few dried currants

1) Heat oil in a soup pot or Dutch oven. Add onion, garlic, ginger, and salt, and sauté over medium heat for about 5 minutes, or until the onion begins to soften.

2) Add the spices, and sauté another 5 minutes over medium heat.

3) Add apples, water, cinnamon sticks, and lemon juice, and bring to a boil. Turn the heat down, mostly cover, and simmer for about 10 minutes, or until the apples are very tender. Remove from heat.

4) Take out the cinnamon sticks, and purée in a blender or food processor — bit by bit, so as not to splash yourself. Return the purée to the pot.

5) Add optional sweetening, and taste to adjust salt. Serve hot or cold, with or without some or all of the toppings. (Even though the toppings are fun and delicious, this soup is also wonderful just plain.)

Preparation time
for each variation:
30 minutes

Yield:
6 servings
per recipe

Variations on a Cream of Tomato

Here are three versions of a perennial favorite, Cream of Tomato, from the richest to the lightest (the third variation contains no oil). To streamline the preparation time, each recipe uses a 28-oz. (1 lb. 12 oz.) can of whole peeled tomatoes. You can also use fresh tomatoes: cut up 2 lbs. of ripe ones, and cook over medium heat with no added liquid for 10 minutes. Whether you use canned or fresh, purée the tomatoes first in a blender or food processor, saving and using all their liquid.

I.

1 Tbs. butter or olive oil
1 ½ cups chopped onion
2 bay leaves
½ tsp. salt

freshly ground black pepper
½ tsp. celery seed
½ tsp. allspice or cloves
2 Tbs. flour

1 28-oz. can tomatoes, puréed
1 tsp. honey
1 cup milk (lowfat or soy ok)
OPTIONAL: small cubes of
    Swiss cheese, for the top

1) Melt the butter or heat the oil in a soup pot or Dutch oven. Add onion, bay leaves, and other seasonings, and sauté over medium heat until the onion is soft (10 minutes or so). Have a whisk ready for the next step.

2) Sprinkle in the flour as you stir constantly with a whisk. Continue stirring and cooking for about 5 minutes more.

3) Stir in tomatoes and honey. Cook over medium heat for about 15 minutes, stirring frequently from the bottom.

4) Turn the heat down to a simmer, and slowly drizzle in the milk. Try to fish out the bay leaves so nobody chokes on them, and serve right away. If you so desire, you can add a few cubes of Swiss cheese to each bowlful of soup. They will soften and become exquisitely chewy.

II.

1 Tbs. olive oil	½ tsp. crumbled rosemary	3 Tbs. dry sherry
1½ cups chopped onion	1 tsp. dried basil	1 tsp. honey
2 large cloves garlic, minced	freshly ground black pepper	4 oz. cream cheese
½ tsp. salt	1 28-oz. can tomatoes, puréed	minced fresh parsley

1) Heat the oil in a soup pot or Dutch oven. Add onion, garlic, salt, herbs, and black pepper, and cook over medium heat until the onion is soft (10 minutes).

2) Add tomatoes, sherry, and honey. Cover and simmer about 15 minutes. Remove the bay leaves (or plan to remind your guests they are there).

3) Cut the cream cheese into the hot soup. Continue cooking, and stir until smooth. (The cream cheese will take a little while to melt thoroughly.)

4) Serve hot, topped with freshly minced parsley.

III.

1½ cups chopped onion	1 28-oz. can tomatoes, puréed	2 tsp. dried basil
1 large potato, unpeeled and thinly sliced	2 large cloves garlic, minced	½ tsp. dried thyme
1 stalk celery, minced	1 tsp. honey	1 cup milk (lowfat or soy ok)
2 cups water	1½ tsp. salt	strips of fresh basil, for garnish—if available
	1 tsp. dried dill	

1) Place onion, potato, celery, and water in a soup pot or Dutch oven. Bring to a boil, cover, and simmer until the potato is soft (15 minutes). Set aside to cool until it is no longer too hot to purée.

2) Purée in several batches with the tomatoes in a blender or food processor.

3) Return to the pot, and heat just to the boiling point. Lower heat; add garlic, honey, and seasonings, and simmer for about 10 minutes. Stir in optional milk just before serving. Garnish with strips of fresh basil, if you have some.

Chinese Mushroom Soup

Preparation time: 40 minutes
(less, if you do the "PRELIMINARY"
well in advance).

Yield: 6 to 8 servings

2 oz. dried black mushrooms
5 cups boiling water

2 Tbs. canola or peanut oil
6 medium cloves garlic, minced
2 Tbs. grated fresh ginger
1 lb. fresh mushrooms, sliced
2 tsp. salt
¼ cup soy sauce
½ cup dry sherry
fresh black pepper to taste

2 Tbs. cornstarch
2 cups additional water
2 Tbs. sugar or honey
2 Tbs. cider vinegar
1 cup minced water chestnuts
12 healthy scallions, minced
   (keep whites and greens separate)
Chinese sesame oil

PRELIMINARY: Place the dried mushrooms in a medium-sized bowl, and
   pour in 5 cups boiling water. Cover with a plate, and let stand for about
   30 minutes while you prepare the other ingredients. Drain the mushrooms in a colander over a bowl, squeezing out and saving all the
   water. Remove and discard the mushroom stems. Thinly slice the caps
   and set aside.

1) Heat the oil in a soup pot or Dutch oven. Add garlic, ginger, fresh mushrooms, and salt, and sauté for 5 minutes over medium heat.

2) Add all remaining ingredients except the scallion greens and sesame oil.
   (Don't forget to include the sliced black mushrooms and their soaking
   water.) Cover and simmer very gently for about 10 minutes.

3) Serve hot, topped with a few minced scallion greens and a drizzle of
   sesame oil.

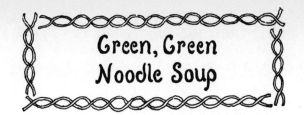

Green, Green Noodle Soup

Preparation time:
35 minutes

Yield: 6 or more
very green servings

Three ♫ Notes:
- ♪ This soup needs some pesto. You can make your own (p. 104) or use a good commercially prepared brand. The preparation time above assumes the pesto is already made.
- ♪ Fresh spinach is delicious in this recipe, but frozen works beautifully too. Use 2 10-oz. packages; defrost and drain before using.
- ♪ You can make the soup up to several days in advance. Just cook the pasta right before serving, and reheat the soup while the pasta is cooking.

2 to 3 Tbs. olive oil
3 cups minced onion
1½ to 2 tsp. salt
1 tsp. dried thyme
1 tsp. dried oregano
6 medium cloves garlic, minced
2 medium zucchini, thinly cut, like this:

 (⅛" thick)

1½ lbs. spinach, minced (or
   2 10-oz. packages frozen chopped
   spinach, defrosted and drained)
6 cups water
freshly ground black pepper
¾ lb. (dry measure) spinach noodles
6 to 8 Tbs. pesto
parmesan for the top

PRELIMINARY: Put up a pot of water to boil (for the noodles).

1) Heat the oil in a soup pot or Dutch oven. Add onion, salt, thyme, and oregano, and sauté over medium heat for about 10 minutes, or until the onion is clear and soft.

2) Add garlic, zucchini, and spinach. Continue to sauté another 5 to 8 minutes over medium heat, stirring frequently, until the spinach is wilted and the zucchini is just tender.

3) Add 6 cups water and bring to a boil. Cover, lower heat, and simmer for about 5 minutes, or until bright green. Season to taste with black pepper and extra salt, if needed. Meanwhile, cook the noodles.

4) Purée approximately half the soup in a blender or food processor, and return it to the unpuréed half.

5) Drain the cooked noodles. Divide them among the serving bowls, adding to each serving approximately 1 Tbs. pesto. Ladle in some hot soup, top with a sprinkling of parmesan, and serve right away.

Potato & Chile Soup

~~~~~~

Preparation time:
40 minutes

Yield:
4 to 6 servings

⚓ ABOUT CHILES: Use fresh Anaheim chiles, if available. Also called
"mild green chiles" (although they are slightly hot), Anaheim chiles
are long, pale green peppers, often available in supermarkets. If
you can't find them, use poblano chiles (smaller, wider, darker),
or open a can of diced green chiles.

⚓ TIME SAVER: Grate the cheese with the grating attachment of the
food processor. Then remove the cheese, change to the steel blade,
and without cleaning the machine, use it again for puréeing
the potatoes.

4 medium (3" diameter) potatoes
3 cups water
1½ cups chopped onion
1 Tbs. olive oil
1½ cups diced bell pepper
1½ cups diced green chiles
1¾ tsp. salt
1 tsp. ground cumin

1 tsp. dried basil
2 medium cloves garlic, minced
fresh black pepper to taste
1 cup milk (lowfat or soy OK)
OPTIONAL: ¾ cup sour cream
          ¾ cup grated jack cheese
          2 scallions, finely minced
          minced fresh cilantro, for
          the top

1) Scrub the potatoes, cut them into small chunks, and cook them in the
water, partially covered, until tender (about 20 minutes). Set aside,
water and all, and cool to room temperature.

2) Meanwhile, begin sautéing the onion in olive oil in a soup pot or Dutch
oven over medium heat. After several minutes, add bell pepper, chiles,
salt, cumin, basil, garlic, and black pepper. Continue to sauté over medium
heat until the vegetables are tender (8 to 10 minutes). Remove from heat.

3) Purée the potatoes in their cooking water, using a blender or a food processor. Add the purée to the potful of sautéed vegetables, and stir in
the milk and optional sour cream. Whisk until well blended.

4) Heat the soup very slowly. When it is hot, stir in the cheese and scallions.
Serve plain or topped with some minced fresh cilantro.

~~~~~~

Potato~Leek Soup

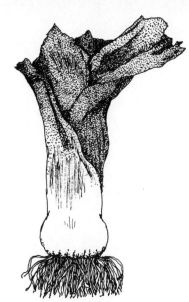

Preparation time:
35 minutes

Yield:
6 servings

Equally delicious hot or cold, this thick, rich-tasting butter- and oil-free soup is very simple to make. If you prefer, you can omit the milk or substitute soy milk. It will still taste wonderful.

3 medium-sized potatoes
3 cups cleaned, chopped leeks
1 medium stalk celery, chopped
1 large carrot, chopped
4 cups water

1½ tsp. salt
1 cup milk (lowfat or soy OK)
freshly ground black pepper
OPTIONAL: snippets of fresh herbs
    (thyme, marjoram, basil)

1) Scrub the potatoes and cut them into 1-inch chunks. Place them in a soup pot or Dutch oven with the leeks, celery, carrot, water, and salt. Bring to a boil, cover, and cook until the potatoes are tender (about 20 minutes). Remove from heat, and let it cool until it's no longer too hot to purée.

2) Purée the soup in a blender or food processor. (You'll probably need to do this in batches.) Return the purée to the pot. Stir in the milk.

3) Add black pepper to taste, and adjust salt, if necessary. Serve hot or cold, possibly topped with a sprinkling of fresh herbs.

The Pumpkin Tureen

Preparation time:
15 minutes to assemble;
about 2 hours to bake.

Yield:
4 to 6 servings

No kettle necessary! This wonderfully filling soup gets baked right inside the pumpkin, and the whole tureen can be brought to the table as an edible centerpiece.

For the broth, you can use homemade stock (p.3), vegetable bouillon, or canned vegetable broth. Water will work, if you are brothless.

1 sincere 6- or 7-lb. pumpkin
　(8-inch diameter)
1 cup finely minced onion
2 slices rye bread, diced
½ cup (packed) grated Swiss cheese
2 tsp. prepared horseradish
2 tsp. Dijon mustard
1½ cups milk (lowfat or soy OK)

1 to 2 cups vegetable broth,
　stock, bouillon, or water
1 tsp. salt
black pepper
cayenne 　} to taste
nutmeg

OPTIONAL TOPPING:
rye croutons
　(see p. 26)

1) Preheat oven to 350°F.
2) Prepare the pumpkin as though you were going to make a jack-o-lantern, but stop short of carving the face. (Cut off the top; remove the seeds and stringy stuff.)
3) Place onion, bread, cheese, horseradish, and mustard inside the pumpkin. Mix with your hands until well combined.
4) Add milk and broth (as much as will fit — you can adjust the amounts) along with the seasonings. Stir it up.
5) Line the pumpkin lid with a piece of foil, and place it on top. Place the filled pumpkin in an ungreased baking pan.
6) Bake until the pumpkin is tender (about 2 hours). To test for tenderness, remove the lid, and gently stick a fork into the side. It should go in easily.

To Serve: Scoop deeply to bring up some pumpkin pieces from the sides and bottom along with the soup. If desired, top with some crunchy rye croutons.

The Enchanted Broccoli Forest (page 223)

Curried Apple Soup (page 11)

Assorted breads (clockwise from top right): Challah (page 73), Squash Double Spiral Roll (page 76 and 82), Carob Swirl Bread (page 79), and Freshly Fruited Bread (page 81)

Greek Pizza (page 140)

Arizona Pumpkin Soup

Preparation time:
30 minutes

Yield:
6 servings

Tart and tangy, this easy pumpkin soup goes beautifully with fresh, warm tortillas and a spinach salad, for a quick and cozy autumn dinner.

You can bake your own pumpkin, but canned works just as well, and will enable you to enjoy a steaming bowlful of soup just 30 minutes after you begin to cook.

NOTE: Baked winter squash or sweet potatoes can substitute for the pumpkin.

3 cups cooked pumpkin, freshly puréed (or a 29-oz. can)
4 cups water
2 to 3 Tbs. olive oil
2 cups minced onion
1 large bell pepper, minced
2 large cloves garlic, minced

2 tsp. salt
1 Tbs. chile powder
2 to 3 Tbs. fresh lime juice
freshly ground black pepper
TOPPINGS:
lightly toasted pumpkin seeds
finely minced scallions

1) Combine the pumpkin and water in a soup pot or Dutch oven. Stir until uniform. Partially cover, and heat gently, stirring often.

2) Heat the oil in a medium-sized skillet. Add the onion and bell pepper, and sauté over medium heat for 5 minutes. Add garlic, salt, and chile powder; stir and cover. Cook over low heat for about 10 more minutes, stirring frequently, until the vegetables are tender.

3) Add the sauté and lime juice to the soup. Stir well, cover, and allow to simmer for about 10 minutes. Season to taste with black pepper, and adjust salt, if necessary. Serve hot, topped with toasted pumpkin seeds and minced scallions.

Galician Garbanzo Soup

Preparation time:
30 minutes to assemble;
30 minutes to simmer.

Yield:
6 servings

<u>NOTE</u>: This recipe calls for canned chick-peas, but if you prefer, you can use dried. Soak 2 cups in water for at least 4 hours, then cook in simmering water until soft (about 1½ hours).

<u>TO PEEL AND SEED A TOMATO</u>: Core the tomato, and drop it into simmering water for about 20 seconds (less, if the tomato is very ripe). Retrieve from the water and pull off the skin. Cut the tomato open; squeeze out and discard the seeds. Chop the remaining pulp.

actual size of
diced whatever

3 15-oz. cans chick-peas
(also known as garbanzo beans)
4½ cups water
2 to 3 Tbs. olive oil
2 heaping cups chopped onion
6 medium cloves garlic, minced
1 small potato, diced (about 1 cup)
1 medium carrot, diced
1 stalk celery, diced
1½ tsp. salt

1 bay leaf
2 tsp. dry mustard
2 tsp. ground cumin
¼ tsp. saffron (optional)
2 tsp. dried basil
fresh black pepper } to taste
cayenne } taste
½ cup peas (fresh or frozen)
3 Tbs. red wine vinegar
1 medium-sized ripe tomato-
peeled, seeded, and minced

1) Rinse and thoroughly drain the chick-peas. Place about ⅔ of them in a food processor or blender with 2 cups of the water. Purée and set aside.

2) Heat the oil in a soup pot or Dutch oven. Add the onion, half the garlic, the potato, carrot, celery, and salt, and sauté over medium heat for about 10 minutes.

3) Add the purée from Step one, plus the remaining water and chick-peas and all of the seasonings. Bring to a boil and lower heat. Cover and simmer for about 30 minutes, stirring occasionally.

4) Stir in the remaining garlic, plus the peas, vinegar, and tomato. Simmer about 5 minutes more, and serve.

White Bean & Escarole Soup

Preparation time:
45 minutes (most
of it simmering time),
after the beans
are cooked.

Yield:
4 to 6
servings

ABOUT THE BEANS: You can use canned white beans (any kind) or cook up some dried beans. If using canned, 2 15-oz. cans should be enough. Rinse them thoroughly before using. If you use dried beans, start with 1½ cups. (Cooking instructions are on pages 276-78.)

ABOUT THE GREENS: The recipe calls for escarole, but you can substitute any green — spinach, kale, chard, collards — or a combination.

2 to 3 Tbs. olive oil
2 cups chopped onion
1 bay leaf
2 stalks celery, minced
2 medium carrots, diced
2 tsp. salt (or more, to taste)
6 cups water

3 to 4 cups cooked white beans
3 Tbs. (about 10 cloves) minced fresh garlic
1½ lbs. escarole, minced
fresh black pepper to taste

freshly grated nutmeg
minced parsley   } toppings
parmesan cheese

1) Heat the oil in a soup pot or Dutch oven; add the onion, bay leaf, celery, carrots, and salt. Cook over low heat for about 10 minutes, then add water. Cover, bring to a boil, lower the heat to a simmer, and cook quietly for about 20 minutes, or until the vegetables are very tender.

2) Add beans, garlic, and as much of the escarole as you can fit. Cover and wait a few minutes. When there is room, add more escarole in batches, waiting between additions for the greens to cook down.

3) Add black pepper to taste (and while you're tasting, adjust the salt). Serve hot, topped with a grating of fresh nutmeg, a little parsley, and a generous sprinkling of parmesan cheese.

Cream of Fresh Green Pea Soup

Fresh herbs comprise the essential magical element of this soup. Use all or some of the list below, or experiment with your own combinations.

1 Tbs. butter

1 cup minced onion

½ tsp. salt

1½ cups water

4 cups peas, fresh or frozen

1 cup milk (lowfat or soy OK)

black or white pepper to taste

MINCED FRESH
(up to 3 Tbs. each or any)
{ mint
basil
dill
tarragon
parsley
chives

1) Melt the butter in a soup pot or Dutch oven. Add onion and salt, and cook over medium heat until the onion is soft (8 to 10 minutes).

2) Add the water and bring to a boil. Lower the heat, cover, and simmer for about 10 minutes. Add the peas, cover again, and remove from heat. Let stand 5 minutes, or until the peas are tender.

3) Purée the soup with the milk in a food processor or blender, then return the purée to the pot.

4) Heat the soup very gently. Add your own personal selection of minced fresh herbs just before serving. NOTE: This soup also tastes wonderful at room temperature or chilled.

Swedish Cabbage Soup

Preparation time:
30 minutes

NOTE: You can substitute Brussels sprouts (coarsely chopped) for all or some of the cabbage.

Yield:
6 servings

2 medium-sized potatoes
7 cups water
2 to 3 Tbs. butter
3 cups chopped onion
2 tsp. caraway seeds
2 tsp. salt
8 cups shredded green cabbage
   (approximately 1 medium head)
fresh black pepper to taste
sour cream or yogurt } OPTIONAL TOPPINGS
minced fresh dill

1) Scrub the potatoes and cut them into small dice. Place them in a large saucepan with the water. Bring to a boil, lower the heat, and simmer, partially covered, for 5 minutes. Set aside.

2) Melt the butter in a soup pot or Dutch oven. Add onion, caraway, and salt, and cook over low heat, stirring occasionally, until the onion is quite soft (about 15 minutes).

3) Add the cabbage—as much as will fit—and cover. Cook over medium heat until there is room in the pot for the rest of the cabbage.

4) Add the remaining cabbage, the potatoes with all their cooking water, and black pepper to taste. Cover and simmer another 15 minutes. Serve hot, topped with a little sour cream or yogurt and some fresh dill.

Curried Peanut Soup

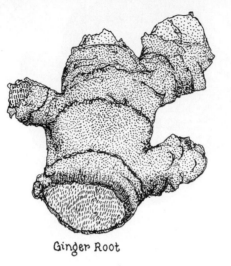

Ginger Root

Preparation time:
45 minutes

Yield:
6 to 8 servings

Filling and very satisfying, this soup can be the focus of a meal. Try it with the Banana Topping, even if it seems strange at first. You won't regret it!

You can make the soup several days ahead. It keeps — and reheats — beautifully.

I. The Soup:

1 cup good plain peanut butter
2 Tbs. honey
4 cups boiling water
1 to 2 Tbs. peanut oil
2 cups minced onion
10 large cloves garlic, minced
2 tsp. salt
2 to 3 Tbs. minced fresh ginger

1 tsp. cinnamon
2 tsp. ground coriander
1 tsp. ground cardamom
½ tsp. ground cloves
2 tsp. turmeric
1 Tbs. ground cumin
1 tsp. dry mustard
up to ½ tsp. cayenne
2 cups buttermilk (room temperature)

1) Place the peanut butter and honey in a medium-sized bowl. Add about 2 cups of the boiling water, and mash with a spoon until it becomes a smooth paste. Whisk in the remaining hot water and set aside.

2) Heat the oil in a soup pot or a Dutch oven. Add the onion, garlic, salt, and ginger. Sauté for about 10 minutes over medium heat, then add all the spices. Continue to cook and stir for about 5 minutes more.

3) Stir in the peanut butter mixture and cover. Bring to a boil, then turn the heat way down, and simmer for about 20 minutes, stirring occasionally. Meanwhile, prepare the topping (recipe follows).

4) Just before serving, whisk in the room temperature buttermilk. Serve hot, with a small spoonful of Banana Topping in each bowl.

II. The Banana Topping:

3 fairly green medium-sized bananas (green as in those
    you bought yesterday to eat 2 days from now)
3 Tbs. fresh lemon juice
2 tsp. canola or peanut oil
a pinch or two of cinnamon
optional: a dash of salt

1) Peel the bananas and slice them at 1/4-inch intervals diagonally. Place the slices in a glass pie pan and drizzle with lemon juice. Allow to stand for about 10 minutes.

2) Heat the oil in a medium-sized heavy skillet. Add the bananas plus all their lemon juice, and sauté on each side for a scant minute. Dust lightly with cinnamon, sprinkle with a tiny bit of salt, stir gently, and remove from heat. (Don't worry if the bananas lose their shape, because they are not that visible in the soup anyway.)

3) If you haven't inadvertently eaten all of these delicious bananas straight from the skillet, add a small spoonful to each bowl of soup. If you couldn't restrain yourself and you have none left, return to Step1 and start over.

Cream of Onion Soup

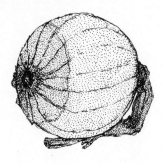

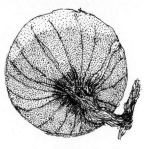

This soup tastes best if served soon after it is made. It thickens considerably if it sits in the refrigerator overnight.

2 cups milk (lowfat or soy OK)
2 to 3 Tbs. butter or oil
5 cups minced onion
2 tsp. dry mustard
1 ½ tsp. salt
2 Tbs. unbleached white flour
3 cups water

a few dashes Worcestershire sauce
1 tsp. prepared horseradish
nutmeg
white pepper } to taste
cayenne

croutons (recipe below) } toppings
minced red bell pepper

1) Heat the milk slowly in a heavy saucepan over very low heat, until it just reaches the boiling point. Remove from heat.

2) Meanwhile, melt the butter or heat the oil in a soup pot or Dutch oven. Add the onion, mustard, and salt. Stir, cover, and cook over low heat until the onions are very soft (about 15 minutes).

3) Stir constantly as you sprinkle in the flour. Add water, hot milk, Worcestershire sauce, and horseradish; season to taste with small amounts of nutmeg, white pepper, and cayenne. Serve hot, topped with croutons and a sprinkling of minced red bell pepper.

Easy Homemade Croutons

4 thick slices of good bread (rye works beautifully)
2 to 3 Tbs. butter or olive oil

① Preheat oven to 325°F. ② Cut the bread into ½-inch cubes. ③ Heat a heavy skillet; add butter or olive oil. ④ Sauté the bread cubes for 5 to 8 minutes, or until they begin to brown. ⑤ Spread the cubes on a baking tray, and bake until crunchy (10 to 15 minutes). ⑥ That's all!

Inspiration Soup

Preparation time:
about 40 minutes

Yield:
6 servings

1 6-oz. jar marinated artichoke hearts
1 cup chopped onion
1 large stalk celery, minced
1 lb. mushrooms, sliced
2 tsp. salt
2 small potatoes (2½-inch diameter),
   scrubbed and thinly sliced
4 medium cloves garlic, minced
1 tsp. dried basil

4 cups water
½ lb. spinach, minced (or a
   10-oz. package frozen chopped
   spinach, defrosted and drained)
2 Tbs. fresh lemon juice
fresh black pepper to taste
1 cup peas (fresh or frozen)
minced fresh parsley

1) Drain the liquid from the marinated artichoke hearts into a soup pot. Chop the hearts coarsely and set aside. Gently heat the artichoke liquid.

2) Add the chopped onion to the artichoke liquid, and sauté over medium heat for 5 minutes.

3) Add celery, mushrooms, salt, potatoes, garlic, and basil. Sauté for 10 minutes over low heat, stirring occasionally.

4) Add water and bring to a boil. Stir, cover, and let it simmer 15 to 20 minutes, until the potatoes are tender.

5) Add the artichoke hearts and spinach. Cover and cook over low heat another 5 minutes. Set aside until just before serving time.

6) Begin heating the soup about 10 minutes before serving. When it is hot, stir in the lemon juice, black pepper, and peas. Allow to cook for a few minutes more, then serve, topped with freshly minced parsley.

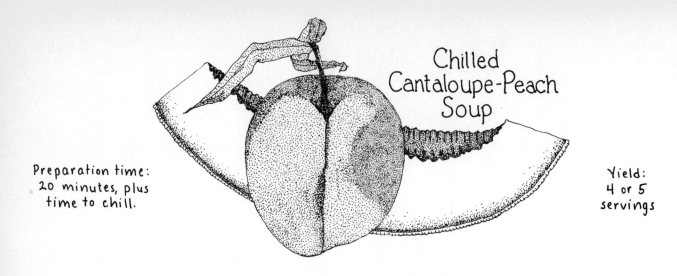

Chilled Cantaloupe-Peach Soup

Preparation time:
20 minutes, plus
time to chill.

Yield:
4 or 5
servings

Good for breakfast!

NOTE: You can cook the peaches up to several days in advance and refrigerate them until you are ready to assemble the soup. The remaining preparations will take just a few minutes.

6 medium-sized (3-inch diameter) very ripe peaches
6 Tbs. fresh lemon juice (about 3 lemons'-worth)
1 Tbs. honey
¼ tsp. cinnamon
a dash of nutmeg
1 medium-sized (5-inch diameter) ripe cantaloupe,
   peeled, seeded, and cut into 1-inch chunks)
1 cup freshly squeezed orange juice
OPTIONAL GARNISHES: a little yogurt or buttermilk
                        fresh blueberries

1) Peel, pit, and slice the peaches. Place them in a medium-sized saucepan with the lemon juice, honey, and spices. Heat to a boil, lower the heat to a simmer, and cook for 5 minutes. Remove from heat, and let it cool down a little before step 2.

2) Use a blender or food processor to purée the peach mixture with the cantaloupe and the orange juice. (You might have to do this in batches.) Purée until very smooth. Transfer to a container with a cover, and chill until very cold.

3) Serve plain or with a little yogurt or buttermilk and/or some exquisite fresh blueberries.

Chilled
Cherry~Plum
Soup

Preparation time: 20 minutes,
plus time to simmer and
to chill.

Yield: 5 or 6 servings

Brace yourself for a stunningly colorful soup!

NOTE I: You can make this soup a day or two in advance. The seasonings intensify the longer it sits around.

NOTE II: You can use frozen unsweetened cherries with great success. The bonus is that they come already pitted. Defrost them first, then use about 3 cups.

1½ lbs. ripe red or purple plums
1 lb. pitted sweet cherries
¼ tsp. salt
1 cup orange juice
1 Tbs. grated fresh ginger
2 tsp. Dijon mustard

1 to 2 Tbs. honey (to taste)
1 tsp. grated orange rind
2 cups yogurt or buttermilk
extra buttermilk ⎫
minced fresh mint ⎬ for the top
thin slices of kiwi ⎭

1) Pit and coarsely chop the plums. Place them in a medium-sized saucepan with the cherries, salt, and orange juice. Heat to boiling, turn heat down, cover, and simmer for 5 minutes.

2) Stir in ginger and mustard. Cover and simmer for 15 minutes.

3) Remove from heat; stir in honey and orange rind. Cool to room temperature, then purée until smooth in a blender or food processor. Transfer to a container with a tight-fitting lid, and chill until very cold.

4) Whisk in the yogurt or buttermilk just before serving. Top each bowlful with a swirl of buttermilk, a scattering of fresh mint, and a few kiwi slices.

✤✤✤ Green Gazpacho ✤✤✤

Preparation time:
15 minutes, plus
time to chill.

(Keeps well for days
if tightly covered
and refrigerated.)

Yield:
4 or 5
servings

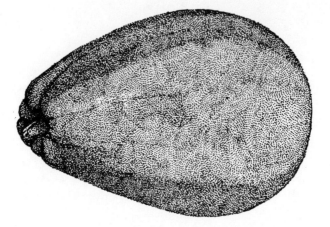

Showcase those underripe tomatoes in this delicious,
gloriously colored Mexican variation on a Spanish
theme.

If you can't find green tomatoes, use the least ripe
ones available.

3 green tomatoes (3-inch
  diameter), cored and chopped
1 medium-sized green
  bell pepper, chopped
1 medium (7-inch) cucumber,
  peeled, seeded, and chopped
a handful of parsley
a handful of cilantro
¼ cup fresh lime juice (about
  2 juicy limes'-worth)
1 medium (4-inch) avocado,
  peeled, pitted, and diced

1 medium clove garlic, minced
1 tsp. salt
1 tsp. ground cumin
1 to 2 Tbs. extra-virgin olive oil
1 Tbs. red wine vinegar
1 tsp. honey or sugar
1 cup cold water
black pepper ⎫
           ⎬ to taste
cayenne   ⎭

OPTIONAL: tortilla chips,
          for the top

1) Combine everything in a large bowl, and mix as well as possible.

2) Purée the soup bit by bit in a blender or food processor, until
   reasonably smooth (it doesn't have to be perfect). Transfer to a
   container with a lid, and chill until very cold.

3) Serve plain or topped with tortilla chips.

Chilled Marinated Mushroom Soup

Preparation time:
  30 minutes,
plus time to chill.

1 lb. mushrooms, minced
½ cup onion, minced
2 large cloves garlic, minced
1 bay leaf
¾ cup dry white wine
1 cup water
1 tsp. salt
freshly ground black pepper

3 to 4 Tbs. fresh lemon juice
1 Tbs. minced fresh basil } or 1 tsp.
1 Tbs. minced fresh dill } dried
½ tsp. dried thyme
2 to 3 Tbs. extra-virgin olive oil
¼ cup minced fresh chives
    or scallions
thin, round slices of lemon } for
small sprigs of fresh thyme } garnish

1) Place mushrooms, onion, garlic, bay leaf, wine, water, salt, and pepper in a medium-large saucepan. Bring to a boil, lower the heat, and simmer, covered, for 15 minutes.

2) Remove from heat, uncover, and let stand for about 10 minutes. Fish out and discard the bay leaf, and stir in all other ingredients except the garnishes. Transfer to a container with a tight-fitting lid, and chill until very cold.

3) Serve topped with delicate rounds of fresh lemon, and a small sprig of fresh thyme, if available.

Chilled Spicy Tomato Soup

Preparation time:
15 minutes, plus
time to chill
(unless the ingredients
are cold to begin with).

Yield:
4 or 5
servings

Easy, refreshing-
with-a-bite...
and 100% fat-free!

NOTE: This soup tastes best served very cold. You can save on chilling time if your ingredients are cold to begin with.

2 medium-sized (3-inch diameter) ripe tomatoes
4 cups tomato juice
2 tsp. Dijon mustard
1 tsp. prepared horseradish
2 Tbs. Worcestershire sauce
10 to 15 drops Tabasco sauce

1 small stalk celery, finely minced
2 Tbs. minced fresh dill (or 2 tsp. dried)
OPTIONAL: 1 to 2 scallions, finely minced (whites and greens)
freshly ground black pepper

1) Bring a medium-sized saucepanful of water to a boil, then lower the heat to a simmer. Core the tomatoes, and drop them in the water for about 20 seconds. Remove from the water and pull off the skins. Cut the tomatoes open, and squeeze out and discard the seeds. Mince the remaining pulp and set aside.

2) In a medium-large bowl, whisk together the tomato juice, mustard, horseradish, Worcestershire sauce, and Tabasco until well mixed. Stir in remaining ingredients (including the minced tomatoes), seasoning to taste with freshly ground black pepper.

3) Cover tightly and chill until very cold.

Salads

SALADS
Table of Contents

"SALAD"

doesn't always mean "tossed green."
Sometimes it means just one perfectly ripe
in-season fresh fruit or vegetable laced with
a splash of good oil and/or vinegar, or drizzled with
a delicious dressing. Other times the fruit or vegetable
(or bean, grain, or pasta) is combined with selected
colleagues and perhaps accented with a pungent cheese,
a contrasting herb, some olives, eggs, nuts, or other
touches.

Vegetables can be cooked and marinated, or
served raw in very thin or small pieces, lightly dressed.
Fruit and vegetables can be sliced, shredded, minced, cut
into chunks, or even hollowed out and stuffed with a
tasty filling and served cold or at room temperature.
All of these things can be called salads. The cook can
define the meal, and the cook is you!

A good salad can be the focal point of a meal,
especially when the weather is warm. Try grouping
several salads together, and your menu planning will
expand into new creative realms.

⁘A Pep Talk for Wilted Saladmakers⁘

WHY DO SOME GREEN SALADS INSPIRE "OOOH" and "AHHH", WHILE
OTHERS CAN'T SEEM TO DRUM UP MUCH MORE THAN "ZZZZZ".....?
  Attention to certain details can really make the difference. Cultivate the
following practices, and your green salads will soar.

1) Buy only the freshest, most perfect lettuces and greens available. Look
   for very fresh prewashed salad mix ("mesclun") as well. If they
   are not prewashed, clean greens leaf by leaf under cold running water.
   Dry them thoroughly in a salad spinner, followed by clean, absorbent
   towels. When they are absolutely dry, store salad greens loosely wrapped
   (or in a salad spinner) in the refrigerator. Use within a day or two.

2) Keep a jar of vinaigrette dressing (p.39) on hand, and store leftover cooked
   beans or chick-peas in there. You can also use dressing to marinate thinly
   sliced mushrooms (or tiny whole ones), leftover cooked vegetables, or small
   cubes of firm tofu. Add drained marinated things to green salads just
   before or after tossing.

3) Greens should be dressed only at the very last minute. Otherwise, sogginess.

4) Keep an assortment of fresh herbs around — or grow them, if possible. Use
   scissors to snip small amounts into green salads. The best ones: chives,
   basil, thyme, marjoram, dill, parsley, tarragon, mint, cilantro, or savory.

5) Extra-virgin olive oil should be your standard for salads. Supplement with
   other flavorful oils (like nut oils) in small amounts.

6) Fresh garlic only!

7) Remember the charms of toasted nuts or seeds; good olives; sweet and
   tiny cherry tomatoes; croutons; freshly shaved parmesan cheese (or crumbled
   goat, blue, or feta cheese); grated fresh beets and carrots; sublimely thin
   slices of celery, radish, mushroom, red onion, or cauliflower; substantial
   slices of apple, pear, orange, grapefruit, or ripe avocado (on top only),
   as well as an assortment of other, less common, vegetables on the next
   two pages.

OTHER SALAD VEGETABLES

Some of these are quite common and even grow wild, but it might take some shopping around at green grocers or farmers' markets to find them. Look in seed catalogues or inquire at a good nursery to see about growing your own, if you have the space and the inclination.

1) <u>ARUGULA</u> (aka "rocket"). These small, notched, bright green leaves are common in southern Italy and France, and becoming more popular in the U.S. as well. The leaves have a strong, deep, peppery flavor. Arugula is commonly found in prewashed salad mixes ("mesclun") in supermarkets.

2) <u>WATERCRESS</u>. A peppery — and very nutritious — green, found year-round in most supermarkets.

3) <u>SORREL</u> (aka "sourgrass"). A lemony green, easy to grow.

4) <u>DANDELION GREENS</u>. These leaves have a far better reputation in the salad bowl than in the lawn. They have a pleasantly bitter flavor and are loaded with iron and vitamins. You can buy a cultivated variety at the green grocer, or pick the ones in your yard while they're still small.

5) <u>RADICCHIO</u>. This beautiful, white-veined, dark red leaf is a member of the chicory family. It has a firm texture and a deep, bitter flavor. It's best when used sparingly in a green salad. Look for it in small heads or in the "mesclun" salad mix in the supermarket.

...also known as "sun choke"...

6) <u>JERUSALEM ARTICHOKE</u>. This vegetable is neither from Jerusalem nor an artichoke. But don't get the wrong impression—it is in every other way upright and honest. It is actually the sweet, crisp tuber of a yellow sunflower. If you plant this hardy perennial, you will have it on hand forever. Scrub or peel, and slice or grate into salads. Or just slice and marinate in lemon juice for a refreshing fat-free snack.

7) <u>NASTURTIUM</u>. Both the greens and blossoms are edible. They have a wonderful spicy flavor and will add wild color to your salads.

8) <u>MÂCHE</u> (aka "lamb's lettuce"). This is one of the sweeter greens—it pairs really well with the many tart varieties. Mâche grows wild but is increasingly available at green grocers. You can recognize it by its small, round, very green leaves.

9) <u>FENNEL</u> (aka "Florence fennel"). It is a bulb with graceful celeryesque stalks and a feathery top, and it has an outstanding flavor, similar to anise, but quite mild. The bulb is the juiciest, most refreshing part. Slice fennel thinly and sprinkle into salads. The top is similar to dill, and can be used with—or in place of— that herb for variety of flavor.

10) <u>BELGIAN ENDIVE</u>. A member of the chicory family, this pale yellow, crunchy vegetable is available in small, tight heads about six inches long. Separate the leaves; chop the larger ones, and leave the smaller ones whole for an elegant addition to any salad.

11) <u>KOHLRABI</u>. These show up most frequently in Chinese produce markets, and since I've never seen one in a Chinese restaurant, I consider them mysterious. Spherical and pale green with a purplish blush, they look like they could have been grown on Mars. The edible part is actually the swollen stem of the plant. Remove the leaves, peel it, and blanch in boiling water for ten minutes. Cool; slice thinly for salads. Kohlrabi has a nice, spunky taste—like a cross between a cabbage and a radish.

Salad Dressings

Garlic & Herb Vinaigrette

Preparation time: 5 minutes

Yield: about ½ cup (easily doubled)

1 medium clove garlic, minced
5 Tbs. extra-virgin olive oil
3 Tbs. red wine vinegar
1 Tbs. fresh lemon juice
¼ tsp. salt
freshly ground black pepper

a pinch of celery seed
¼ tsp. dry mustard
1 Tbs. each (or any):
   minced fresh dill, basil,
   chives and/or marjoram
   (or 1 tsp. each, dried)

Combine everything in a small jar with a lid. Cover tightly and shake until well blended. This keeps indefinitely in the refrigerator. Shake well before using.

Creamy Mustard Dressing

Preparation time: about 2 minutes

Yield: 1 cup

2 Tbs. Dijon mustard
¼ cup dry white wine
½ cup extra-virgin olive oil
3 Tbs. red wine vinegar

salt to taste (optional)
freshly ground black pepper
a dash of cayenne
¼ cup firm yogurt

Combine everything in a medium-small bowl. Whisk until uniform. Store in a tightly lidded container in the refrigerator.

Orange & Sesame Dressing

Preparation time: 5 minutes

Yield: a scant 2 cups

1 cup orange juice
¼ cup red wine vinegar
½ cup canola oil
2 Tbs. Chinese sesame oil
1 Tbs. soy sauce

½ tsp. salt
½ tsp. dry mustard
1 Tbs. minced fresh dill
  (1 tsp. dried)
1 large clove garlic, minced

Combine everything in a small jar with a lid. Cover tightly and shake until well blended. Refrigerate; shake well before using.

Apple Vinaigrette

Preparation time: 5 minutes   Yield: 2 cups

NOTE: Wasabi is Japanese green horseradish paste. It comes in a tube in most Asian groceries.

2 cups apple juice
1/3 cup vinegar (cider or red wine)
2 tsp. wasabi or Dijon mustard

1 medium clove garlic, minced
1/2 tsp. salt

Combine everything in a medium-sized jar with a lid. Cover tightly and shake until well blended. This keeps for weeks in the refrigerator. Whisk from the bottom before each use.

Tofu Dressing

Preparation time: 5 minutes   Yield: 1 1/2 cups

NOTE: Silken tofu is an ultrasmooth variety that comes vacuum-packed in 10-oz. boxes. Look for it in natural foods stores, Asian groceries, and in many supermarkets.

1 box (12-oz.) silken tofu
3 Tbs. cider vinegar
1 Tbs. fresh lemon juice
2 Tbs. soy sauce
1 Tbs. minced fresh dill
    (or 1 tsp. dried)

fresh black pepper to taste
1/2 tsp. salt
1 medium clove garlic, minced
1/4 cup minced bell pepper
1/4 cup minced fresh parsley

Combine everything in a blender and purée until smooth. Store in a tightly lidded container in the refrigerator. This will keep for up to 2 weeks.

Buttermilk & Cucumber Dressing

Preparation time: 5 minutes   Yield: 2 1/2- plus cups

1 medium (7-inch) cucumber—
    peeled, seeded, and chopped
1 1/2 cups buttermilk
1 medium clove garlic, minced
1/2 tsp. salt
2 Tbs. red wine vinegar
2 tsp. prepared horseradish

1 Tbs. minced fresh dill
    (or 1 tsp. dried)
2 Tbs. minced fresh mint
    (or 2 tsp. dried)
2 Tbs. minced red onion
1/2 tsp. mild paprika

Combine everything in a food processor or blender and purée until smooth. This dressing will keep for 1 to 2 weeks if stored in a tightly lidded container in the refrigerator.

Chilled Marinated Cauliflower

Preparation time:
  25 minutes
plus time to chill.

Yield:
4 to 5
servings

Serve this with a picnic supper on a warm day. It is dramatically refreshing.

This recipe is easy: cauliflower pieces are cooked directly in a marinade, then chilled. Just before serving, a few snippets of fresh herbs and vegetables are added, providing touches of color, flavor, and crunch.

⅓ cup olive oil
¼ cup red wine vinegar
½ cup water
3 large cloves garlic, minced
¾ tsp. salt
1 tsp. whole peppercorns
2 bay leaves

1 medium (6- to 7-inch diameter)
  cauliflower, in bite-sized florets
½ cup finely minced red onion
½ cup minced fresh parsley
a handful minced fresh basil
  (1 to 2 tsp. dried)
1 medium carrot, grated

1) Combine oil, vinegar, water, garlic, salt, peppercorns, bay leaves, and caulifowerets in a large saucepan or a Dutch oven. Bring to a boil, reduce heat, cover, and simmer for about 15 minutes, or until the cauliflower is tender but not too soft.
2) Transfer to a serving bowl. Cool to room temperature, then cover tightly and chill.
3) Shortly before serving, stir in the onion, parsley, basil, and carrot. Mix well and serve.

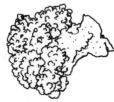
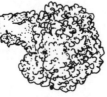
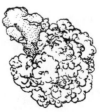

Russian Beet Salad

Preparation time:
About 30 minutes,
plus time to stand
and to chill.

Yield:
4 or 5
servings

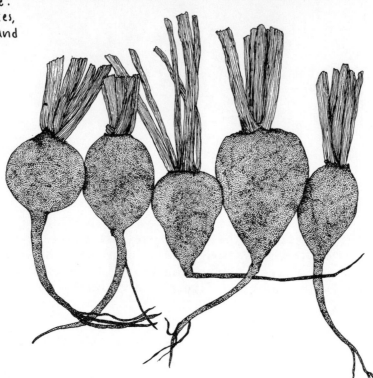

8 healthy (2½-inch diameter) beets
¼ cup cider vinegar
1 medium clove garlic, minced
1 to 2 tsp. honey
½ tsp. salt
½ cup minced red onion
2 scallions, minced (whites and greens)

1 medium cucumber — peeled,
    seeded, and minced
2 hard-boiled eggs, chopped
2 Tbs. minced fresh dill (or
    2 tsp. dried)
1 cup firm yogurt (optional)
freshly ground black pepper

1) Trim the beets of their stems and greens, and place the beets in a medium-large saucepan. Cover them with water and bring to a boil. Cook for about 25 minutes, or until tender enough for a fork to slide in easily.
2) Meanwhile, combine the vinegar, garlic, honey, and salt in a medium-large bowl.
3) Rinse the cooked beets under cold running water as you rub off their skins. Chop into ½-inch bits, and add them, still warm, to the vinegar mixture. Stir and let stand about 30 minutes.
4) Add the remaining ingredients, seasoning to taste with black pepper. Mix well, cover tightly, and chill until very cold.

Swiss Green Beans

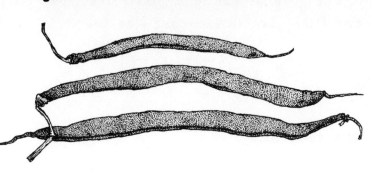

Preparation time:
30 minutes, plus
at least 2 hours
to marinate.

Yield:
4 or 5
servings

If you make this a day ahead and let it marinate overnight, it will be most delicious. Leave out the lemon juice and vinegar until shortly before serving, so the green beans can retain their color. (The acid causes fading.)

1½ lbs. fresh whole green beans (slender as possible), cleaned and trimmed

2 large cloves garlic, minced
¼ cup extra-virgin olive oil
1 tsp. dried tarragon
1 Tbs. minced fresh dill (or 1 tsp. dried)
½ tsp. salt (more, to taste)
fresh black pepper to taste
2 tsp. Dijon mustard
½ cup minced fresh parsley

⅓ lb. Swiss cheese, in thin strips
½ cup chopped ripe olives (or whole tiny ones, like Niçoise)
1 small green bell pepper, sliced
1 small red bell pepper, sliced
3 to 4 Tbs. fresh lemon juice (to taste)
1 Tbs. red wine vinegar
½ cup chopped, toasted almonds

1) Steam the green beans until just tender. Remove from heat, and immediately rinse under cold running water. Drain well.

2) Combine everything else except the lemon juice, vinegar, and almonds in a large bowl.

3) Add the drained beans to the bowl. Toss until everything is well distributed. Cover tightly and let marinate, at room temperature or refrigerated, for at least 2 to 3 hours. (Longer is fine.)

4) Stir in the lemon juice and vinegar within about 10 minutes of serving. Serve cold or at room temperature, topped with almonds.

Here are two wonderful, easy tomato salads. Chilling is optional. They both taste good at room temperature, too. NOTE: The ingredients — and their amounts — are flexible.

Bulgarian Salad

6 medium-sized ripe tomatoes
½ cup thinly sliced red onion
1 medium clove garlic, minced
1 small bell pepper (any color), thinly sliced
1 small cucumber: peeled if necessary,
   seeded, and minced
1 Tbs. minced fresh oregano or marjoram
   (1 tsp. dried)
3 Tbs. minced fresh mint (3 tsp. dried)
a handful of Kalamata (Greek) olives
3 Tbs. extra-virgin olive oil } more, to
2 Tbs. red wine vinegar   taste
freshly ground black pepper
⅓ lb. feta cheese, crumbled
salt to taste (optional)

Israeli Salad

6 ripe medium-sized tomatoes
½ cup minced red onion
2 small cucumbers: peeled if necessary,
   seeded, and diced
6 radishes, sliced
2 scallions, minced (include greens)
1 small bell pepper (any color), diced
1 large dill or half-sour pickle, minced
½ cup sliced green olives (optional)
a handful of minced fresh parsley
3 Tbs. extra-virgin olive oil
salt and pepper to taste
½ cup firm yogurt (optional)

Preparation time:
about 10 minutes

Instructions:

1) Cut the tomatoes in half. Squeeze out and discard the seeds. Cut the tomatoes into 1-inch chunks, and transfer to a medium-large bowl.

2) Add everything else, and toss gently until well mingled. Taste to adjust seasonings.

3) Serve at room temperature or cold.

moroccan orange-walnut salad

Preparation time:
about 10 minutes

6 large oranges
1 Tbs. honey
½ tsp. cinnamon
1 lb. mixed salad greens -
   cleaned, dried, and chilled
½ small red onion, thinly sliced
10 radishes, thinly sliced
6 Tbs. extra-virgin olive oil
salt to taste
freshly ground black pepper to taste
1 cup chopped, toasted walnuts

1) Peel and section the oranges, using a sharp paring knife or a serrated knife. To do this, first cut off the polar ends of the peel, then slice the peel off the sides. With a gentle sawing motion, cut in one side of the membrane and out the other, releasing each orange section into a bowl. Squeeze all excess juice from the remaining membrane into the bowl as well, and pick out the seeds, if necessary. Discard the membrane.

2) Drizzle honey and sprinkle cinnamon into the orange slices. Stir gently to mix, cover, and set aside until serving time.

3) Shortly before serving, toss the greens in a large bowl with the onion, radishes, and olive oil. Season to taste with salt and freshly ground black pepper.

4) To serve, bring the orange sections, the tossed greens, and the walnuts to the table in separate containers. Let each person assemble his or her own salad, by piling some greens on a plate, spooning over some oranges-au-jus, and sprinkling a few walnuts on top.

Cucumber Salads

Each of these salads takes only about 10 minutes to prepare (plus time to chill), contains no oil, and yields approximately 4 to 6 servings.

1. Wilted Cucumbers:

Make this at least a day ahead, so the cucumbers can fully absorb their marinade. In this case, "wilted" doesn't mean tired, it means <u>relaxed</u>. This keeps beautifully in the refrigerator for two weeks or longer.

$2/3$ cup vinegar (wine or cider)
$1/3$ cup water
4 Tbs. honey or sugar
1 tsp. salt
$1/2$ cup thinly sliced red onion

4 medium-sized cucumbers, peeled, seeded, and thinly sliced
fresh black pepper to taste
2 Tbs. minced fresh dill (or 2 tsp. dried)

1) Combine the vinegar, water, honey or sugar, and salt in a small saucepan. Heat just to the boiling point, then remove from heat.
2) Place the onion and cucumber slices in a medium-large bowl, and add the hot liquid. Cool to room temperature; add pepper and dill.
3) Transfer to a jar with a tight-fitting lid. Chill until cold.

2. Tsatsiki (Greek Cucumbers)

...Very simple and refreshing. Serve as a salad, appetizer, or dip.

4 medium-sized cucumbers
$3/4$ tsp. salt (more, to taste)
$1\frac{1}{2}$ cups firm yogurt

1 to 2 small cloves garlic, minced
fresh black pepper to taste
3 Tbs. minced fresh mint

1) Peel, seed, and coarsely grate the cucumbers. Place in a colander over a sink, sprinkle with the salt, and let stand 10 minutes. Squeeze out the extra liquid and transfer to a medium-sized bowl.
2) Add remaining ingredients, mix well, and taste to adjust seasonings. Cover tightly and chill until cold.

Eggplant Salads

Each of these variations keeps well and goes beautifully on crackers or in toasted miniature pitas as an appetizer. Preparation time for each: 30 minutes. Yield for each: 4 to 6 servings.

Roumanian

1 1½-lb. eggplant	2 medium cloves garlic, minced	water, as needed
1 tsp. salt	fresh black pepper to taste	3 Tbs. fresh lime juice
2 Tbs. olive oil	3 Tbs. tahini	1 Tbs. minced fresh dill
1 cup minced onion	3 Tbs. hot water	⅓ cup minced parsley

1) Peel the eggplant (or not) and cut it into ½-inch cubes. Place them in a bowl, toss with ½ tsp. of the salt, and set aside.

2) Meanwhile, heat the oil in a large, deep skillet or a Dutch oven. Add the onion, and sauté over medium heat for 5 minutes. Add the garlic and pepper and sauté 5 minutes more. Stir in the eggplant and remaining salt. Cover and cook over medium heat while you do the next step.

3) Combine the tahini and water in a small bowl, and stir until it becomes a uniform paste. Add this to the eggplant, along with small amounts of water, as needed, to prevent sticking. Stir, cover, and continue to cook until the eggplant is very tender (15 to 20 minutes).

4) Transfer to a bowl, and stir in lime juice and dill. Cover and chill until cold. Stir in the parsley shortly before serving.

Israeli

1 1½-lb. eggplant	2 medium cloves garlic, minced
1 tsp. salt	water, as needed
2 Tbs. olive oil	fresh black pepper to taste
1½ cups minced onion	1 to 2 Tbs. red wine vinegar

1) Cut the eggplant into ½-inch cubes (peeling is optional). Place them in a bowl and toss with ½ tsp. of the salt. Set aside.

2) Meanwhile, heat the oil in a large, deep skillet or Dutch oven. Add the onion, and sauté over moderate heat for 5 minutes. Add the garlic, and sauté for 5 minutes more.

3) Stir in eggplant and remaining salt. Cover and cook until the eggplant is very tender (15 to 20 minutes), adding water, as needed, to prevent sticking.

4) Remove from heat, and season to taste with black pepper and vinegar. Serve at room temperature or cold.

More ☞

❧ ❧ ❧ ❧ ❧ Indian ❧

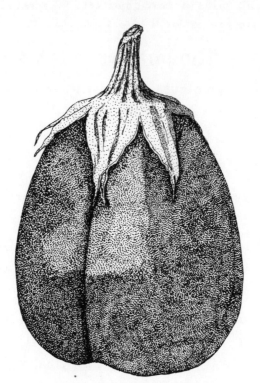

1 1½-lb. eggplant
1 tsp. salt
2 tsp. mustard seeds
2 tsp. cumin seeds
2 Tbs. sesame seeds
1 Tbs. peanut oil
1½ cups minced
   onion

2 large cloves garlic, minced
water, as needed
3 Tbs. fresh lemon juice
2 medium-sized ripe
   tomatoes, peeled and
   seeded (see Step 3,
   opposite page)—
   and minced
cayenne to taste

1) Cut the eggplant (peeling is optional) into ½-inch cubes. Place them in a bowl, toss with ½ tsp. of the salt, and set aside.

2) Toast all the seeds together in a small skillet or toaster oven for a minute or two, or until aromatic. Transfer to a spice grinder or a mortar and pestle, and grind to a coarse powder. (If you lack these utensils, you can just leave the seeds whole.)

3) Heat the oil in a large, deep skillet. Add onion and garlic, and sauté over medium heat for about 5 minutes, or until the onion softens.

4) Add the seeds, eggplant, and remaining salt, and stir well. Reduce heat, cover, and cook until the eggplant is soft. Stir occasionally, and add small amounts of water, as needed, to prevent sticking. This will take about 15 to 20 minutes.

5) Transfer to a bowl; stir in the lemon juice and minced tomato. Add cayenne to taste. Serve warm, at room temperature, or cold.

Italian

- 1 1½-lb. eggplant
- 2 Tbs. olive oil
- 1 cup minced onion
- 2 large cloves garlic, minced
- ½ tsp. salt
- 1 medium stalk celery, minced
- 3 medium-sized ripe tomatoes
- 2 to 3 Tbs. red wine vinegar
- 2 Tbs. tomato paste
- 2 Tbs. minced fresh basil (2 tsp. dried)
- freshly ground black pepper
- ¼ cup minced fresh parsley
- 2 to 3 Tbs. capers } optional
- ½ cup toasted pine nuts

1) Peel the eggplant or not, and cut it into ½-inch cubes. Steam the cubes in a vegetable steamer over boiling water until tender (10 to 15 minutes). Transfer to a medium-large bowl. Meanwhile, put up a medium-sized saucepanful of water to boil.

2) Heat the olive oil in a medium-sized skillet. Add the onion, garlic, and salt, and sauté for about 5 minutes over medium heat. Add the celery, and sauté for another 5 minutes.

3) Meanwhile, core the tomatoes, and gently drop them into the panful of boiling water from Step 1. Turn off the heat, and count slowly to 15. Remove the tomatoes from the water, and pull off their skins. Cut the tomatoes in half, and squeeze out and discard the seeds. Dice the remaining tomato pulp, and add this to the sauté. Cook for a few more minutes— until the celery is tender.

4) Add the sauté to the eggplant, along with all remaining ingredients. Mix well, and taste to adjust seasonings. Serve cold or at room temperature, on crackers or crusty bread.

Kind & Unusual Potato Salads

Good news! Two lowfat potato salads!

1.

Dill Pickle Potatoes

Preparation time:
20 minutes, if you
sauté the vegetables
while the potatoes cook.

Yield:
6 servings

6 medium (2½-inch diameter) potatoes
2 Tbs. canola oil
1 cup thinly sliced onion
1 large carrot, sliced into thin rounds
2 tsp. caraway seeds
1½ tsp. salt
2 large dill pickles, minced
1 cup dill pickle juice (from the jar)
fresh black pepper } to taste
cayenne
1 cup peas, lightly steamed (fresh or frozen)

1) Scrub the potatoes (no need to peel), and chop them into 1-inch cubes.

2) Place the potato chunks in a large pot, cover them with water, and bring to a boil. Lower heat and cook until the potatoes are tender but not mushy. Drain and transfer to a large bowl.

3) Heat the oil in a medium-sized skillet, and cook the onion and carrot with the caraway seeds and ½ tsp. of the salt over medium heat for 8 to 10 minutes, or until the vegetables are tender.

4) Add the cooked vegetables, along with the pickles, pickle juice, and remaining salt to the potatoes and mix well. Stir in black pepper and cayenne to taste.

5) Serve warm, at room temperature, or cold, topped with peas.

2.

Very-Much-Marinated Potatoes

Preparation time:
10 minutes of doing
things, then about
15 minutes for the
potatoes to cook
while you do some-
thing else.

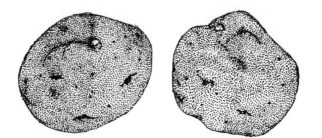

Yield:
6 to 8
servings

The potatoes are cooked right in their marinade, which infuses them with intense flavor. The ingredients are not unusual, but somehow the result far surpasses the sum of its parts.

If you have any of these potatoes left over, try adding them to a panful of sautéed onions and heating them up for breakfast. These just might be the best homefries you've ever had!

14 medium (2½-inch diameter) potatoes,
  unpeeled and diced
1 cup red wine vinegar
5 cups water

8 medium cloves garlic, peeled
  and sliced in half lengthwise
2 tsp. salt
1 cup thinly sliced red onion
fresh black pepper to taste

OPTIONAL ADDITIONS:
a drizzle of extra-virgin olive oil
small amounts of minced fresh parsley, basil, and/or chives
very thinly sliced bell pepper
Niçoise olives
sliced cherry tomatoes } for the top

1) Place the potatoes, vinegar, water, garlic, and salt in a large pot. Bring to a boil, lower heat to a simmer, and cook uncovered until the potatoes are tender but not mushy (about 15 minutes).

2) Drain and transfer to a medium-large bowl. Stir in the red onion while the potatoes are still hot, and season to taste with black pepper. Allow to cool to room temperature.

3) If desired, drizzle with extra-virgin olive oil to taste, and stir in some herbs and sliced bell pepper. Serve at room temperature or cold, plain or garnished with olives and/or cherry tomatoes.

Alfalfa~Romaino Salad

Preparation time:
- 5 minutes to make the dressing
- 10 minutes to prepare the lettuce
- 5 minutes to assemble

Yield: 4 to 6 servings

Adapted from the traditional Caesar, this delicious, spicy salad makes a great lunch entrée.

You can use commercially prepared croutons (many bakeries make terrific ones) or create your own. There's a recipe at the bottom of page 26.

6 Tbs. extra-virgin olive oil
1 large clove garlic, minced
1 Tbs. Dijon mustard
1 Tbs. Worcestershire sauce
1 tsp. prepared horseradish
   (more, to taste)
3 to 4 Tbs. fresh lemon juice
   (to taste)

1 head romaine lettuce (about 1½ lbs.),
   cleaned, dried, and chilled
a handful of alfalfa sprouts
¼ cup grated parmesan cheese
freshly ground black pepper

croutons
extra parmesan (freshly shaved, if possible) } TOPPINGS

1) Combine oil, garlic, mustard, Worcestershire sauce, horseradish, and lemon juice in a small bowl, and whisk until uniform.

2) Shortly before serving, break the lettuce into bite-sized pieces into a large bowl. Use your fingers to separate the sprouts into the lettuce. Sprinkle in the parmesan, and toss until well combined.

3) Just before serving, whisk the dressing vigorously, and drizzle it into the salad. Toss until the lettuce is thoroughly coated. Grind in a generous amount of fresh black pepper, add a handful of croutons, and toss again.

4) Serve immediately, topped with extra croutons and freshly shaved parmesan, if available.

Chilled Asparagus in Dilled Mustard Sauce

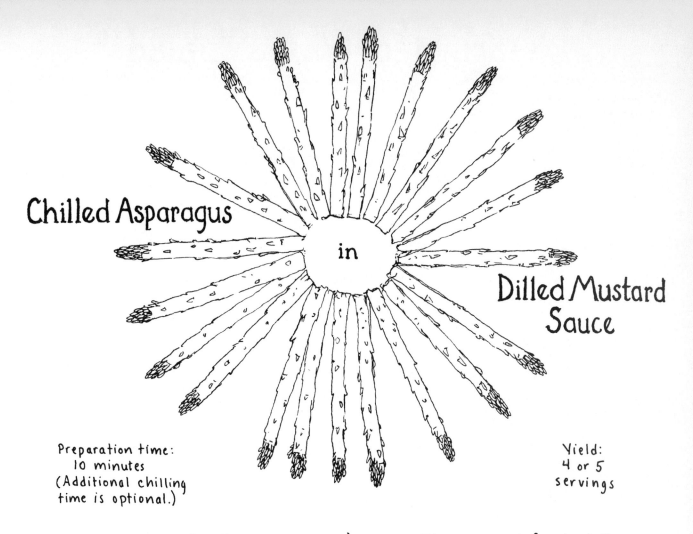

Preparation time:
    10 minutes
(Additional chilling
time is optional.)

Yield:
4 or 5
servings

1 lb. asparagus (as thin as possible)
1 cup firm yogurt
¼ cup mayonnaise (optional)
2 Tbs. Dijon mustard

2 Tbs. minced fresh dill
2 Tbs. minced fresh chives
salt to taste (optional)
fresh black pepper to taste

1) Snap off and discard the tough bottom ends of your elegantly
thin asparagus.

2) Steam the spears over boiling water until just tender. Remove
them immediately from the heat, rinse under cold running water,
and drain well. (At this point, you can leave them at room
temperature or chill until serving time.)

3) In a small bowl, combine yogurt, optional mayonnaise, mustard,
and herbs, and whisk until smooth. Season to taste with salt (or not).

4) To serve, arrange the asparagus in a shallow dish, drizzle on the
dressing, and grind some fresh black pepper over the top. That's it!

Marinated Pasta Salad

Preparation time:
about 30 minutes.
(Add time to chill
if you're serving
it cold.)

Yield:
4 to 6
servings

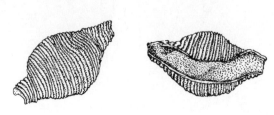

Fresh basil is the ingredient that sends this
pasta salad over the top.

½ lb. uncooked shells (the size of the
  illustration) or orecchiette ("little ears")

3 Tbs. extra-virgin olive oil
2 Tbs. red wine vinegar
¾ tsp. salt
2 to 3 medium cloves garlic, minced
1 cup finely minced red onion
¼ cup grated parmesan
1 medium-sized bell pepper (any color), minced
1 medium-sized cucumber – peeled, seeded, and minced
a handful of minced fresh basil leaves
a handful of minced fresh parsley
fresh black pepper to taste

GARNISHES: { tiny cherry tomatoes (very ripe)
small olives (oil-cured or Niçoise)
a few toasted pine nuts
small cubes of fresh mozzarella

1) Cook the pasta in plenty of boiling water until al dente (just tender).
   Drain well and transfer to a medium-large bowl.
2) Add the oil, vinegar, salt, garlic, onion, and parmesan to the hot
   pasta. Mix well, and allow to come to room temperature.
3) Add remaining ingredients (except garnishes) and mix thoroughly.
4) Serve at room temperature or chilled, lavishly garnished.

Eggless Egg Salad
(made with Tofu)

Preparation time:
15 minutes,
plus time to chill.

Yield:
4 to 6
servings

I know what you're probably thinking, but try this anyway. It's surprisingly similar to the real thing, and it's very good! This might just become one of your favorite crowd-pleasing lunch entrées.

Serve as you would ordinary egg salad—on a bed of greens with olives, tomatoes, and vegetable garnishes—or in a sandwich. This goes especially well in pita bread.

3/4 lb. very firm tofu

3 scallions, minced (whites and greens)

1 medium carrot, grated

1 medium stalk celery, finely minced

1/2 small bell pepper, finely minced

1/4 cup toasted sunflower seeds

1 batch Tofu Mayonnaise (recipe below)

1/2 tsp. salt (or more, to taste)

fresh black pepper to taste

1) Cut the tofu into small dice, and place in a medium-sized bowl.

2) Add remaining ingredients, and mix gently. Season to taste.

3) Cover tightly and chill until cold.

TOFU MAYONNAISE:

NOTE: Silken tofu is a very smooth variety that comes vacuum-packed (usually unrefrigerated) in a 10-oz. box. It is available in natural foods stores, Asian groceries, and in some supermarkets. Use soft or firm—both work perfectly. This mayonnaise will keep up to a week if kept tightly covered in the refrigerator.

1 12-oz. box silken tofu

2 tsp. Chinese sesame oil

1 to 2 Tbs. cider vinegar

1/2 tsp. (and possibly more) dry mustard

1/2 tsp. salt

1 tsp. soy sauce

1) Whip everything together in a blender. Transfer to a small bowl.

2) Taste to adjust seasonings. Cover and refrigerate until cold.

······Cold Stuffed Things······

A cold, stuffed vegetable or fruit can make an oasis out of a hot summer day's lunch. Preparation time is brief, no cooking is involved, yet the result is beautiful and elegant — and <u>COOL</u>.

* * * * * * * * *  * * * * * * * * * *

Freshly-Herbed Cottage Cheese

Combine cottage cheese or very fresh ricotta with small amounts of minced fresh herbs, and you have an easy, perfect filling for hollowed-out cucumbers or bell peppers. Use an assortment of fresh herbs, minced with scissors or a very sharp knife. For each cup of cottage cheese, use about ¼ cup minced herbs (increasing to taste). RECOMMENDED: any combination of dill, basil, thyme, marjoram, mint, parsley, chives, cilantro, or chervil.

* * * * * * * * * * * * * * * ## Cold Stuffed Peppers *

& Cucumbers

Fresh, small bell peppers and cucumbers are perfect containers for herbed cottage cheese. They're tender, yet sturdy, so you can pick them up and eat them with your hands for a refreshing, light lunch-on-the-run.

Choose small vegetables for stuffing. Slice in half lengthwise, and remove the pepper's stem, seeds, and membranes — or the cucumber's seeds. Lay each half on its back, and stuff with as much filling as will fit. Cover tighty and refrigerate — or eat right away.

* * * * * * * * * * * * * * Tomato Fans * * * * * * * * * * * * * *

Preparation time:
15 minutes

Yield:
4 servings

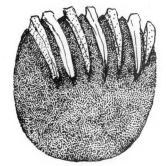

4 perfectly ripe medium-sized tomatoes
1 equally ripe medium-sized avocado, thinly sliced
2 hard-boiled eggs, sliced into thin rounds
salad greens for the plates
Creamy Mustard Dressing (p. 39)
freshly ground black pepper

1) Core the tomatoes, and make a series of parallel slices lengthwise, cutting about 2/3 of the way down, at ¼-inch intervals.
2) Gently insert slices of avocado and egg — alternately — in the crevices.
3) Place the filled tomatoes on small individual plates lined with salad greens. Drizzle lightly with dressing, grind some fresh pepper over the top, and serve.

* * * * * * * * Stuffed * * * * * * * * * * * * * *
Cantaloupe

Preparation time:
10 minutes

Yield:
2 servings
(easily multiplied)

1 small (5-inch diameter) cantaloupe
2 Tbs. fresh lemon
  or lime juice (to taste)
1 cup firm yogurt
2 to 3 Tbs. real maple syrup

1½ cups fresh
  (or frozen/defrosted) berries
  (leave smaller berries whole;
  slice larger ones)
OPTIONAL: toasted coconut
          fresh mint leaves

1) Cut the cantaloupe in half around the equator, and scoop out the seeds. Slice a small piece from each end, so the halves can stand upright. Place each half on a plate, and drizzle the open surface with lemon or lime juice.
2) Combine the yogurt, maple syrup, and berries in a medium-sized bowl and stir gently. Divide this mixture between the melon halves. If desired, sprinkle with a little coconut, and garnish with a mint leaf.

Fancy Stuffed Pears

Preparation time:
15 minutes

Yield:
6 servings

Serve these as a luncheon treat, with fresh pumpernickel bread and a green salad. Or wrap individual Stuffed Pears tightly in plastic wrap, and pack them in your family's lunchboxes.

3 medium-sized ripe pears
2 Tbs. fresh lime juice

FILLING:
½ cup ricotta or cottage cheese
⅓ cup (packed) grated sharp cheddar
2 Tbs. finely minced fresh parsley
2 Tbs. finely minced fresh chives or scallions
⅓ cup minced toasted nuts
    (walnuts or pecans)
2 Tbs. Worcestershire sauce (optional)
1 Tbs. fresh lime juice
salt to taste (optional)

5 or 6 dried apricots, for garnish

1) Slice the pears in half lengthwise. Carefully cut out the cores, and generously brush the open surfaces with lime juice. Set aside.

2) In a medium-sized bowl, whisk together the ricotta or cottage cheese and the cheddar. Add the remaining filling ingredients and mix well.

3) Generously spoon a mound of filling onto each pear half, and smooth the top surface with a dinner knife.

4) Cut the apricots into little strips, and decorate the top of each filled pear with an inspired floral design. (See helpful diagram below for inspiration.)

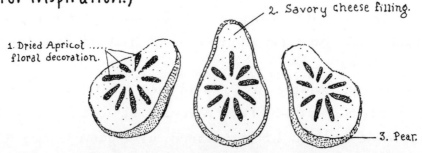

1. Dried Apricot floral decoration.
2. Savory cheese filling.
3. Pear.

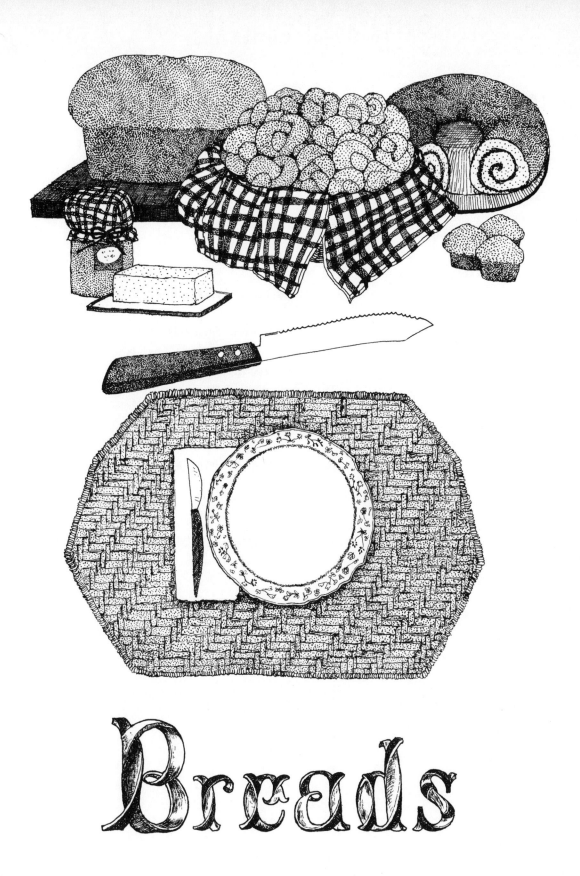

Breads

BREADS
Table of Contents

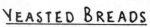
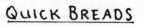

Bread baking is easy, sensuous, and fun — and it can transform the atmosphere in your home. It is very rewarding to get truly physical with food, and to be able to work in such a basic way with one's hands. You might ask: "But isn't it time-consuming and impractical?" The answer is yes and no. Yes, it is time-consuming in that a yeasted bread dough needs several hours to rise and bake. But the actual hands-on time is relatively brief and very enjoyable. If you are going to be at home anyway, doing other things, making bread can be easily incorporated into your day. Impractical? Sure, it would be more efficient to just go to the bakery or use a bread machine.* But you will be missing out on a creative, personal adventure.

This chapter begins with "An Illustrated Guide to the Baking of Yeasted Bread", which takes you step-by-step through that process. If you are new to this, or if yeast has been intimidating to you in the past, I hope this simplified presentation will encourage you to go ahead and try it. Following the Illustrated Guide is a question-and-answer article that gives more technical details. After a batch of yeasted bread recipes, you will find some for quick breads, muffins, and other treats. You might find yourself acquiring a new hobby (not to mention a great-smelling kitchen).

RECOMMENDATION: Once you get really serious about baking bread, treat yourself to a copy of The Village Baker by Joe Ortiz (Ten Speed Press, 1993). You will learn all about time-honored bread-baking traditions from European and American master bakers (including the best sourdough methods).

*If you are in love with your electric bread machine and will never be motivated otherwise, the best — and most complete — book is Bread Machine Baking — Perfect Every Time by Lora Brody and Millie Apter (Morrow '93). It tells you how to adapt all kinds of recipes to all kinds of machines.

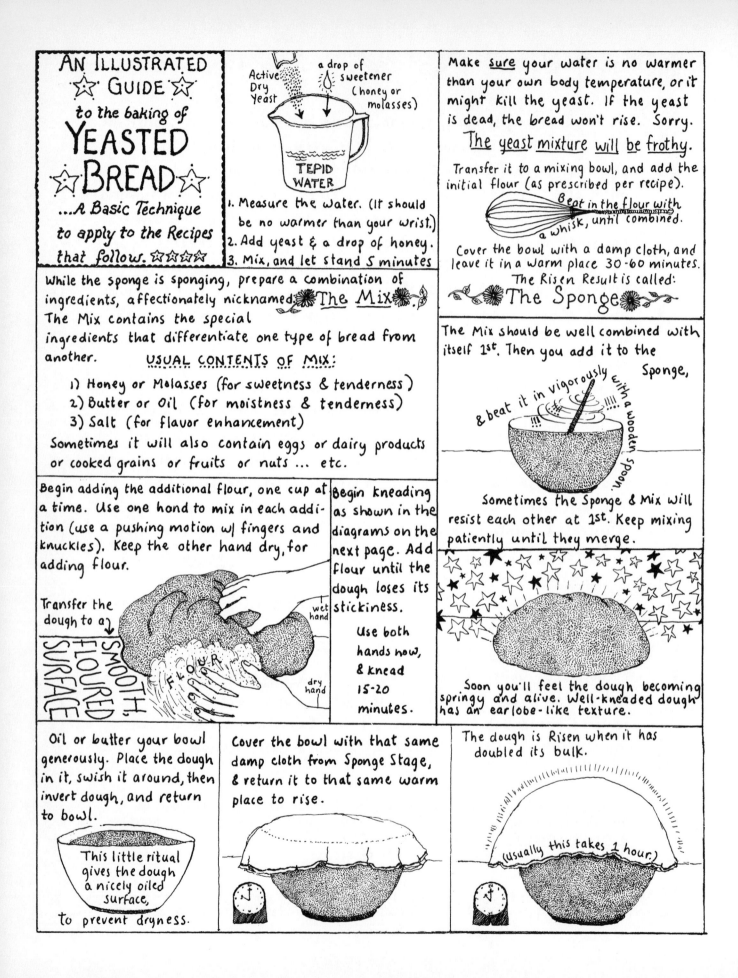

AN ILLUSTRATED ☆ GUIDE ☆ to the baking of YEASTED ☆ BREAD ☆

...A Basic Technique to apply to the Recipes that follow. ☆☆☆☆

Active Dry Yeast — a drop of sweetener (honey or molasses)

TEPID WATER

1. Measure the water. (It should be no warmer than your wrist.)
2. Add yeast & a drop of honey.
3. Mix, and let stand 5 minutes

Make **sure** your water is no warmer than your own body temperature, or it might kill the yeast. If the yeast is dead, the bread won't rise. Sorry.

<u>The yeast mixture will be frothy.</u>

Transfer it to a mixing bowl, and add the initial flour (as prescribed per recipe). Beat in the flour with a whisk, until combined.

Cover the bowl with a damp cloth, and leave it in a warm place 30-60 minutes.

The Risen Result is called:
❀❀ The Sponge ❀❀

While the sponge is sponging, prepare a combination of ingredients, affectionately nicknamed ❀ The Mix ❀. The Mix contains the special ingredients that differentiate one type of bread from another.

USUAL CONTENTS OF MIX:

1) Honey or Molasses (for sweetness & tenderness)
2) Butter or Oil (for moistness & tenderness)
3) Salt (for flavor enhancement)

Sometimes it will also contain eggs or dairy products or cooked grains or fruits or nuts ... etc.

The Mix should be well combined with itself 1st. Then you add it to the Sponge, & beat it in vigorously with a wooden spoon.

Sometimes the Sponge & Mix will resist each other at 1st. Keep mixing patiently until they merge.

Begin adding the additional flour, one cup at a time. Use one hand to mix in each addition (use a pushing motion w/ fingers and knuckles). Keep the other hand dry, for adding flour.

Transfer the dough to a SMOOTH FLOURED SURFACE

FLOUR

wet hand
dry hand

Begin kneading as shown in the diagrams on the next page. Add flour until the dough loses its stickiness.

Use both hands now, & knead 15-20 minutes.

Soon you'll feel the dough becoming springy and alive. Well-kneaded dough has an earlobe-like texture.

Oil or butter your bowl generously. Place the dough in it, swish it around, then invert dough, and return to bowl.

This little ritual gives the dough a nicely oiled surface, to prevent dryness.

Cover the bowl with that same damp cloth from Sponge Stage, & return it to that same warm place to rise.

The dough is Risen when it has doubled its bulk.

(usually this takes 1 hour.)

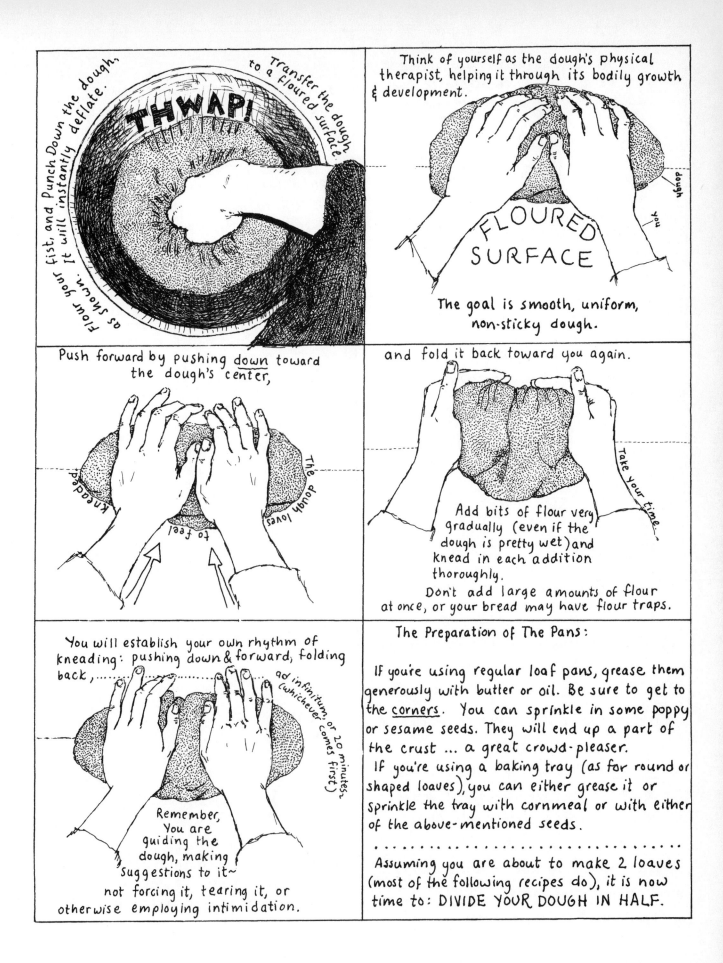

Panel 1 (top left):

Flour your fist, and Punch Down the dough. It will instantly deflate. as shown.

Transfer the dough to a floured surface.

THWAP!

Panel 2 (top right):

Think of yourself as the dough's physical therapist, helping it through its bodily growth & development.

dough

you

FLOURED SURFACE

The goal is smooth, uniform, non-sticky dough.

Panel 3 (middle left):

Push forward by pushing down toward the dough's center,

Kneaded

to feel

The dough loves

Panel 4 (middle right):

and fold it back toward you again.

Take your time.

Add bits of flour very gradually (even if the dough is pretty wet) and knead in each addition thoroughly.

Don't add large amounts of flour at once, or your bread may have flour traps.

Panel 5 (bottom left):

You will establish your own rhythm of kneading: pushing down & forward, folding back, ...

ad infinitum, or 20 minutes (whichever comes first)

Remember, You are guiding the dough, making suggestions to it~

not forcing it, tearing it, or otherwise employing intimidation.

Panel 6 (bottom right):

The Preparation of The Pans:

If you're using regular loaf pans, grease them generously with butter or oil. Be sure to get to the <u>corners</u>. You can sprinkle in some poppy or sesame seeds. They will end up a part of the crust ... a great crowd-pleaser.

If you're using a baking tray (as for round or shaped loaves), you can either grease it or sprinkle the tray with cornmeal or with either of the above-mentioned seeds.

. . . .

Assuming you are about to make 2 loaves (most of the following recipes do), it is now time to: DIVIDE YOUR DOUGH IN HALF.

To loaf: Use rolling pin or palms of your hands to gently persuade the dough that it wants to be a 7-inch-wide-at-center Oval, ½-1 inch thick, w/ all air pockets expelled.

Snugly roll up the oval lengthwise, and when you get to the other end, pinch the seam tightly, and pat the loaf firmly into a Decent Shape.

Lateral View

side-view

front-view

To make a <u>Round</u> loaf, roll it 1st, as described in preceding square, then shape it with your hands, pushing it around on your work surface. Round loaves get baked on baking trays or low, flat pans.

<u>To make a regular bread-pan loaf:</u>
Place the dough into the greased pan, press it hard into the corners & floor of the pan, take the dough out again, and return it upside-down. This gives the bread a handsomely shaped surface.

You may also wish to try some fancy shapes.

Here are 2 nice ones:

5 snakes + 1 ball =

Seal the pieces together with water.

·OR:

2 curved snakes + =

Place these on a flat tray to rise & bake.

Look through this chapter for more shape ideas.

BEFORE

AFTER

Once again, cover the dough with a damp cloth, and put it in a cozy place to rise.

It is ready to bake when its bulk has doubled. (This final rising often goes more quickly than the others.) Preheat the oven (usually to 375°F) 15 minutes before baking.

🌼 CRUSTS 🌼

<u>Butter</u> - melted butter brushed onto the top right before baking, and applied once more when the bread is done, gives a <u>SOFT</u> crust.

<u>Milk</u> - brushed on before baking makes the top brown evenly & nicely.

<u>Beaten Egg</u> - before baking, makes it shiny & rich. <u>Yolk Alone</u> (or with a little water) makes it richer & darker. <u>White Alone</u> makes a very crisp crust.

<u>Water</u> - sprayed on intermittently during baking (use plant mister) gives a crisp, French Bread-type crust.

A hot oven causes a thicker crust. If desired, preheat the oven to 425°, & leave it there for the 1st 10 min. (then turn oven down)

The bread is done if it gives off a hollow sound when thumped. Most common baking time: 40 minutes.

Remove the bread from its pan right away, and cool it on a rack. It slices more easily if it has been allowed to cool at least 10 minutes first.

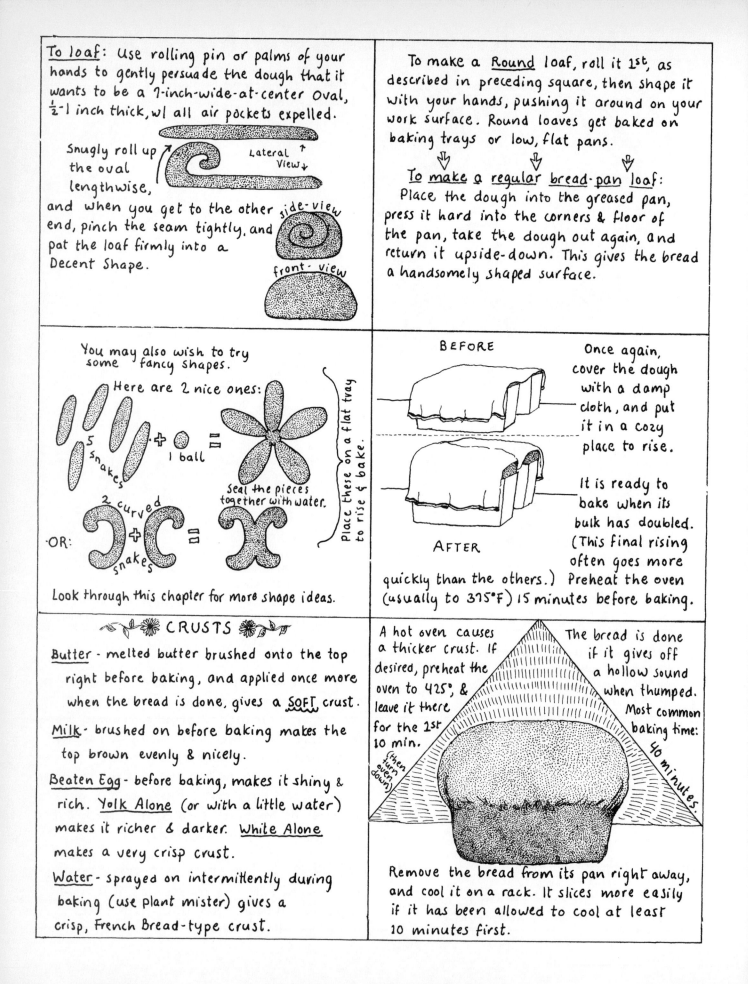

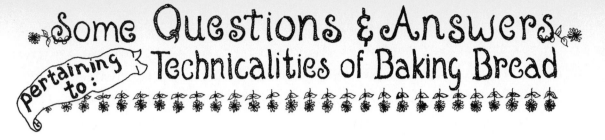

Some Questions & Answers
pertaining to: Technicalities of Baking Bread

What are the differences between yeasted and quick breads?

❀ *Technically* ~ Quick breads are leavened <u>chemically</u>, with baking powder and/or soda. Yeasted breads are leavened <u>biologically</u> by yeast, a live organism. Yeasted rising depends on the activation and development of the yeast, and mostly takes place before the bread bakes. It takes much longer than chemical rising, which occurs during baking only. In yeasted breads, the oven heat serves mostly to finalize the rising that has already taken place.

❀ *Texturally* ~ The texture of quick bread is cakey and crumbly. Yeasted bread is breadier, chewier, more durable. These differences are due to the greater development of gluten in the yeasted dough.

❀ *Nutritionally* ~ Since neither baking soda nor baking powder has any nutritional value, and active dry yeast (not to be confused with Brewer's or nutritional yeast) has only a trace, the nutritional value of any bread comes from other ingredients (grains, eggs, milk, nuts, etc.).

What is the yeast actually doing in there?

❀ It is coming to life from a dry, dormant state. This happens when it first comes into contact with moisture (i.e., when you add it to the water). As the yeast awakens, it surges with Life Impulse. Wanting to grow, it gets hungry for starches and sugars. This is your cue to add sweetener and flour. The yeast actually feeds on these.

❀ As the yeast eats, it grows. It also gives off waste products, one of which is carbon dioxide, a gas, which expands the dough. This is the rising.

❀ Unfortunately, the yeast must be forced to cash in its chips at a certain point, otherwise the dough might expand forever and take over the universe. Yeast prefers human body temperature and will survive refrigeration, but it can't survive baking temperature. After one final, noble gesture of expansion, it dies in the oven. The loaf retains its shape because the gluten holds it up.

What is gluten, anyway?

❀ Gluten is a group of proteins in the wheat kernel. It remains, in both whole wheat and white flours alike, after the wheat is processed into flour.

What is gluten "development", and what has it to do with kneading?

✿ When the flour comes into contact with moisture and agitation, the gluten becomes activated and its physical form alters. Think of preactivated gluten as wool freshly shorn from a sheep. It gets converted into strands when spun, and is greatly rearranged when woven or knitted. The form is changed (it is now a sweater instead of a sheepsuit) but its substance is unchanged (it is still wool). Mixing and kneading dough are analagous to spinning and weaving wool. Kneading changes random gluten blobs into long, interlocking strands that prevent the carbon dioxide from escaping from the yeast. So, the yeast causes the rising, and the gluten contains the risenness.

Why is a "sponge", and not the complete dough, put up for the first rise?

✿ A sponge is advantageous for whole grain breads and/or breads with dense ingredients, because:

✿ → It gives the yeast a head start by allowing it a first rise free from obstruction by heavier materials. (A sponge is just water, yeast, a drop of sweetener, and a small amount of flour.)

✿ → Extra ingredients, the densest part of the dough (the "mix" and the additional flour), are more easily incorporated into a risen sponge than when they are combined with all the other ingredients at the outset.

✿ → There is also a straight dough method, where all the ingredients are combined before the first rise (as in the Challah recipe, p. 73). This method has one less rising period than the sponge method. It works well for white breads without a lot of additional rich ingredients.

What does punching down accomplish?

✿ Punching down interrupts the rising immediately. If the rising isn't stopped in time, the strands of gluten will break like a rubber band stretched beyond its limit. Since broken gluten strands can't be reunited, the result will be a coarse loaf. ✿ Punching down also expels waste products given off into the dough by the growing yeast. An accumulation of these could give the bread a bitter flavor.

Can caked yeast be substituted for active dry yeast?

✿ Yes. One commercially packaged unit of one is interchangeable with ditto of the other. The equivalent in bulk yeast is a scant tablespoon.

Why do some yeasted doughs work with no kneading?

🌸 They simply end up with less gluten development, and the difference is textural. Bready breads are those that have been kneaded more and have risen a lot. Cakey breads result from less kneading and rising.

How do the available wheat flours differ?

🌼 _Whole Wheat "Bread" Flour_ has a higher gluten content than other whole wheat flours. I recommend it for all yeasted bread recipes.

🌸 _Whole Wheat "Pastry" Flour_ is more finely milled and lower in gluten than bread flour. The lower gluten content makes it a better choice for flaky, light results — pie crusts, quick breads, cakes, pancakes, cookies, etc. — in short, most baked goods other than yeasted breads. (NOTE: Whole wheat pastry flour is often referred to simply as "whole wheat flour".)

🌸 _Bleached =vs= Unbleached White Flour_: Bleached white flour contains traces of its chemical bleaching agents, bromine and chlorine. Unbleached white flour is cleaner and has a fresher taste.

Can flour get stale? What is a good storage method?

🌸 All flours can get stale. Whole grain flours contain oil, so they can get rancid. You can tell by the smell. Buy small quantities frequently for insurance.

Store whole-grain flours in a cool, dry place such as the refrigerator. The humble brown paper bag, believe it or not, is one of the best flour storage containers. It is slightly porous, and keeps the flour fresh by allowing it to breathe. Wrap the paper bag loosely in an unsealed plastic bag to keep it dry.

You can also store flour in glass jars whose tops have been delicately punctured (again, for respiratory purposes).

What are the best bread pans made of?

🌸 The best pans for baking bread are made either from unglazed stoneware or from aluminized steel (such as the Professional Bakeware line from Calphalon). Another good choice is old-fashioned heavy, dark-tinned steel pans. You can also bake bread directly on unglazed tiles or a baking stone in any oven, for a crusty "artisan" loaf.

Where is the best place for dough to rise? What should be done if the dough gets too hot during rising?

❀ The best rising temperature is human body temperature. Remember, yeast is a living organism that needs comfort to grow. Pick a nice, warm spot in your kitchen. If it's a very cold day, you could let the dough rise in a slightly warmed oven with a kettleful of boiling water sitting near it. (Just be sure the oven isn't <u>hot</u>, because that could kill the yeast.) The symptoms of too much heat are: too quick a rise (say, if the yeast looks like it's going to double its bulk in 45 minutes or less) and/or a partially cooked or crusted bottom. Remedy: punch down the dough, remove it from the bowl, and knead it for several minutes. Put it in a different bowl if the first one is encrusted, and put it up to rise again in a cooler spot. It will likely bounce back — bread dough has a resilient disposition.

Which ingredients help the dough rise? Which ones slow it down?

DOUGH HELPERS

Eggs are agents to rising, especially when beaten first. They also make the bread richer and higher in protein. A large egg equals a scant ¼ cup liquid, and can be added to most yeasted bread doughs, if desired.

The <u>correct</u> <u>amount</u> <u>of</u> <u>sweetening</u> is also an agent to rising, because it feeds the yeast. Too much sweetening, however, might retard rising. It causes the yeast to overeat and get sluggish.

<u>*Warmth*</u> is an agent to rising. The warmer your kitchen, the faster the dough will rise. You also contribute your own warmth through your hands as you knead.

DOUGH RETARDERS

<u>*Salt*</u> is a retarder, because it interferes metabolically with the yeast.

<u>*Oil*</u> (or butter) is a retarder, because it lubricates the strands of gluten, making it more difficult for them to adhere together.

Although they are retarders, salt and oil (or butter) are necessary, respectively, for flavor and tenderness. They get added to the yeast a little later (after the sponge stage), so the sponge can have an unencumbered first rise.

<u>*Cold*</u> is a retarder. If your kitchen is chilly, rising will take longer.

Can yeasted dough be refrigerated overnight?

❀ Yes. The rising will still occur, but it will take 2 to 3 times longer. If you refrigerate it overnight, place the bowl of dough in a large, sealed plastic bag. Dough can be refrigerated like this for up to several days, if it is periodically punched down and the surface is re-oiled. Unbaked loaves can also be refrigerated while rising. Be sure they are in large, sealed plastic bags which leave them plenty of room to expand. (If you have a choice between refrigerating at the dough stage or the loaf stage, choose the latter — it works better.)

Is it possible to over- or underknead?

❀ Old cookbooks used to recommend that each kneading session last 45 minutes to an hour. So if you are kneading by hand, you won't overdo it.

❀ However, if you use a mixer with a dough hook, you _can_ overknead, causing overdeveloped gluten and a toughened loaf. With a dough hook, use low speed and watch it carefully. The dough is amply kneaded when it feels like an earlobe.

❀ It is definitely possible to underknead, and the resulting loaf might be mistaken for a brick. Average kneading time, if you are an average person, is about 10 minutes of concerted activity. Try the earlobe test if you are unsure.

Why do bread recipes often have indefinite instructions (about final amounts of flour, rising time, baking time, etc.)?

❀ There are many variables in your kitchen and ingredients that can affect the dough. Some examples: temperature, humidity, altitude (see below), age of the yeast, texture of the flour, etc. Experienced bread bakers learn to make adjustments, and experience comes quickly with practice.

How should one accommodate altitude in yeasted baking?

❀ The higher you are, the quicker the rise. A too-quick rise can deprive the yeast and gluten of their full maturation time. Remedies: Use less yeast and/or refrigerate the dough during some or all of the rising. Also, try to give the dough extra rising periods of shorter duration (e.g., two 45-minute rises instead of a single 1½ hour rise). Punch down in between.

A BASIC BREAD RECIPE

Here is a sample recipe for a plain loaf of part white, part whole wheat bread. It's a good one to start with if baking bread is new to you. Or, if you're already comfortable with the craft, but you'd like to experiment and improvise for the first time, use this recipe as a sturdy base for your increasingly bold and exotic forays into spontaneity.

ABOUT THE ORGANIZATION OF THIS YEASTED BREAD SECTION: Since the Illustrated Guide (pages 62-64) goes into the techniques of yeasted bread baking in some detail, all of the recipes that follow the one below will rely on your having read the Guide beforehand. Also, there are no "preparation time" notices posted at the tops of the yeasted bread recipes. The general idea is, choose to bake yeasted bread on a day when you are planning to be at home anyway. The actual hands-on time is fairly brief; you can do lots of other activities while the dough rises and bakes.

Yield: 2 loaves

The Sponge:
- 2 cups wrist-temperature water
- 1 package (a scant Tbs.) active dry yeast
- a drop of honey or molasses
- 1½ cups whole wheat bread flour

The Mix:
- 4 Tbs. melted butter (canola oil also ok)
- ⅓ cup honey or molasses
- 1 Tbs. salt

Additional Flour: (approximate)
- 3 more cups whole wheat bread flour
- 4 cups unbleached white flour

You'll Also Need:
- a little butter or oil for the bowl and the pans
- FOR POSSIBLE CRUSTS: more butter or a little milk, or some beaten egg, or a little water

1) Place the water in a large bowl and sprinkle in the yeast. Add the drop of sweetener and let it stand for about a minute or two.

2) Beat in 1½ cups whole wheat bread flour with a whisk, cover the bowl with a clean tea towel, and put it in a warm place to rise for 35 to 40 minutes.

3) Beat in the mix.

4) Add the additional flour 1 cup at a time, graduating from wooden spoon to floured hand as the dough thickens. When all the flour is added, turn out the dough onto a clean, floured surface.

5) Knead the dough for about 10 to 15 minutes, adding extra flour, as necessary, to combat stickiness.

6) Oil (or butter) the bowl, and roll the kneaded dough in it so its surface gets nicely coated. Cover with a towel, and let it rise until its bulk has doubled. (This will take about 1½ to 2 hours.)

7) Punch down the risen dough, return it to the floured surface, and knead for another 5 to 10 minutes, adding flour if necessary. Divide in half and form 2 loaves. Oil (or butter) 2 bread pans or baking trays, place the loaves in or on them, and cover with the towel. Let rise until doubled in bulk one more time. (This time it will rise more quickly.) Meanwhile, preheat the oven to 375°F.

8) If desired, brush the loaves with butter, milk, egg, or water for various effects on the crust (see bottom of p. 64). Bake for about 40 minutes, or until the loaves sound hollow when tapped resolutely on the bottom. Remove the breads from the pans or tray right away, and cool on a rack, so the crust will crispen. Wait at least 30 minutes before slicing.

OPTIONAL ADDITIONS (and good ones to begin with if you are new to improvisation):

an egg . . . . . . beaten in with the mix (reduce water by ¼ cup).
wheat germ . . . up to 1 cup (replaces 1 cup additional flour).
seeds . . . . sesame, sunflower, poppy (or a combination)
                    up to ½ cup ~ added with additional flour.

chopped dried fruit ⎫
chopped nuts   ⎬ add up to 1 cup each to mix
cooked grains (any ⎭
      kind)

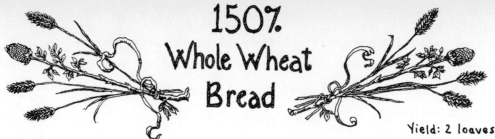

150%
Whole Wheat
Bread

Yield: 2 loaves

<u>Order of events:</u>

1) Make mix and let it cool to room temperature.
2) Put up the sponge while the mix cools.
3) When it is cool enough, beat the mix into the risen sponge.
4) Add flour and knead; let rise, etc. (Review method pages 62-64).

<u>The Mix:</u>

1 cup uncooked bulgur
1 cup boiling water
1 Tbs. salt
4 Tbs. butter or canola oil
4 Tbs. molasses
1½ cups golden raisins
OPTIONAL: 1 cup cooked wheat berries
(see page 215.)

Combine bulgur and water in a medium-small bowl. Cover with a plate and let stand 30 minutes. Add remaining ingredients, cover again, and let stand until room temperature.

<u>The Sponge:</u>

1 package (a scant Tbs.) active dry yeast
1 cup wrist-temperature water
a drop of molasses
1½ cups whole wheat bread flour

Dissolve yeast in water in a large bowl. Add molasses. Beat in flour, cover, let rise 30 to 45 minutes.

<u>Other Ingredients:</u>

3 to 4 cups additional whole wheat bread flour
a little butter or oil for the bowl and baking pans or tray
OPTIONAL: melted butter for the crust

Add flour to the risen sponge a cup at a time. Knead, let rise, etc.

After you've formed loaves and they've risen, brush with melted butter, if desired, and bake for about 40 minutes at 375°F (until the bread sounds hollow when thumped on the bottom).

Remove from pans or tray; cool 30 minutes on a rack before slicing.

CHALLAH

2½ cups wrist-temperature water
1 package (a scant Tbs.) active dry yeast
½ cup sugar or honey
4 Tbs. canola oil or melted butter
3 eggs (1 for the crust)

1 Tbs. salt
½ cup raisins (optional)
8 to 9 cups unbleached white flour
a little oil for the baking trays
poppy or sesame seeds (optional)

1) Place the water in a large bowl. Sprinkle in the yeast. Beat in the sugar or honey, oil or butter, 2 eggs, and salt with a wire whisk.

2) Stir in optional raisins, then add flour a cup at a time, whisking after each addition. Graduate from whisk to wooden spoon to a floured hand as the dough thickens. Knead the dough in the bowl for a few minutes — until smooth, elastic, and no longer sticky. Cover with a clean cloth, and set the bowl in a warm place for about 1½ hours, or until the dough doubles in bulk.

3) Punch down the risen dough, and turn it out onto a floured surface. Divide it in half, and knead each half for about 5 minutes, adding flour as needed, if it gets a little sticky. Divide each half into thirds, and roll each third into a long snake about 1½ inches in diameter. Line up 2 sets of 3 snakes, each, and braid from the middle like this:

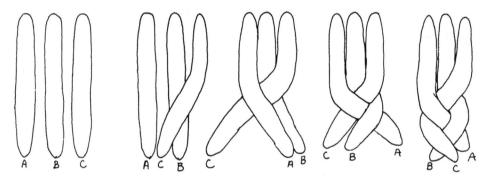

A B C   A C B   C   A B   C B   A   B   A
                                                          C

Pinch the ends together very firmly.

4) Lightly oil 2 baking trays, and place a finished braid on each. Cover with a towel, and let rise another hour, or until doubled in bulk again. Meanwhile, preheat the oven to 375°F.

5) Beat the remaining egg in a small bowl. Brush a generous amount over each braid, and sprinkle lightly with seeds. Bake for about 40 minutes, or until the breads give off a hollow sound when thumped on the bottom. Remove from the trays right away and cool on a rack for at least 30 minutes before eating.

Cashew-Barley Bread

Review the method, pages 62-64.   Yield: 2 loaves

NOTE: You can buy barley flour in most natural foods stores. You can also grind your own in the blender. For 2 cups flour, use 1 cup whole barley (hulled or pearl). It will take about 5 to 10 minutes to grind it (and it will be noisy) but it will work.

PRELIMINARIES (DO THESE TWO STEPS AHEAD OF TIME):

I. 3/4 cup uncooked barley (hulled or pearl)
2 cups water

} Place barley and water in a saucepan. Bring to a boil, turn heat down to a simmer, cover, and cook until tender but still chewy (1½ hours for pearl barley; slightly longer for hulled). Remove from heat; cool to room temperature.

II. 1½ cups cashews, ground in the blender in a few quick spurts
2 cups barley flour

} Toast together in a 350°F oven for 15 to 20 minutes (or in a cast-iron skillet over medium heat for 10 to 15 minutes). Cool to room temperature.

TO MAKE THE BREAD:

Sponge:
2 cups wrist-temperature water
1 package (a scant Tbs.) active dry yeast
a drop of honey
2 cups unbleached white flour

Mix:
about 2 cups cooked barley (from "I", above)
the toasted cashews and barley flour ("II", above)
3 Tbs. honey
2 Tbs. Chinese sesame oil
1 Tbs. canola oil
1 Tbs. salt

Additional flour: 5 to 6 cups unbleached white flour

1) Combine the sponge ingredients in a big bowl. Mix well, cover, and let rise 30 to 45 minutes.
2) Beat in the mix ingredients.
3) Add the flour, a cup at a time, stirring between additions. Proceed with the method, as described on pages 62-64. Bake the risen loaves at 375°F for about 45 minutes, or until they sound hollow when thumped. Cool on a rack for at least 30 minutes before slicing.

Review pages 62-64.

Yield: 2 loaves

SUNFLOWER·MILLET BREAD

I. THE MIX:
1½ cups water
1 cup uncooked millet
4 Tbs. (½ stick) butter
4 Tbs. honey
2½ tsp. salt

II. THE SPONGE:
1 package (a scant Tbs.)
  active dry yeast
1 cup wrist-temperature water
a drop of honey
1 cup unbleached white flour

III. FURTHERMORE:
1 cup sunflower seeds (more, if desired)
2 cups whole wheat bread flour
2 to 3 more cups unbleached white flour

RECOMMENDED CRUST:
melted butter

1) PREPARE THE MIX: (Do this ahead so the millet can cool.)
Bring 1½ cups water to a boil in a medium-sized saucepan. Add the millet, cover, and turn the heat to very low. Cook for 15 minutes, or until all the water is absorbed and the millet is tender. Fluff with a fork, add the remaining mix ingredients, and stir until well combined. Let it cool to room temperature before adding it to the sponge. (NOTE: If using leftover cooked millet, use 3½ cups. Melt the butter and honey together, then stir that mixture into the millet, along with the salt.)

2) PREPARE THE SPONGE: As per usual. Let rise 30 to 45 minutes.

3) ASSEMBLE THE DOUGH: Beat the mix into the sponge, along with the sunflower seeds. Add the flour, a cup at a time. Carry on as usual with kneading, rising, punching, shaping, etc.

4) BAKE THE RISEN LOAVES: About 40 minutes at 375°F (until the loaves are nicely browned and give off a hollow sound when thumped on the bottom). Cool on a rack for at least 30 minutes.

Review pages 62-64.

Squash Bread

Golden & Sweet

Yield:
2 loaves

You will need 2½ cups mashed, cooked acorn or butternut squash. Bake 2 medium squash in advance: split them lengthwise, remove seeds, and place them face down on a lightly oiled tray. Bake at 350°F for about 35 minutes, or until very soft. Cool and scoop out the insides. Mash, (or purée in a food processor) and measure out 2½ cups.

SPONGE:

2 cups wrist-temperature water
1 package (a scant Tbs.) active dry yeast
a drop of molasses
1½ cups unbleached white flour
1 cup whole wheat bread flour

Place water in large bowl. Add yeast and molasses. Beat in flour. Cover and let rise 30 to 45 minutes.

MIX (make sure it is room temperature before adding):

2½ cups well-mashed cooked squash
3 Tbs. molasses
4 Tbs. melted butter
1 rounded Tbs. salt
OPTIONAL: 1 tsp. cinnamon
          ½ tsp. ground cloves

Mix together until well combined. Beat into risen sponge.

ADDITIONALLY:

about 3 more cups whole wheat bread flour
about 4 more cups unbleached white flour
a little butter or oil for bowl and pans
    or tray

Add flour to risen sponge a cup at a time. Proceed to knead, let rise, form loaves, etc. as per pages 62-64.

Bake at 375°F for 40 to 45 minutes—until it sounds hollow when thumped. Remove from pans or tray and cool for at least 30 minutes before slicing.

for Potato Bread

Make these substitutions:
{ mashed potatoes instead of squash
  honey instead of molasses
  ½ cup minced chives instead of spices

Vegetable-Flecked Bread

☆ ☆ ☆ ☆ ☆ ☆ ☆ ☆ ☆ ☆ ☆ ☆

The vegetable flecks make this savory, delicious bread beautiful. The dough takes a little extra kneading – but it's well worth it.

Review the method, pages 62-64.

I. THE MIX:

4 Tbs. butter, olive oil, or canola oil

1 cup minced red onion

3 medium cloves garlic, minced

½ cup sunflower seeds

½ cup sesame seeds

1 cup grated zucchini

1 cup grated carrot

¾ cup minced red bell pepper

1 Tbs. plus 1 tsp. salt

a handful of minced fresh parsley

3 Tbs. honey or brown sugar

2 Tbs. fresh lemon juice

1 cup mung bean sprouts (optional)

freshly ground black pepper

1) Melt the butter or heat the oil in a medium-sized skillet. Add onion and sauté over medium heat for 2 minutes.

2) Add garlic, seeds, zucchini, and carrot; sauté for 2 minutes more.

3) Remove from heat. Stir in remaining ingredients. Set aside to cool to room temperature.

II. THE SPONGE:

1½ cups wrist-temperature water

1 package (a scant Tbs.) active dry yeast

a drop of honey

1½ cups whole wheat bread flour

Place the water in a large bowl; add yeast and honey. Whisk in flour. Cover, and let rise 30 to 45 minutes.

III. ADDITIONALLY:

1 more cup whole wheat bread flour

about 4 cups unbleached white flour

cornmeal for the baking tray (you can also use rolled oats)

water for the crust

Beat in, then knead in, the flour. Proceed as per the method on pages 62-64. Sprinkle the baking tray with cornmeal or rolled oats. Brush the risen loaves with water.

→ Bake in a 350°F oven for 50 to 60 minutes, or until a loaf sounds hollow when thumped on the bottom. Cool for at least 30 minutes on a rack before slicing.

✳ ✳ ✳ ✳ ✳ Carob Pumpernickel ✳ ✳ ✳ ✳ ✳
☽ ☽ ☽ ☽ ☽ ☽ ☽ ☽ ☽ ☽ ☽ ☽ ☽

Review
pages 62-64.

Yield:
2 loaves

NOTE: Make the mix first, so it has time to cool.

I. THE MIX:

½ cup carob powder
¼ cup Postum or Caffix or instant coffee granules
1 cup hot water
5 Tbs. molasses
OPTIONAL: 2 Tbs. brown sugar (if using instant coffee)
3 Tbs. butter or canola oil
1 Tbs. salt
OPTIONAL: 1 tsp. caraway seeds
1 cup raisins

1) Combine everything except the caraway seeds and raisins, and mix until it forms a uniform paste. (A blender does this well.)
2) Stir in the optional caraway seeds and raisins, and set aside to cool to room temperature.

II: THE SPONGE:

2 cups wrist-temperature water
1 package (a scant Tbs.) active dry yeast
a drop of molasses
1½ cups whole wheat bread flour

Place water in large bowl. Add yeast and molasses. Whisk in flour. Cover and let rise 30 to 45 minutes.

III. ADDITIONALLY:

3 cups rye flour
about 4 more cups whole wheat bread flour
cornmeal for the baking tray
egg yolk for the crust

Add the flour to the risen sponge a cup at a time. Beat with a wooden spoon until thick, then mix with a floured hand. Knead, let rise, punch down, etc. (pages 62-64). Place the completed loaves on corn meal-dusted trays, brush the loaves with egg yolk, and bake at 375°F for 40 minutes. Cool on a rack for at least 30 minutes before slicing.

CAROB SWIRL BREAD

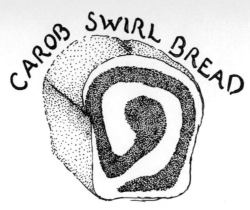

☆ This bread requires 2 doughs: one dark and one light.

Review the method, pages 62-64.

☆ The sponges are identical, but the mixes are different.

Yield: 2 good-sized loaves

I.) PRELIMINARY: Make the 2 mixes ahead of time, so they can properly cool:

DARK MIX
½ cup carob powder
1 cup hot water
3 Tbs. molasses
1 Tbs. butter or canola oil
2 tsp. salt

Combine in a small bowl.

LIGHT MIX
1⅓ cups hot milk (lowfat or soy OK)
3 Tbs. honey
2 Tbs. butter or canola oil
2 tsp. salt

Combine in another small bowl.

Set both mixes aside to come to room temperature.

II.) Make 2 identical sponges:
1 package (a scant Tbs.) active dry yeast
2 cups wrist-temperature water
a drop of honey for each bowl
2 cups unbleached white flour

Take 2 large bowls. Put half the yeast, 1 cup water, a drop of honey, and 1 cup flour in each. Mix, cover, and let rise for 30 to 45 minutes.

III.) Make the bread:

DARK DOUGH
1 sponge (above)
the dark mix (above)
about 4 cups whole wheat bread flour

LIGHT DOUGH
the other sponge (above)
the light mix (above)
about 4 cups unbleached white flour

RECOMMENDED CRUST: milk (soy OK)
a little butter or oil for the pans

1) Beat each mix into a sponge. Add the appropriate flour a cup at a time; knead to make 2 beautiful doughs. Let rise, punch down, etc.

2) To make the loaves, knead the doughs well; divide each in half. Roll each dough with a rolling pin to make a neat oval about ¾ inch thick. (Try to get all the ovals roughly the same dimensions.) Place the dark on top of the light, and roll them together tightly. Lightly grease 2 medium-sized loaf pans, and fit 1 roll into each. Let rise for an hour, then brush with milk and bake in a 375°F oven for 40 minutes. Cool before slicing.

♥ 2 Loaves ♥

Light Swedish Rye

I. SPONGE:

1 package (a scant Tbs.) active dry yeast
1½ cups wrist-temperature water
a drop of molasses
1 cup whole wheat bread flour
} Combine everything in a large bowl. Cover and let rise 30 to 45 minutes.

II. MIX: ½ cup orange juice   1 tsp. fennel seeds
1 Tbs. salt   2 tsp. grated orange rind
4 Tbs. melted butter   5 Tbs. molasses
} Mix everything together; beat into risen sponge.

III. IN ADDITION: 1½ cups rye flour
1½ cups whole wheat bread flour
4½ cups unbleached white flour (as needed)
} Knead in. Make round loaves.

IV. AND FINALLY: cornmeal for the baking tray.
1 egg yolk + 1 Tbs. water, for the crust
} Brush with yolk mixture after final rise.

Bake for 40 minutes at 375°F. Cool for at least 30 minutes before slicing.

♥ 2 Loaves ♥

Cumin-Garbanzo Bread

This is a variation of the Light Swedish Rye recipe above. Just make the following changes:

1) Increase the water in the sponge to 2 cups.
2) Omit the orange juice and orange rind.
3) Add 1 15-oz. can chick-peas (aka garbanzo beans), rinsed and drained, to the mix. (That's approximately 1½ cups cooked chick-peas.)
4) Replace the fennel seeds with 2 tsp. cumin seeds.
5) Replace the butter with olive oil.
   – Everything else is the same.

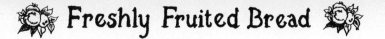# Freshly Fruited Bread

Tart & refreshing.   Review pages 62-64.   Yield:
2 loaves

THE SPONGE:
1 cup wrist-temperature water
2/3 cup orange juice
1 package active dry yeast
a drop of honey
2 cups unbleached white flour

} Combine water and juice in a large bowl. Add yeast and honey; beat in the flour. Cover; let rise for 30 to 45 minutes.

THE MIX:
1 cup finely minced cranberries (fresh or dried)
1 large, ripe banana, mashed
1 packed cup grated, peeled apple
1 Tbs. grated orange rind
1 Tbs. grated lemon rind
½ cup sugar or honey
1 Tbs. plus 1 tsp. salt
3 Tbs. melted butter
OPTIONAL: 1½ cups finely minced nuts
            up to 1½ cups minced dried fruit

} Beat into risen sponge. (No need to precombine.)

ADDITIONALLY:
2 cups whole wheat bread flour
approximately 4 to 5 more cups unbleached white flour
a little butter or oil for the pans or baking tray
OPTIONAL: a little milk for the crust

Add the flour a cup at a time, beating at first with a wooden spoon, then kneading it in with a floured hand. Knead, let rise, punch down, etc. (per pages 62-64). If desired, brush the risen loaves with a little milk before baking. Bake at 350°F for 40 to 50 minutes, or until it sounds hollow when thumped on the bottom. Cool for at least 30 minutes on a rack before slicing.

Some Shapes for Rolls

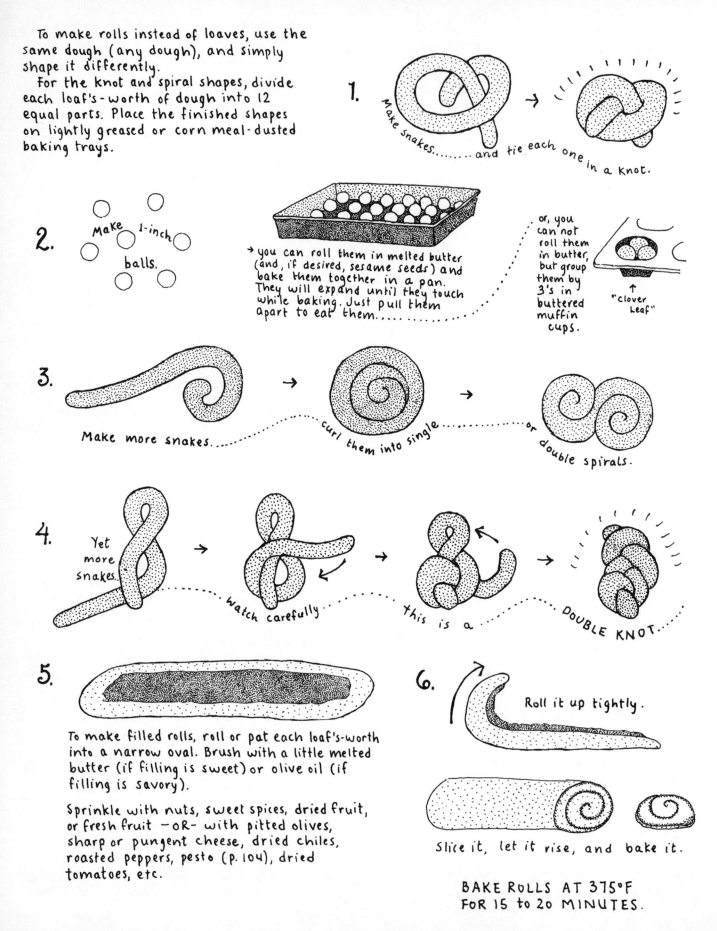

To make rolls instead of loaves, use the same dough (any dough), and simply shape it differently.

For the knot and spiral shapes, divide each loaf's-worth of dough into 12 equal parts. Place the finished shapes on lightly greased or corn meal-dusted baking trays.

1. Make snakes.......... and tie each one in a knot.

2. Make 1-inch balls.

→ you can roll them in melted butter (and, if desired, sesame seeds) and bake them together in a pan. They will expand until they touch while baking. Just pull them apart to eat them..........

or, you can not roll them in butter, but group them by 3's in buttered muffin cups.

↑ "clover Leaf"

3. Make more snakes.......... curl them into single.......... or double spirals.

4. Yet more snakes. .... watch carefully .... this is a .... DOUBLE KNOT..........

5. To make filled rolls, roll or pat each loaf's-worth into a narrow oval. Brush with a little melted butter (if filling is sweet) or olive oil (if filling is savory).

Sprinkle with nuts, sweet spices, dried fruit, or fresh fruit —OR— with pitted olives, sharp or pungent cheese, dried chiles, roasted peppers, pesto (p. 104), dried tomatoes, etc.

6. Roll it up tightly.

Slice it, let it rise, and bake it.

BAKE ROLLS AT 375°F FOR 15 to 20 MINUTES.

Stuffed Artichokes (page 228)

White Bean & Escarole Soup (page 21)

Mushroom Pie with Spinach Crust (page 134)

Cherry-Berry Pie (page 248)

Quick Breads

also known as "Batter Breads"

Each of these quick bread recipes is very easy and produces a single medium-sized loaf. You can easily double any of them.

Sweet Whole Wheat~Nut Bread

15 minutes to prepare;
40 minutes to bake.

Yield: 1 medium-sized loaf

a little butter or oil for the pan

⅓ cup lightly toasted cashews

1 cup water

1 egg

1 tsp. vanilla extract

⅓ cup sugar

1 cup unbleached white flour

1 cup whole wheat flour

2 tsp. baking powder

½ tsp. baking soda

½ tsp. salt (rounded measure)

½ tsp. cinnamon

a dash each: ground ginger and nutmeg

⅓ cup minced almonds

⅓ cup minced pecans

1) Preheat oven to 350°F. Lightly grease a medium-sized loaf pan.

2) Place cashews and water in a blender and purée until you have a fairly smooth cashew milk. Add the egg and vanilla and blend.

3) Place the sugar in a medium-sized mixing bowl. Sift in the flours, baking powder, baking soda, salt, and spices. Make a well in the center, and pour in the cashew mixture. Stir with a rubber spatula or wooden spoon, adding the almonds and pecans along the way, until the batter becomes fairly uniform.

4) Transfer to the prepared pan, and bake about 40 minutes – until a knife inserted all the way into the center comes out clean. Cool for about 10 minutes, then remove the bread from the pan and cool for at least 30 minutes longer before slicing.

Savory Nut Bread

30 minutes
to prepare,
50 minutes
to bake.

Yield:
1 medium-sized
loaf

a little butter or oil for the pan
4 Tbs. butter
½ cup finely minced onion
½ cup finely minced walnuts
½ cup finely minced pecans or almonds
1½ cups unbleached white flour
1 cup whole wheat flour
2 tsp. baking powder
½ tsp. baking soda
½ tsp. salt
⅓ cup sugar
1½ cups buttermilk or yogurt
2 eggs
½ cup chopped pitted black olives

1) Preheat oven to 350°F. Lightly grease a medium-sized loaf pan.

2) Melt the butter in a small skillet. Add the onion, and sauté over medium heat for about 5 minutes, or until the onion begins to soften. Add the nuts and sauté for 5 to 8 minutes more — until the onion is very soft and the nuts are lightly browned. Remove from heat.

3) Sift together the flours, baking powder, soda, and salt into a large bowl. Stir in the sugar, and make a well in the center.

4) Combine the buttermilk or yogurt and the eggs in a separate bowl. Beat until frothy, and pour into the well in the dry ingredients. Add the olives, onion, and nuts, and stir until completely blended.

5) Spread into the prepared pan, and bake for about 50 minutes, or until a knife inserted all the way into the center comes out clean. Cool in the pan for about 10 minutes, then rap sharply and remove. Cool on a rack for about 30 minutes more, or else the bread will crumble.

Yogurt & Herb Bread

15 minutes to prepare;
40 to 45 minutes to bake.

Yield:
1 medium-sized loaf

a little butter or oil
  for the pan
1 cup unbleached white flour
1 cup whole wheat flour
1 tsp. baking powder
½ tsp. baking soda
¾ tsp. salt
1 cup firm yogurt
5 Tbs. melted butter
2 eggs
⅓ cup honey or sugar
2 Tbs. minced fresh dill
  (or 2 tsp. dried)
1 tsp. dried oregano
1 tsp. dried thyme
1 tsp. dried basil

1) Preheat oven to 350°F. Lightly grease a medium-sized loaf pan.

2) Sift together the flours, baking powder, baking soda, and salt into a medium-large bowl. Make a well in the center.

3) In a separate container, beat together the yogurt, melted butter, eggs, and honey or sugar. Pour this mixture into the dry ingredients, along with the herbs. Mix with a wooden spoon until thoroughly blended.

4) Spread into the prepared pan, and bake for 40 to 45 minutes, or until a knife inserted all the way into the center comes out clean. Let it sit for about 5 minutes, then rap the pan sharply to remove the bread. Cool on a rack for at least 20 minutes before slicing.

Apple Bread

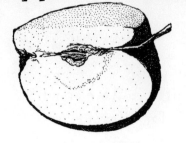

20 minutes to prepare;
50 minutes to bake.

Yield: 1 medium-sized
loaf

NOTE: Use a food processor to grate the apples, and this delicious bread will take no time to throw together.

a little butter or oil for the pan
1½ packed cups peeled, grated tart apple
3 Tbs. fresh lemon juice
½ tsp. grated lemon rind
½ cup light brown sugar
4 Tbs. melted butter
1 egg
2 cups unbleached white flour
2½ tsp. baking powder
½ tsp. baking soda
½ tsp. salt
1 tsp. cinnamon
1 tsp. vanilla extract
½ cup minced nuts

1) Preheat oven to 350°F. Lightly grease a medium-sized loaf pan.

2) Combine the grated apple, lemon juice, and lemon rind in a medium-sized bowl. Beat in the sugar, butter, and egg.

3) Sift together the flour, baking powder, baking soda, salt, and cinnamon into another medium-sized bowl. Make a well in the center, and add the apple mixture, along with the vanilla and the nuts. Stir with a rubber spatula or a wooden spoon until just combined.

4) Spread into the prepared pan. Bake for about 50 minutes, or until a knife inserted all the way into the center comes out clean. Cool in the pan for about 10 minutes, then rap the pan sharply and remove the bread. Cool on a rack for about 30 minutes before slicing.

Cottage Cheese~Dill Bread

15 minutes to prepare;
about 50 minutes to bake.

Yield: 1 medium-sized loaf

Good with a little cream cheese and thin slices of cucumber.
Also very good lightly toasted and spread with raspberry preserves.

a little butter or oil for the pan
2 cups unbleached white flour
2 tsp. baking powder
½ tsp. baking soda
a scant ½ tsp. salt
1 cup cottage cheese
2 eggs
6 Tbs. milk
¼ cup honey or sugar
4 Tbs. melted butter
3 Tbs. minced fresh dill
  (or 1 Tbs. dried)

1) Preheat oven to 350°F. Lightly grease a medium-sized loaf pan.

2) Sift together the flour, baking powder, baking soda, and salt into a medium-large bowl. Make a well in the center.

3) Combine the cottage cheese, eggs, milk, sweetening, and melted butter in a separate bowl and beat well. Add this to the dry ingredients along with the dill, and mix just enough to thoroughly blend. The batter will be fairly stiff.

4) Take your time as you spread it evenly into the prepared pan. Let it bake for 50 minutes, or until a knife inserted all the way into the center comes out clean. Remove from the pan after about 10 minutes, and cool on a rack for another 30 or so before slicing.

Zucchini ∞ Spice Bread

20 minutes to prepare;
50 to 60 minutes to bake.
(Use a food processor to
grate the zucchini.)

Yield:
1 medium-sized
loaf

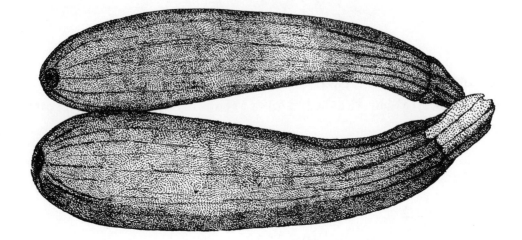

a little butter or oil for the pan

2 cups (packed) coarsely grated
    zucchini
6 Tbs. melted butter
⅓ cup sugar
2 eggs
1½ tsp. vanilla extract

1 cup unbleached white flour
1 cup whole wheat flour
¾ tsp. salt
2½ tsp. baking powder
¼ tsp. nutmeg
¾ tsp. allspice
1 tsp. cinnamon
½ tsp. ground ginger

½ cup chopped nuts
½ cup currants

1) Preheat oven to 350°F. Lightly grease a medium-sized loaf pan.
2) Place the grated zucchini in a colander in the sink. Let it stand for about
   10 minutes, then squeeze out all excess moisture.
3) Beat together the butter, sugar, eggs, and vanilla in a large bowl.
4) In a separate medium-sized bowl sift together the dry ingredients.
5) Add the sifted dry ingredients, alternately with the zucchini, to the butter-
   egg mixture, beginning and ending with the dry. Stir in nuts and currants.
6) Spread the batter into the prepared pan. Bake 50 to 60 minutes, or until a
   knife inserted all the way into the center comes out clean. Remove from
   the pan after about 10 minutes, then cool on a rack for another 30 before
   slicing.

Green Chile & Cheese
Corn Bread

10 minutes to assemble;
30 to 35 minutes to bake.

NOTE: You can use ¼ cup diced
canned green chiles instead of
fresh. Sauté for about 2 minutes.

a little butter or oil for the pan
3 Tbs. butter or olive oil
1 medium-sized poblano or Anaheim chile, seeded and minced
½ cup unbleached white flour
2 tsp. baking powder
1 tsp. baking soda
½ tsp. salt
1½ cups yellow cornmeal
¼ cup light-colored honey
1 egg
1 cup firm yogurt
⅓ cup (packed) grated jack cheese

1) Preheat oven to 350°F. Lightly grease an 8-inch square pan or its equivalent.

2) Melt 3 Tbs. butter (or heat 3 Tbs. olive oil) in a small skillet. Add the minced chile and sauté over medium heat for about 5 minutes, or until tender. Remove from heat and set aside.

3) Sift the flour, baking powder, baking soda, and salt into a medium-sized mixing bowl. Stir in the cornmeal, and make a well in the center.

4) In a separate bowl, beat together the honey, egg, and yogurt. Pour this mixture into the well in the center of the dry ingredients. Add the sautéed chiles with all their butter or oil, and sprinkle in the grated cheese. Mix with a wooden spoon, blending as well as possible with a few quick strokes.

5) Spread into the prepared pan, and bake for 30 to 35 minutes, or until the center springs back when touched. Cool for 10 minutes before serving.

Cranberry Brown Bread

20 minutes to prepare:
40 to 45 minutes to bake.

Yield: 1 medium-sized loaf.

a little butter or oil for the pan
½ cup (1 stick) butter
½ tsp. cinnamon
1½ cups cranberries, coarsely chopped
⅓ cup minced walnuts
1 cup whole wheat flour
1 cup unbleached white flour

2 tsp. baking powder
½ tsp. baking soda
½ tsp. salt
2 eggs
½ cup orange juice
½ tsp. vanilla extract
⅓ cup molasses
⅓ cup brown sugar

1) Preheat oven to 350°F. Lightly grease a medium-sized loaf pan.

2) Melt ½ cup butter in a medium-sized skillet. Add cinnamon, cranberries, and walnuts, and cook over medium heat, stirring often, for 8 to 10 minutes. Remove from heat and set aside.

3) Sift together flours, powder, soda, and salt into a medium-large bowl.

4) Combine eggs, orange juice, vanilla, molasses, and brown sugar in a separate bowl and beat well. Add this mixture to the dry ingredients, along with the cranberries (be sure to scrape in all the butter). Stir until completely combined.

5) Spread into the prepared pan, and bake for 40 to 45 minutes, or until a knife inserted all the way in comes out clean. Cool in the pan for 10 minutes, then rap the pan sharply to remove. Cool at least 30 minutes on a rack before slicing.

Oatmeal~Maple Bread

20 minutes to prepare;
50 to 60 minutes to bake.

Yield: 1 medium-sized loaf

Lemony and just sweet enough, this bread could double as a light cake for tea or dessert.

a little butter or oil for the pan
1½ cups rolled oats
2 cups unbleached white flour
½ tsp. baking soda
1½ tsp. baking powder
3/4 tsp. salt
2 eggs

½ cup real maple syrup
1 cup buttermilk or yogurt
1 tsp. vanilla extract
½ tsp. grated lemon rind
2 Tbs. fresh lemon juice
4 Tbs. melted butter

1) Preheat oven to 350°F. Lightly grease a medium-sized loaf pan.

2) Place the oats in a blender, and grind to a coarse flour (about 20 seconds at medium speed). Set aside.

3) Sift together the flour, soda, powder, and salt into a medium-large bowl. Stir in the ground oats, and make a well in the center.

4) In a separate container, beat together the eggs, maple syrup, buttermilk or yogurt, vanilla, lemon rind, lemon juice, and melted butter. Pour this mixture into the well in the dry ingredients, and mix with a rubber spatula or wooden spoon until well combined.

5) Turn into the prepared pan, and bake for 50 to 60 minutes, or until a knife inserted all the way into the center comes out clean. Cool in the pan for 10 minutes, then remove by rapping the pan sharply. Cool 30 more minutes before slicing, or it will seriously crumble.

Muffins

Just-baked muffins have a way of instantly putting everyone in a good mood. As you linger in bed some morning when you don't have to be anywhere too early, consider this: fresh muffins could be emerging from your own oven in less than 40 minutes. What a mind-boggling revelation! Assuming you have the ingredients, all you have to do is get up and put them together.

Corn & Molasses Muffins

10 minutes to prepare;
15 to 20 minutes to bake.

Yield:
about 1 dozen
2½-inch muffins

a little butter or oil for the pan
   (if not nonstick)
1½ cups unbleached white flour
½ tsp. baking soda
2 tsp. baking powder
a scant ½ tsp. salt
1 cup yellow corn meal

1½ cups milk
   (lowfat or soy OK)
1 egg
5 Tbs. melted butter
4 Tbs. dark molasses
3 Tbs. sugar
a dash of cinnamon

1) Preheat oven to 375°F. Lightly grease 12 muffin cups, unless they're nonstick.

2) Sift together flour, soda, powder, and salt into a medium-sized bowl. Stir in the corn meal, and make a well in the center.

3) In a separate container, beat together the remaining ingredients. Pour this mixture into the dry ingredients, and stir just enough to combine thoroughly.

4) Fill the muffin cups just up to the edge of the pan. Bake for 15 to 20 minutes, or until a toothpick inserted all the way into the center comes out clean. Remove the muffins from the pan right away, and cool on a rack for at least 10 minutes before eating.

Pecan-Oat Muffins

20 minutes to prepare;
15 to 20 minutes to bake.

Yield:
about a dozen
2½-inch
muffins

a little butter or oil for the pan
   (if it's not nonstick)
¾ cup minced pecans
1 cup rolled oats
1½ cups unbleached white flour
½ tsp. baking soda
1½ tsp. baking powder
¼ tsp. salt (rounded measure)
1 cup buttermilk or yogurt
1 egg
4 Tbs. melted butter
6 Tbs. brown sugar
½ tsp. vanilla extract

1) Preheat oven to 350°F. Lightly grease 12 muffin cups, if they're not nonstick.

2) Place the pecans and oats in a medium-sized cast-iron skillet, and dry-roast over low heat for about 10 minutes, stirring frequently. When the oats are lightly browned and the mixture smells engagingly toasty, remove from heat and set aside.

3) Sift together flour, soda, powder, and salt into a medium-sized bowl. Stir in the toasted oats and pecans, and make a well in the center.

4) In a separate container, beat together the remaining ingredients, and pour this mixture into the well. Mix just enough to blend.

5) Fill the muffin cups ⅔ full, and bake for 15 to 20 minutes, or until a toothpick inserted all the way into the center comes out clean. Remove the muffins from the pan right away, but for optimal flavor and texture, wait about 10 minutes before eating.

✿ ✿ ✿ Orange~Date Muffins ✿ ✿ ✿

20 minutes to prepare;
15 to 20 minutes to bake.

a little butter or oil for the pan
   (if it's not nonstick)

1 medium-sized seedless orange
1½ cups unbleached white flour
½ cup whole wheat flour
½ tsp. baking soda
1 tsp. baking powder
¼ tsp. (rounded measure) salt

1½ cups buttermilk or yogurt
1 egg
3 Tbs. melted butter
3 Tbs. brown sugar
½ tsp. vanilla extract
½ cup chopped, pitted dates
OPTIONAL: ½ cup minced nuts

1) Preheat oven to 375°F. Lightly grease 12 muffin cups, unless they're nonstick.

2) Grate enough of the orange rind to fill ½ teaspoon. Set this aside; remove and discard the remaining orange peel. Section the orange into a small bowl, and cut the sections into smaller pieces. Save all the juice.

3) Sift together the flours, soda, powder, and salt into a medium-sized bowl, and make a well in the center.

4) Beat together the buttermilk or yogurt, egg, melted butter, sugar, and vanilla in a separate container. Add this to the dry ingredients, along with the orange pieces (plus all their juice), the grated orange rind, the dates, and optional nuts. Stir until thoroughly combined.

5) Fill the muffin cups just to the rim, and bake for 15 to 20 minutes, or until a toothpick inserted all the way into the center comes out clean. Remove the muffins from the pan right away, and cool on a rack for at least 10 minutes before eating.

Blueberry Muffins

10 minutes to prepare;
15 to 20 minutes to bake.

Yield: about a dozen
2½-inch muffins

a little butter or oil for the pan
   (if it's not nonstick)
1½ cups unbleached white flour
½ tsp. baking soda
1 tsp. baking powder
½ tsp. salt
½ tsp. grated lemon rind
⅓ cup sugar
4 Tbs. melted butter
¾ cup milk (lowfat ok)
1 egg
3 Tbs. fresh lemon juice
1 cup blueberries (fresh or
   unsweetened frozen,
   defrosted and drained)

1) Preheat oven to 350°F. Lightly grease 12 muffin cups, unless they're nonstick.

2) Sift together the flour, baking soda, baking powder, and salt into a medium-sized bowl. Make a well in the center.

3) In a separate container, beat together all remaining ingredients except the berries. Pour this mixture into the well, and stir gently until blended, gradually adding the berries. Fill the muffin cups just to the rim.

4) Bake 15 to 20 minutes, or until a toothpick inserted all the way into the center comes out clean. Remove the muffins from the pan right away; cool on a rack for 10 minutes before devouring.

Apricot-Bran Muffins

15 minutes to prepare;
15 to 20 minutes to bake.

Yield:
about 1 dozen
2½-inch muffins

a little butter or oil for the pan
   (if it's not nonstick)
1 cup unbleached white flour
a scant ½ tsp. salt
½ tsp. baking soda
1 tsp. baking powder
1 cup unprocessed wheat bran
1 cup buttermilk or yogurt
1 egg
4 Tbs. melted butter
3 Tbs. brown sugar
⅓ cup chopped dried apricots (the plump kind,
   not the very dry, shriveled ones)
OPTIONAL: ¼ cup minced walnuts
              ¼ cup raisins
              1 cup peeled, chopped tart apple

1) Preheat oven to 350°F. Lightly grease 12 muffin cups, unless they're nonstick.

2) Sift together the flour, salt, baking soda, and baking powder into a medium-sized bowl. Stir in the bran, and make a well in the center.

3) In a separate container, beat together the liquid ingredients and the sugar, and pour this into the well in the dry mixture. Add the fruit and nuts, and stir just enough to thoroughly combine.

4) Fill the cups just to the rim. Bake 15 to 20 minutes, or until a tooth-pick inserted all the way into the center comes out clean. Remove the muffins from the pan right away, and cool on a rack for about 10 minutes before eating.

Glazed Lemon Muffins

15 minutes to prepare;
15 to 20 minutes to bake.
(Add another 10 minutes
for glazing.)

Yield:
about 1 dozen
2½-inch muffins

a little butter or oil for the pan
(if it's not nonstick)

6 Tbs. brown sugar
4 Tbs. melted butter
1 cup yogurt
1 egg
¼ cup fresh lemon juice
½ tsp. grated lemon rind
2 cups unbleached white flour
a few dashes of nutmeg
¾ tsp. baking soda
2 tsp. baking powder
¼ tsp. salt

DELIGHTFUL OPTIONAL
ADDITIONS:
½ cup minced nuts
1 cup raspberries (fresh,
or frozen unsweetened—
defrosted and drained)

GLAZE:
5 Tbs. granulated sugar
¼ cup fresh lemon juice
½ tsp. grated lemon rind

1) Preheat oven to 375°F. Lightly grease 12 muffin cups, if they're
   not nonstick.
2) Combine the brown sugar, melted butter, yogurt, egg, lemon juice,
   and lemon rind in a medium-sized bowl and beat well.
3) In a separate medium-sized bowl, sift together the dry ingredients.
   Make a well in the center, and pour in the wet mixture. Stir briefly, in quick, decisive strokes. If you so desire, stir in the optional
   nuts and/or raspberries.
4) Fill the muffin cups just up to the rim. Bake for 15 to
   20 minutes, or until a toothpick inserted all the way into the
   center comes out clean. Remove the muffins from the pan right
   away, and cool on a rack for about 10 minutes before glazing.
5) To prepare the glaze, combine the glaze ingredients in a small saucepan. Bring to a boil and lower heat to a simmer. Let it cook for
   5 minutes, then remove from heat and let it cool for 5 minutes.
   Spoon about 1 to 2 tsp. glaze onto the top of each muffin —it
   will soak in. Let the glazed muffins stand for about 10 minutes
   before serving.

OLIVE-STUDDED FOCCACIA

Preparation time:
About 2 hours
(mostly rising time)

Yield:
4 to 6
servings

1 cup wrist-temperature water
1 ½ tsp. active dry yeast
1 tsp. salt
2 Tbs. olive oil, plus extra for the bowl and the dough
approximately 3 cups unbleached white flour
2 to 3 Tbs. dried rosemary
extra flour for handling the dough and for the baking tray
1 cup pitted Kalamata (Greek) olives

1) Place the water in a medium-sized bowl and sprinkle in the yeast. Let it stand for 5 minutes. (It will become foamy.)

2) Stir in the salt and 2 Tbs. olive oil.

3) Add the flour, one cup at a time, beating it in with a whisk. Crumble in the rosemary with the last cup of flour. As the dough thickens, switch from the whisk to a wooden spoon and, eventually, your hand. Knead the dough right in the bowl for a few minutes, adding small amounts of additional flour, as needed, to prevent stickiness. When the dough is smooth, oil both the bowl and the top surface of the dough. Cover the bowl with a clean tea towel, and let the dough rise in a warm place for an hour or so, or until doubled in bulk.

4) Punch down the dough, and transfer it to a clean, floured surface. Let it rest for about 10 minutes, then gently stretch the relaxed dough into an oval about 14 inches long and 9 inches wide. Let it rest for another 10 minutes or so. In the meantime, preheat the oven to 400°F. Sprinkle a baking tray with flour.

5) Transfer the oval of dough to the floured baking tray, and stretch or pull the dough back into shape, if necessary. Brush the top surface with olive oil, then scatter the olives over the top, poking each one into the dough with your finger.

6) Bake for 20 to 30 minutes, or until lightly browned. Serve hot, warm, or at room temperature.

chappatis

This simple Indian flatbread is basically the same as a Chinese Mushu pancake or a flour tortilla, except that a Chappati is usually made with the addition of some whole wheat flour.

In India, experienced chappati-makers can slap the dough into thin, supple pancakes with their bare hands. For most of us Westerners, however, a rolling pin is necessary.

Traditional Indian meals consist of numerous courses served all at the same time. Chappatis are a standard bread, appropriately served with any combination of Indian dishes. (See pages 199 - 201.) You can make the dough and roll the pancakes in advance, and cook them shortly before serving, so they'll be fresh and hot.

½ cup unbleached white flour, plus extra for handling the dough
½ cup whole wheat pastry flour
a scant ½ tsp. salt
½ cup water
peanut oil or canola oil for the pan
2 Tbs. melted butter

1) Place ½ cup of each kind of flour in a medium-sized bowl. Sprinkle in the salt, and mix it in.

2) Add the water, and stir until fairly well combined. The dough will be soft.

3) Transfer the dough to a clean, floured surface. Knead it for a few minutes, sprinkling on extra flour, as necessary, to keep it from becoming too sticky.

4) Divide the dough into 4 equal balls, and roll each one into a very thin circle (about ⅛ inch thick). Use a lot of flour, both on the work surface and on the rolling pin.

5) Heat a heavy skillet or a griddle for a few minutes. Add a small amount of oil (easiest to brush it on), and cook the chappatis, one or two at a time, for about 3 minutes on the first side. Flip the chappatis over, and cook for only 1 to 2 minutes on the second side, so they won't become too crisp. Brush on both sides with melted butter, and serve right away.

Whole Wheat-Buttermilk
Biscuits

30 minutes
to prepare;
10-12 minutes
to bake.

Yield: 3 dozen.

Preheat oven to 450°F.

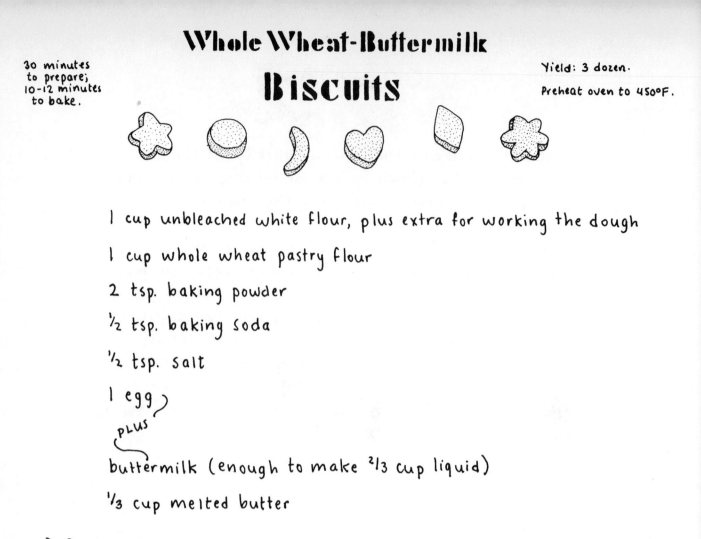

1 cup unbleached white flour, plus extra for working the dough

1 cup whole wheat pastry flour

2 tsp. baking powder

½ tsp. baking soda

½ tsp. salt

1 egg

PLUS

buttermilk (enough to make ⅔ cup liquid)

⅓ cup melted butter

1) Preheat oven to 450°F.

2) Combine the dry ingredients in a medium-sized bowl. Make a well in the center.

3) Break the egg into a liquid measuring cup, and beat the egg until frothy. Add enough buttermilk to make ⅔ cup.

4) Pour the buttermilk-egg mixture into the well in the dry ingredients, and add the melted butter as well. Stir until all the dry ingredients are dampened, then turn out onto a floured surface, and knead the dough briefly until it is uniform and smooth.

5) Flour the work surface again, then roll or pat the dough into a large oval about ½ inch thick. Use a knife or large cookie cutters to cut the dough into your desired shapes.

6) Bake on an ungreased tray for 10 to 12 minutes, or until puffy and lightly browned. Serve hot.

Sauces, Dips, and Spreads

SAUCES, DIPS, & SPREADS
Table of Contents

 **Light meals**

are becoming a way of life for more and more people. The recipes in this chapter are intended to give you some fresh and, I hope, inspiring suggestions for making complete meals out of plain cooked pasta, beans, or grains, as well as raw or steamed vegetables, whole grain crackers, and breads. A dip, sauce, or spread will be all you need to transform these things into quick, satisfying, light lunches or suppers. (The dips also make great healthy snacks for any time of day.) Everything in this chapter is easy to prepare and will keep for at least several days (and in many cases longer).

Pesto

Sweet Basil

10 minutes to prepare.

This most famous version of pesto is a powerful-tasting paste made from fresh basil and garlic, moistened with olive oil, sharpened by the presence of cheese, and —if desired— subtly textured with pulverized nuts. It is most commonly used as a sauce for pasta, yet it lends itself beautifully to many other dishes as a seasoning (see index). Pesto keeps well in the refrigerator for up to several weeks, so you can keep it on hand to use spontaneously.

> 3 packed cups fresh basil leaves
> 3 to 4 large cloves garlic
> 1/3 cup lightly toasted pine nuts
>   or walnuts (optional)
> 1/3 cup olive oil
> 1/3 cup grated parmesan
> salt   } to taste
> freshly ground black pepper

1) Place the basil leaves and garlic in a food processor or blender, and mince well.

2) Add the nuts, if desired, and continue to blend until the nuts are finely ground.

3) Keep the machine running as you drizzle in the olive oil. When you have a smooth paste, transfer to a bowl, and stir in the parmesan. Season to taste with salt and pepper.

4) To serve on pasta, place room-temperature Pesto in a warmed serving bowl. Add hot pasta and toss thoroughly. (Allow 2 to 3 Tbs. Pesto per serving.)

Marinated Tomato Sauce

10 minutes to prepare, plus at least 30 minutes to marinate.

Yield: Enough for 5 or 6 servings of pasta (3/4 to 1 lb. dry pasta) — or 5 or 6 appetizer servings.

Here is a simple uncooked tomato sauce to celebrate the peak of the harvest. Spoon room-temperature sauce over hot pasta or rice. Or just serve it as an appetizer, accompanied by some fresh crusty bread to mop up the juices.

BASIC SAUCE:
2 to 3 lbs. ripe tomatoes
1/2 tsp. salt
1 large clove garlic, minced
3 to 4 Tbs. extra-virgin olive oil
1 to 2 Tbs. red wine or balsamic vinegar
12 to 15 leaves fresh basil, minced
freshly ground black pepper

OPTIONAL ADDITIONS & EMBELLISHMENTS:

Use all, some, or none.
- 1/2 lb. fresh mozzarella cheese, in small cubes
- a handful of Niçoise olives
- 1/2 cup finely minced red onion
- 1/2 cup minced fresh parsley
- 1 to 2 Tbs. minced anchovies
- 1 to 2 Tbs. capers
- 3 to 4 Tbs. lightly toasted pine nuts

1) PEEL AND SEED THE TOMATOES (optional—not necessary for smaller ones): Bring a medium-sized saucepanful of water to a boil, then lower heat to a simmer. Core the tomatoes, and drop them into the water for a slow count of 20 (less, if the tomatoes are very ripe). Retrieve them, and peel off the skins. Cut them open, and squeeze out and discard the seeds. Coarsely chop the remaining pulp. NOTE: If you are using smaller tomatoes, or you've chosen not to peel and seed larger ones, just cut the tomatoes into bite-sized pieces and place them in a medium-large bowl.

2) Add all other ingredients and stir gently. Cover and let marinate—in the refrigerator or at room temperature—for at least 30 minutes.

Pepper Sauce

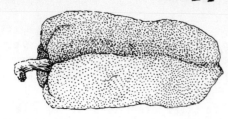 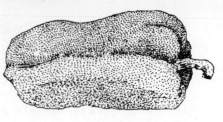

15 minutes to prepare.

Yield: 6 servings
(Enough for 1 lb. pasta)

Serve this sauce hot, with freshly cooked pasta or with rice. This also tastes good at room temperature or cold, spooned over thick slices of toasted sourdough bread.

NOTE: If you're serving Pepper Sauce over pasta, the ideal coordination between sauce and pasta preparation is to have the pasta water boiling as you begin the sauce. Cook the pasta as you sauté the peppers. Everything should be ready at the same time.

6 medium-sized bell peppers (assorted colors)
3 Tbs. olive oil
½ tsp. salt
½ tsp. dried oregano
2 tsp. dried thyme
1 large clove garlic, minced
freshly ground black pepper ⎱
crushed red pepper   ⎰ to taste
1 to 2 Tbs. red wine or balsamic vinegar

1) Cut the peppers in half lengthwise. Remove the stems, seeds, and membranes. Slice the peppers into thin strips.

2) Heat the olive oil in a large, deep skillet or a Dutch oven. Add the peppers, salt, and herbs, and cook over medium heat for about 5 minutes, or until the peppers are just barely tender. Add the garlic, and cook for 5 minutes longer.

3) Stir in black pepper, crushed red pepper, and vinegar to taste. Remove from heat and serve.

Artichoke Sauce
with
mushrooms & greens

15 minutes to prepare.

Yield: 5 or 6 servings
(Enough for 1 lb. pasta.)

Serve this luxurious sauce over pasta, plain cooked rice, or baked potatoes.

NOTE: Use any kind of leafy green in addition to (or in place of) kale or collard greens. (Try spinach, escarole, or chard.)

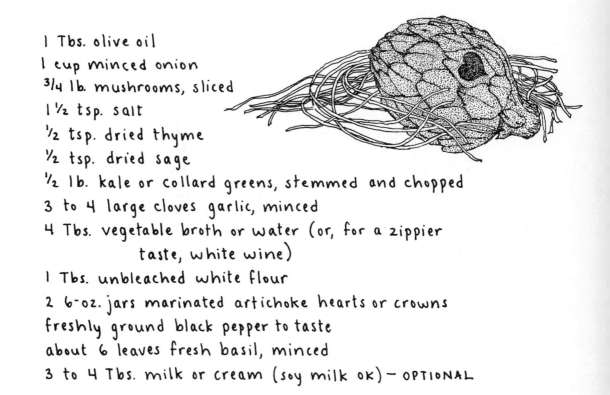

1 Tbs. olive oil
1 cup minced onion
3/4 lb. mushrooms, sliced
1½ tsp. salt
½ tsp. dried thyme
½ tsp. dried sage
½ lb. kale or collard greens, stemmed and chopped
3 to 4 large cloves garlic, minced
4 Tbs. vegetable broth or water (or, for a zippier
                    taste, white wine)
1 Tbs. unbleached white flour
2 6-oz. jars marinated artichoke hearts or crowns
freshly ground black pepper to taste
about 6 leaves fresh basil, minced
3 to 4 Tbs. milk or cream (soy milk ok) — OPTIONAL

1) Heat the olive oil in a large, deep skillet or Dutch oven. Add the onion and sauté for about 2 minutes over medium heat. Add the mushrooms, ½ tsp. salt, thyme, and sage. Stir and cook over medium heat for about 5 minutes, then add the greens, garlic, and remaining salt. Stir, cover, and cook another 5 minutes over medium heat.

2) Add the broth, water, or wine, and wait until it bubbles. Sprinkle in the flour, stirring as you sprinkle. Cook uncovered for another minute or two, stirring constantly. The liquid will thicken.

3) Cut the artichokes into bite-sized pieces. Add these to the skillet, along with all the liquid from the jars. Grind in some black pepper, stir in the basil, and, if desired, stir in the milk or cream. Remove from heat and serve.

Spiked Mushroom Sauce

30 minutes to prepare.

Yield: about 2½ cups

3 Tbs. butter or canola oil
1 lb. mushrooms, thinly sliced
½ tsp. salt (more, to taste)
3 Tbs. brandy or dry sherry
3 Tbs. unbleached white flour
1½ cups warmed milk
   (lowfat or soy OK)
freshly ground black pepper

1) Melt the butter or heat the oil in a medium-sized skillet. Add mushrooms and salt, and cook over medium heat for about 10 minutes, stirring occasionally.
2) Add brandy or sherry, and cook for 5 minutes more.
3) Gradually sprinkle in the flour as you whisk the mushroom mixture. Whisk and cook for another 5 minutes over medium heat.
4) Stir in the warmed milk. Cook over low heat, stirring often, until thickened and smooth (about 5 more minutes). Season to taste with black pepper and additional salt, if necessary.

Dilled Horseradish Sauce

10 minutes to prepare.

Yield: about 1½ cups

2 Tbs. butter or canola oil
1 to 2 Tbs. unbleached white flour
   (depending on desired thickness)
1¼ cups warmed milk
   (lowfat or soy OK)

1 Tbs. prepared horseradish
a scant ½ tsp. salt
1 Tbs. minced fresh dill
   (or 1½ tsp. dried)
freshly ground black pepper to taste

1) Melt the butter or heat the oil in a medium-small saucepan. Whisk in the flour, and cook over low heat, whisking often, for about a minute.
2) Whisk in the milk, and continue to cook over low heat, whisking frequently for another 5 minutes. Stir in horseradish and salt, and remove from heat. Stir in the dill and black pepper just before serving.

Miso-Walnut Sauce

Warning: This exquisite, unusual, and very easy sauce could become habit-forming!

15 minutes to prepare.   Yield: about 2 cups

❧   Good on plain cooked greens, or on a variety of steamed vegetables over grains or noodles.

❧   You have the option of making this with apple juice or with mirin (Japanese cooking sake, available in most Asian groceries and in the imported foods section of many supermarkets). Miso-Walnut Sauce tastes more intense and slightly sweeter if made with mirin, but is very good made either way. (You can also make it with half apple juice and half mirin – very yummy!)

❧ NOTE: This keeps a long time if stored in a covered container in the refrigerator. Reheat very gently before using.

❧ ABOUT MISO: Miso is a paste made from aged, fermented soybeans and grains. There are many varieties, and any of them can be used in this recipe. Miso is sold at most Asian groceries and at natural foods stores. It keeps almost indefinitely.

2 cups mirin or apple juice

4 Tbs. miso

2 cups chopped, toasted walnuts

1 Tbs. cider or rice vinegar
   (increase slightly if using mirin)

2 small cloves garlic, minced

salt

cayenne } to taste

1) Place the mirin or apple juice in a small saucepan and bring to a boil. (If using mirin, let it simmer uncovered for about 5 minutes to let the alcohol partially evaporate.) Remove from heat, add the miso, and whisk until it is mostly dissolved. (It doesn't have to be absolutely uniform.) Transfer to a blender or food processor.

2) Add the toasted walnuts, and purée until fairly smooth. Transfer to a medium-sized bowl.

3) Stir in the vinegar and garlic. (If you are using mirin, you might want to add an extra 2 tsp. vinegar to cut the sweetness a little.) Add salt and cayenne to taste.

4) Serve the sauce warm or at room temperature over hot, freshly steamed vegetables and/or cooked grains and/or noodles.

DIPS

Dips: foods mashed with seasonings to a harmonious consistency— readily spreadable or pick-up-able with raw or steamed vegetables or crackers or chips. Dips as appetizers or lunches .... dips as dinner. These are very easy to make and even easier to eat.

Almond-Orange Dip

10 minutes
to prepare.

Yield:
about
3 cups

NOTE: Silken tofu is a very smooth variety that comes packed in 10-oz. boxes. Look for it in natural foods stores, in Asian groceries, and in many supermarkets.

1 12-oz. box silken tofu
1 cup almond butter
2/3 cup orange juice
2 tsp. grated fresh ginger
1 medium clove garlic, minced
1 tsp. soy sauce

2 Tbs. minced fresh parsley
2 Tbs. minced fresh chives
1/2 tsp. grated orange rind
3/4 tsp. salt
fresh black pepper } to taste
cayenne

1) Combine all ingredients in a blender or food processor and purée until smooth.

2) Season to taste, cover, and refrigerate until cold.

PEANUT DIP WITH TOFU

10 minutes to prepare. ...Mild and light. Yield: 2 cups

NOTE: Silken tofu is explained in the introduction to Almond-Orange Dip (opposite page).

⅓ cup good peanut butter

¼ cup hot water

1 10-oz. box silken tofu

2 Tbs. cider vinegar

1 Tbs. soy sauce

1 medium clove garlic, minced

½ tsp. salt

2 tsp. grated fresh ginger

cayenne to taste

about 2 Tbs. minced cilantro

a little honey or sugar to taste

½ cup finely minced toasted peanuts

} OPTIONAL

1) Put everything except the optional minced peanuts in a blender or food processor and purée until smooth and uniform. Transfer to a bowl or a container with a lid, and taste to adjust seasonings. Cover and chill.

2) Top with minced peanuts, if desired, just before serving. Serve with raw and/or lightly steamed vegetables.

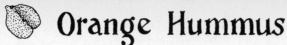 # Orange Hummus

Hummus is a staple in Middle Eastern cuisines. It is a chick-pea purée with tahini, garlic, and lemon. This variation adds some subtle twists: orange juice and vinegar instead of lemon juice, and a medley of what I like to call "the red and yellow spices".

NOTE: Use fresh-squeezed orange juice, if available, and this dip will soar.

2 15-oz. cans chick-peas,
   rinsed and drained

ground cumin
ground coriander
ground ginger   ⎫
dry mustard   ⎬ ½ tsp. each
turmeric   ⎭
mild paprika

¾ cup orange juice
⅓ cup tahini
½ tsp. salt
3 Tbs. cider vinegar
3 medium cloves garlic, minced
1 tsp. soy sauce
cayenne to taste

1) Combine everything in a food processor and purée until smooth. Transfer to a bowl or a container with a lid, cover tightly, and chill.

2) Serve as a dip, surrounded by an array of raw and/or lightly steamed vegetables — or simply with crackers. This also goes beautifully in a toasted pita pocket with minced salad greens and chopped ripe tomatoes.

Mexican Bean Dip

Less than 10 minutes
to prepare.

NOTE 1: A 15-oz. can of beans is equal to approximately 2 cups cooked beans.

NOTE 2: To peel and seed a tomato, lower it into simmering water for 10 to 20 seconds. Retrieve and pull off skin; cut open and squeeze out seeds.

1 15-oz. can pinto beans,
   rinsed and drained
2 Tbs. fresh lime juice
1 medium-sized tomato,
   peeled and seeded
      (See "NOTE", above)
1 to 2 medium cloves garlic

parsley }
cilantro } a handful of each
3/4 tsp. ground cumin
1 scallion, coarsely chopped
1/4 to 1/2 tsp. salt
freshly ground black pepper
cayenne

1) Place everything except the salt, black pepper, and cayenne in a food processor or blender and purée until smooth.

2) Transfer to a bowl, and season to taste. Cover tightly and chill. Serve with chips, vegetables, crackers, or warmed flour tortillas.

Pesto-Bean Dip

5 minutes to prepare.

Yield: 1 1/2 cups

Quick, quick, quick! Instant lunch!

1 15-oz. can white beans (pea or navy), rinsed and drained
3 Tbs. pesto (recipe on p. 104 – or use a good commercial brand)
1 Tbs. red wine or cider vinegar
salt
freshly ground black pepper } to taste
a handful or two of cherry tomatoes,
   halved or quartered (optional)

1) Place the beans, pesto, and vinegar in a food processor or blender, and blend to a paste.

2) Transfer to a bowl, and season to taste with salt and pepper. Stir in the tomatoes, if desired. Cover tightly and chill. Serve as described in Mexican Bean Dip, above.

Tahini Dip

10 minutes
to prepare.

Yield: 1½ cups
(easily doubled)

Tahini is a paste made from sesame seeds. Unlike sesame butter, which is made from toasted whole seeds, tahini is made from hulled raw seeds, giving it a very earthy and pure flavor. This dip (also a spread) is very simple to make and utterly delicious. It will keep for weeks in a tightly covered container in the refrigerator.

1 cup tahini

⅓ cup apple juice

3 Tbs. cider vinegar

2 medium cloves garlic, minced

½ tsp. salt

½ tsp. ground cumin

¼ tsp. cinnamon

¼ tsp. cayenne

1) Place the tahini in a medium-sized mixing bowl. Beat it at high speed with an electric mixer for 5 minutes. Gradually drizzle in the apple juice and vinegar during this time.

2) Stir in the remaining ingredients and adjust seasonings to taste.

3) Serve at room temperature or cold, with raw or lightly steamed vegetables, crackers, and/or wedges of toasted pita bread. This is also a wonderful sandwich spread!

Savory Vegetable Cheesecake (page 202)

Szechwan Tofu Triangles in Triple Pepper Sauce (page 182)

Moroccan Orange-Walnut Salad (page 45)

Coconut & Almond Macaroon Torte (page 257)

PURÉED VEGETABLE DIP

... Very tasty!

30 minutes to prepare,
plus time to chill.

Yield: about
3½ cups

2 Tbs. olive oil
2 cups chopped onion
½ tsp. salt
1½ cups chopped broccoli
1 cup chopped zucchini or summer squash
1 medium-sized bell pepper, diced
2 tsp. dried basil
2 medium cloves garlic, minced
2 Tbs. red wine or balsamic vinegar
freshly ground black pepper to taste
¼ cup toasted sunflower seeds
¼ cup toasted sesame seeds
1 cup finely minced pitted black olives
        (any kind)

1) Heat the oil in a large skillet. Add onion and salt, and sauté over medium heat for about 2 minutes, or until the onion begins to soften.

2) Add broccoli and continue to sauté for another 5 minutes. Add the zucchini or summer squash, bell pepper, basil, and half the garlic, and cook for 5 minutes longer. Remove from heat, stir in the vinegar, and black pepper, and let it sit for about 10 minutes.

3) Add the remaining garlic, transfer to a food processor or blender, and purée until smooth. (Or relatively smooth. It will retain some texture.)

4) Transfer to a bowl, stir in the toasted seeds and minced olives, cover tightly, and chill.

5) Serve with raw and/or steamed vegetables, crackers, and/or chips. Or spread it on bread for a memorable sandwich.

CHUTNEY

Here are some potent condiments to liven up any plain rice-and-bean dinner. These chutneys—the first one hot and tart, the next two sweet and tangy— also go perfectly with any curry. They're quick and simple to make, impressive to eat, and keep for a long time in the refrigerator.

 ## PARSLEY~MINT CHUTNEY

... pungent & potent ...

10 minutes to prepare.   Yield: about 1 potent cup

2 packed cups fresh parsley   ½ tsp. salt
1 Tbs. grated fresh ginger   1 Tbs. fresh lemon juice
5 medium cloves garlic   ½ cup firm yogurt
½ cup fresh mint leaves   cayenne to taste

1) Combine everything except the yogurt and cayenne in a food processor or blender, and purée until it is smooth.

2) Transfer to a bowl and stir in the yogurt. Add cayenne to taste. Cover tightly and refrigerate.

Date & Orange Chutney

35 minutes to prepare.   Yield: about 1 cup

1 medium-sized seedless orange   ⅓ cup cider vinegar
1 packed cup chopped, pitted dates 1 to 2 Tbs. honey (to taste)
1 Tbs. minced or grated fresh ginger cayenne to taste
½ cup water

1) Cut the orange, skin and all, into 1-inch pieces. Place them in a medium-sized saucepan with all the other ingredients except the honey and cayenne.

2) Bring to a boil, then lower the heat to a simmer. Partially cover, and cook over low heat for about 30 minutes, stirring occasionally.

3) Allow to cool for about 20 minutes, then add honey and cayenne to taste. Cover tightly and refrigerate.

Apricot~Lime Chutney

Preparation time:
a few minutes to assemble,
plus 30 minutes to cook.

½ lb. dried apricots (about 2 cups)

1½ cups water (possibly more)

½ cup fresh lime juice

1 tsp. grated lime rind

3 Tbs. honey or brown sugar

a 1-inch knob fresh ginger, thinly sliced

1) Cut the apricots into thin strips. Place them in a medium-sized saucepan with all the other ingredients.

2) Bring to a boil, then lower the heat to a simmer. Partially cover, and cook quietly for 30 minutes. (NOTE: If the apricots are excessively dry, you might want to add a little extra water during the cooking.)

3) Allow to cool for about an hour, then transfer to a lidded container, cover tightly, and refrigerate.

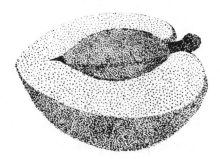

Raita

Preparation time: up to 10 minutes, depending on how many optional ingredients get added.

Yield: about 2½ cups (enough for 4 to 6)

Raita, a lightly spiced yogurt preparation, laced with small touches of minced vegetables, is a traditional side dish in Indian cuisine. Served alongside hotter (both in temperature and in seasoning), heavier dishes, it provides a refreshing contrast. You can serve Raita with just about anything — its use isn't limited to curries and other Indian dishes. It can even be the main dish for a light lunch. Just put in a few extra vegetables, and scoop it up with toasted pita bread.

This is a basic recipe for Raita. All ingredients and amounts are flexible. You can improvise in any direction.

NOTE: To intensify the flavor, you can lightly toast the seeds in a small skillet or toaster oven before adding them to the yogurt.

2 cups firm yogurt
1 tsp. cumin seeds
1 tsp. fennel seeds
salt and cayenne

MANY POSSIBLE ADDITIONS:
minced ripe tomato (seed it first *)
minced or grated cucumber (peel and seed it first)
minced bell pepper (any color)
minced red onion or scallion
minced fresh herbs (cilantro, mint, parsley, chives)
grated carrot
grated beet   } These look beautiful on top.
minced spinach

1) Place the yogurt in a medium-sized bowl. Stir in the seeds; add salt and cayenne to taste.
2) Add as many of the optional additions (or not) as you prefer. Stir it well, and taste to adjust salt. Cover and refrigerate until serving time. Add toppings just before serving.

*TO SEED A TOMATO: Cut it in half and squeeze out the seeds. That's it!

Heated Cheeses

Plain, good cheese is a noble food—simple and sophisticated at the same time. Take this same plain, good, cold or room temperature cheese, and heat it — either to a melted state or just to slightly warmed softness— and watch it acquire the elusive ability to transmit psychological comfort to the person eating it. Cold cheese feels like a snack, but warmed cheese feels like a <u>meal</u>. Melt cheese on bread or steamed vegetables or a baked potato or cooked grains — or melt cheese by itself, and dunk bread into it. (See Greek Melt, below.) Even semisoft cheeses like chèvre, Brie, Camembert, or Rondelé can be heated gently (wrapped in foil, in a low oven for 10 to 20 minutes) and served with bread and/or wedges of fresh fruit. (Try perfectly ripe cantaloupe or pears.)

When you have little else but cheese in the house, and you sense a feeling of deprivation coming on, the answer is: heat the cheese. Chances are you will feel much better.

GREEK MELT

10 minutes to prepare.   Yield: 2 servings (easily multiplied)

> 1 Tbs. olive oil
> ¼ lb. Kasseri (or any medium sharp) cheese, cubed
> 1 medium clove garlic, minced
> 1 to 2 tsp. fresh lemon juice
> Some warm, crusty bread

1) Heat the olive oil in a small, heavy skillet—nonstick, if possible.

2) Distribute the cheese as evenly as possible over the hot oil. Cook over low heat until the cheese is thoroughly melted and beginning to bubble.

3) Sprinkle the cheese with minced garlic and lemon juice. Bring the skillet to the table, set it down on a trivet and serve immediately with some warm, crusty bread.

Swiss Rarebit

Preparation time:
about 30 minutes.

Yield: 4 to 6 servings

This is a delicious mushroom-wine-cheese sauce with a touch of tarragon. Serve it over pumpernickel toast, topped with sprinklings of nutmeg and black pepper, for a comforting lunch or supper.
NOTE: The amount of cheese is flexible.

2 Tbs. butter or olive oil
¾ lb. mushrooms, sliced
½ tsp. salt
3 Tbs. unbleached white flour
1½ cups dry white wine
½ tsp. dried tarragon
5 medium-sized scallions, minced
up to 1 cup grated Swiss cheese (up to ¼ lb.)
thick slices of toasted pumpernickel
freshly grated nutmeg   } to taste
freshly ground black pepper

1) Melt the butter or heat the oil in a large skillet or medium-large sauce-pan. Add the mushrooms and salt, and cook for about 10 minutes over medium heat, stirring frequently.

2) Gradually sprinkle in the flour, stirring constantly. Cook and stir for about 1 minute, then stir in the wine and tarragon. Cover and simmer for about 15 minutes.

3) Shortly before serving, stir in the scallions and cheese. Keep cooking over low heat, stirring, until the cheese is completely melted.

4) To serve, place 4 generous slices of pumpernickel toast on 4 separate plates or in shallow soup bowls. Spoon the Rarebit over the top, grind on some fresh nutmeg and black pepper, and it's ready to eat.

Entrées

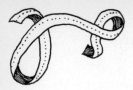

ENTRÉES
Table of Contents

This is a broad unit, therefore it has been divided into sections. The boundaries overlap to some degree (for example, casseroles appear in the "Beans & Grains" section as well as under the "Casseroles, Mélanges, and Other Groupings" heading). However, each section has its own "Table of Contents", so you should be able to find what you're seeking. (For further assistance, check the Appendix (pp. 282-84) and/or the Index (beginning on p. 285). The following page numbers refer you to the tables of contents for all "Entrées" sections:

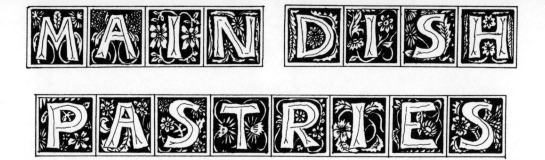

MAIN DISH PASTRIES

AND

Many people assume that quiche-making is a difficult process—for experts only. But this couldn't be further from the truth! A quiche is really a simple, straightforward concoction: a pie crust filled with a few vegetables, some cheese, and an egg custard. It is then baked until firm and served hot, warm, at room temperature, or even cold—for breakfast, brunch, lunch, casual supper, or elegant dinner.

If you can make a pie crust, you can make a quiche. But maybe it's the crust itself, shrouded in mystique, that is intimidating. In the following pages you will find recipes for a variety of both traditional and fanciful pie crusts, spelled out in full detail, so that even the least confident beginner can quickly become proficient.

In the quiche department, instead of giving you an exact recipe, I'm presenting a list of fillings plus custard instructions. This can be a guide for your own improvisations: a formula, wherein you can fill in the blanks. It's more fun and flexible this way, and you can exercise your creative genius (and use up leftover cheeses and vegetables from your refrigerator) in the process.

Following the quiche formula are some recipes for vegetable pies. So what is the difference between a quiche and a vegetable pie? A quiche is built around an egg custard, while a vegetable pie emphasizes other things, like sautéed vegetables (Russian Carrot Pie or Mushroom Pie), vegetable purée (Curried Sweet Potato Pie), or even eggs and potatoes (Devilled Egg Pie with Mashed Potato Crust). These pies can be served as a first course or as a main-dish for a delicious light meal. All the recipes can easily be doubled.

Numerous Pie Crusts

Here, and on the pages that follow, are some pie crusts designed for savory fillings. We begin with a basic pie crust (below), and variations on that theme (next page). Following these are a Coconut Crust plus some unusual ones made with vegetables. These can all be patted into the pan with a fork or fingers, and don't require rolling.

Basic (Regular) Pie Crust

Preparation time: 15 minutes.

Yield: a 9- or 10-inch crust

6 Tbs. cold butter, cut into small pieces
1½ cups flour (can be up to ¼ whole wheat)
about 4 Tbs. cold water, milk, or buttermilk
extra flour for rolling the dough

1) Use a pastry cutter, two forks, or a food processor to cut together the butter and flour until they make a uniform mixture resembling coarse cornmeal. (The food processor will accomplish this in just a few short bursts.)

2) As you stir with a fork (or as the food processor briefly runs) add the liquid, a little at a time, until the dough holds together. The varying humidity will affect the amount of liquid needed.

3) You can now wrap the dough and chill it to roll out later, or you can roll it immediately, using extra flour, as needed, to prevent sticking. Transfer carefully to a 9- or 10-inch pie pan, and form a crust with an edge. If not filling and baking soon, refrigerate until use.

Nut Crust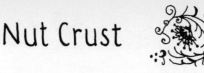

6 Tbs. cold butter, cut into small pieces
1¼ cups flour (use mostly white with
    a little whole wheat)
½ cup finely minced*nuts-of-your-choice
¼ tsp. salt
about 3 to 4 Tbs. cold water

Follow the instructions for Basic Pie Crust (preceding page). Add the nuts and salt in Step 1, and proceed exactly the same.

    * Defining note: "Finely minced" means just this side of ground. Use a blender or food processor in short bursts. (Go lightly, so you don't end up with nut butter.)

 # Cheese Crust

6 Tbs. cold butter, cut into small pieces
1½ cups flour (can be up to ¼ whole wheat)
½ cup grated sharp cheddar
about 4 Tbs. cold water, milk, or buttermilk

Follow the instructions for Basic Pie Crust (preceding page). Stir in the cheese just before adding the liquid in Step 2. Proceed exactly the same with everything else.

 # Poppy Seed-Cheese Crust

Make the Cheese Crust (above) and add 2 Tbs. poppy seeds when you add the cheese.

other additions along these lines:
- Other kinds of hard cheese, grated
- sesame seeds instead of poppy
- Caraway or cumin seeds instead of poppy
- a combination of some or all of the above-mentioned seeds

 # Coconut Crust

Preparation time:
15 minutes

Yield:
a
9- or 10-inch
crust

1 cup flour
5 Tbs. butter
¼ tsp. salt
⅓ cup shredded, unsweetened
   coconut, lightly toasted
2 to 3 Tbs. coconut milk

Follow the instructions for Basic Pie Crust (p.125). Add the salt and coconut in Step 1, and proceed exactly the same.

NOTE: This crust works beautifully for both sweet and savory pies.

 # Spinach Crust

15 minutes to prepare;
15 minutes to bake.

Yield: a 9- or 10-inch
crust

a little oil for the pan
2 Tbs. butter or canola oil
¾ lb. fresh spinach, finely minced
¾ tsp. salt
¾ cup unbleached white flour
¾ cup wheat germ or fine bread crumbs
a few gratings — or dashes — of nutmeg

1) Preheat oven to 375°F. Lightly oil a 9- or 10-inch pie pan.
2) Melt the butter or heat the oil in a large skillet. Add the spinach and salt, and sauté quickly over fairly high heat until the spinach is limp.
3) Remove from heat; add remaining ingredients and mix well.
4) Pat into the oiled pie pan. Use a fork at first, and then your fingers, to mold the crust. Prebake for 15 minutes ~ no need to cool before filling.

MAIN DISH PASTRIES   127

Golden Vegetable Crust

Special Guest Star: PARSNIP! This surprisingly sweet and mild vegetable is often underrated, if not overlooked altogether. Discover it here, and you might find yourself grating it into your salads as well.

a little butter or oil for the pan
2 packed cups grated yellow
    summer squash
½ tsp. salt
½ cup grated carrot

½ cup peeled, grated parsnip
2 Tbs. olive oil or melted butter
    (plus extra to brush on top)
⅓ cup unbleached white flour

1) Preheat oven to 375°F. Lightly grease a 9- or 10-inch pie pan.

2) Place the grated squash in a colander in the sink. Sprinkle with the salt and let it stand 10 minutes. Squeeze out all excess moisture, and transfer to a medium-sized bowl.

3) Add remaining ingredients and mix well. Transfer to the pie pan, and sculpt an attractive crust with a fork (and possibly your fingers).

4) Bake for 40 minutes. Midway through the baking, brush with a little extra olive oil or melted butter. You don't need to cool it before filling.

Mashed Potato Crust

Preparation time: 1 hour, including baking.

(Filling can be made while crust bakes.)

Yield: a 9- or 10-inch crust

4 Tbs. butter, melted (for the
    pan and the top of the crust)
2 large potatoes (about 1 lb.)

2 Tbs. butter
½ tsp. salt
black pepper to taste
½ cup minced onion

1) Preheat oven to 375°F. Brush the bottom of a 9-inch pie pan or springform pan with about half the melted butter.

2) Scrub or peel the potatoes, cut them into chunks, and boil until soft. Drain and transfer to a medium-sized bowl.

3) Add 2 Tbs. butter, salt, pepper, and onion, and mash well.

4) Using a spoon and/or rubber spatula, form a thick crust in the buttered pan.

5) Bake 25 minutes, then brush the top surface with the rest of the melted butter. Bake for 20 minutes longer. You don't need to cool the crust before filling it.

A Quiche Formula

After you have prepared the crust (see preceding pages), there are three more steps involved before the quiche is ready to bake. These are: ① the cheese, ② the filling, and ③ the custard — and they are all easy. Once the crust is prepared, the most difficult part is done.

THE CHEESE:

This is the first layer, which gets deposited (diced or grated) directly on the crust. There is a reason why the cheese goes in first: when it melts, it forms a moisture-resistant barrier between the filling and the crust. This helps to keep the crust flaky and crisp. Recommended cheeses: Swiss varieties (especially Gruyère) and cheddar (sharp or medium-sharp). Use about ¼ to ⅓ pound, depending upon whether it's diced or grated and the size/shape of your pan. (A straight-sided quiche pan is roomier than a pie pan.)

THE FILLING:
(Distribute over the cheese.)

a) **SPINACH** (½ lb. – chopped and steamed), with sautéed onions, dry mustard, and nutmeg

b) **MUSHROOMS** (½ lb. – sliced), sautéed with scallions, oregano, and thyme

c) **ASPARAGUS** (8 to 10 slim stalks – chopped and steamed), with tarragon

d) **BROCCOLI** (1 large stalk, chopped), sautéed with garlic

e) **TOMATO** (1 medium), sliced and sprinkled with basil and dill

f) **FRESH HERBS** (marjoram, thyme, basil, parsley, dill, chives...), small amounts in various combinations, snipped in with scissors

g) **MARINATED ARTICHOKE HEARTS**, drained and chopped

h) You get the idea (it's hard to go wrong).

THE CUSTARD:

Beat together 3 eggs and 1 cup milk. (NOTE: Lowfat or soy milk work fine, as do yogurt or buttermilk.) Pour this over the filling. Dust the top with paprika, and bake at 375°F for 35 to 40 minutes, or until firm. Cool for at least 10 minutes before slicing, and serve at any temperature.

CURRIED SWEET POTATO PIE

WITH COCONUT CRUST

Preparation time:
CRUST = 15 minutes
FILLING = 30 minutes
BAKING = 45 minutes

TOTAL = 1½ hours

Yield:
4 to 5
servings

1¾ lbs. sweet potatoes
⅓ lb. green beans
1 to 2 Tbs. butter
¾ cup minced onion
2 tsp. curry powder
1¼ tsp. salt
½ cup minced Anaheim chiles (2 medium)

2 eggs
½ cup coconut milk
3 to 4 Tbs. fresh lime juice
black pepper, to taste
1 Coconut Crust (p. 127), unbaked in a 10-inch pie pan
3 Tbs. shredded, unsweetened coconut
½ cup minced pecans (optional)

1) Peel the sweet potatoes, and cut them into large chunks. Boil until very soft, drain, and transfer to a medium-large bowl. Mash well and set aside.

2) Trim the green beans, and cut them into ½-inch pieces. Place them in a steamer over boiling water, and cook until just tender. Transfer to a colander in a sink, refresh under cold running water, and set aside to drain. Meanwhile, preheat the oven to 350°F.

3) Melt the butter in a medium-sized skillet. Add the onion, curry powder, and salt, and cook over medium heat, stirring often, until the onion is soft (5 to 8 minutes). Add the chiles, and cook for about 5 minutes longer, or until the chiles wilt. Transfer this mixture to the sweet potatoes, and mix well.

4) Beat together the eggs and coconut milk. Add this to the sweet potatoes, along with the green beans. Add lime juice and black pepper to taste. Mix well, then spread the filling into the unbaked pie crust.

5) Bake for 25 minutes, then sprinkle with coconut and, if desired, minced pecans. Bake another 20 minutes after adding the toppings. Serve hot, warm, or at room temperature.

Russian Carrot Pie

Preparation time:
CRUST = 15 minutes*
FILLING = 30 minutes
BAKING = 45 minutes

TOTAL = 1½ hours

Yield:
4 servings

*NOTE: The crust can be made days ahead and stored in the refrigerator.

1 Tbs. butter
1 cup finely minced onion
½ tsp. salt
1 lb. slender carrots, thinly sliced
2 medium cloves garlic, minced
2 Tbs. fresh lemon juice
1 Tbs. unbleached white flour
1½ cups firm cottage cheese

1 egg
3 Tbs. fine bread crumbs
freshly ground black pepper
3 Tbs. minced fresh dill } or 1½ tsp. dried
3 Tbs. minced fresh mint

1 Nut Crust (p. 126), unbaked
paprika, for the top

1) Preheat oven to 375°F.

2) Melt the butter in a large skillet. Add the onion and salt, and cook over medium heat, stirring frequently, until the onion is soft (about 5 to 8 minutes).

3) Add the carrots, garlic, and lemon juice. Cook and stir until the carrots are tender but not mushy - about 8 more minutes. Sprinkle in the flour, mix well, and cook for about 2 minutes more. Remove from heat.

4) Beat together the cottage cheese and egg in a large bowl. Stir in bread crumbs, black pepper to taste, and fresh herbs. Add the cooked carrot mixture (OK if it's still hot) and mix well. Spread into the crust and dust the top with paprika.

5) Bake for 15 minutes at 375°F., then turn the heat down to 350°F. and bake another 30 minutes. Let it cool for at least 5 minutes before slicing. Serve hot, warm, or at room temperature.

Onion Pie

with **Walnut Crust**

Preparation time:
CRUST = 15 minutes *
FILLING = 30 minutes
BAKING = 1 hour

TOTAL = 1¾ hours

Yield:
4 or 5
servings

*NOTE: The crust can be made days ahead and refrigerated until use.

1 Tbs. canola oil
4 cups thinly sliced onion
1 medium-sized red bell pepper, cut into thin strips
¾ tsp. salt
2 tsp. dry mustard
3 Tbs. fresh lemon juice
3 Tbs. unbleached white flour
3 to 4 Tbs. water, as needed

¾ cup sour cream (lowfat OK)
¾ cup firm yogurt
2 eggs (ok to delete yolks)
1 Tbs. prepared horseradish
2 Tbs. minced fresh parsley
freshly ground black pepper
1 unbaked Nut Crust (p. 126), made with walnuts
2 tsp. caraway seeds
paprika } for the top

1) Preheat oven to 375°F.

2) Heat the oil in a large skillet. Add onion, bell pepper, salt, mustard, and lemon juice. Cook, stirring frequently, over medium heat until the onion softens (about 8 minutes).

3) Sprinkle in the flour, stirring constantly. Stir and cook another 8 to 10 minutes over medium heat, adding water, as needed, to prevent sticking. Remove from heat.

4) In a medium-sized bowl, beat together the sour cream, yogurt, eggs, horseradish, and parsley. Stir this into the pepper-onion mixture and season to taste with black pepper.

5) Pour the filling into the crust, and sprinkle caraway seeds and paprika on top. Bake for 1 hour. Let sit at least 10 minutes before serving. Serve hot, warm, or at room temperature.

Devilled Egg Pie

with mashed potato crust

- Preparation time: 1½ hours
  (less if using hard-boiled eggs)
- Make the filling while the
  crust bakes.

Yield:
about 4
servings

You can make this pie two ways:
1) Bake fresh eggs right in the pie, or
2) Add hard-boiled eggs, and broil it.

1 Mashed Potato Crust (p. 128)	½ tsp. salt for the sauce
2 Tbs. butter	black pepper to taste
4 Tbs. unbleached white flour	1 Tbs. minced fresh dill
1½ cup hot milk (lowfat OK)	4 eggs, fresh or hard-boiled
2 tsp. prepared horseradish	salt, pepper, and paprika
1 tsp. dry mustard	for the top

1) Make and prebake the crust. Set aside. Leave oven on, set to 375°F.

2) Melt the butter in a medium-sized saucepan. Sprinkle in the flour, and cook, whisking over low heat, for about a minute.

3) Gradually drizzle in the hot milk, whisking continuously. Add horseradish, mustard, ½ tsp. salt, and pepper. Whisk steadily, and continue cooking over medium heat until it thickens (5 to 8 minutes). Scrape the bottom and sides intermittently with a rubber spatula. Remove the thickened sauce from the heat, and stir in the fresh dill.

4) If using fresh eggs, preheat the oven to 350°F. If using hard-boiled eggs, preheat the broiler. In either case, spread the sauce in the crust.

FOR FRESH EGGS: Crack open each egg, and arrange them side-by-side on top of the sauce. Sprinkle with a little salt, pepper, and paprika, and bake for 20 to 30 minutes, or until the eggs are set. Serve hot.

FOR HARD-BOILED EGGS: Peel the eggs, then cut them in half lengthwise. Place the halves yolk side up in the filling in a circular design. Sprinkle lightly with salt, pepper, and paprika, and broil for just 3 to 5 minutes, until the sauce is bubbly. Serve hot.

Mushroom Pie

with Spinach Crust

Preparation time:
CRUST = 30 minutes
FILLING = 30 minutes
BAKING = 30 minutes

TOTAL = 1½ hours

Yield:
4 servings

1 Tbs. butter or canola oil
1 cup minced onion
1 tsp. salt
¾ lb. mushrooms, sliced
2 Tbs. fresh lemon juice
3 Tbs. unbleached white flour
2 tsp. dry mustard
1 tsp. dried basil
½ tsp. dried thyme

1 egg
1 cup firm yogurt
fresh black pepper to taste
½ cup grated Swiss cheese (optional)
½ cup minced fresh parsley
1 Spinach Crust (p. 127), prebaked

extra Swiss cheese (optional) } for the top
paprika

1) Preheat oven to 350°F.

2) Melt the butter or heat the oil in a large, deep skillet. Add onion and salt, and cook until the onion begins to soften (5 to 8 minutes).

3) Add the mushrooms and lemon juice. Cook, stirring often, over medium heat about 5 to 8 minutes more.

4) Gradually sprinkle in the flour, mustard, and herbs, stirring as you go. Cook and stir over medium heat another 5 minutes. Set aside.

5) Beat together the egg, yogurt, black pepper, cheese, and parsley in a medium-large bowl. Beat in the mushroom sauté.

6) Pour the filling into the prebaked crust. Top with extra cheese, if desired, and dust with paprika. Bake for 30 minutes. Allow to cool for at least 10 minutes before cutting. Serve hot or warm.

Working with Strudel~Leaf Pastry

Strudel dough (also called filo or phyllo leaves) is available commercially in many groceries, especially those emphasizing Mediterranean cuisine. Filo comes frozen or refrigerated in long, rectangular one-pound packages. Once thawed, unwrapped, and unrolled, the package becomes a neat stack of about 20 soft, dry, white sheets. To make pastries, the thin leaves are layered with oil or melted butter, filled with something delicious, and baked until golden, flaky, and crisp. Filo appears delicate, but it is actually quite sturdy and cooperative if handled correctly. Here's how:

a) Defrost the whole package, still wrapped. If you unwrap and unroll it too soon, the leaves will break into a thousand tiny pieces, causing you to throw them angrily into the garbage. (This type of dough can't be stuck together again.).

b) Unwrap just before using. Unroll, and take out the amount you will need. (The following recipes will use the entire package. However, many other recipes use only half a pack.)

c) Immediately rewrap the unused portion, if any, by rolling it in waxed paper first. Then seal the roll, airtight, in a plastic bag. Refrigerate or freeze until your next strudel adventure.

d) Filo dries out very quickly, once unwrapped. Keep the leaves all piled up as you use them; take one sheet at a time from the top of the pile, and work steadily.

e) No matter what shape your finished pastry will become, the initial treatment of the filo leaves will always be the same — i.e., the dough will be layered, and each leaf will be brushed with oil or melted butter (or sprayed with oil spray) before the next one is placed on top. This procedure strengthens the dough, seals it against the moisture from the filling, and gives the finished product its characteristic brown color and exquisite crispness.

continued....

f) Before you begin, always have the filling ready, along with everything else needed for assembly (oil, brush, baking pan, etc.).

g) Don't worry if a leaf of pastry puckers or tears. The layering (and in some cases the rolling and folding over) will compensate.

A VERY IMPORTANT CONVENIENCE NOTE:
Once assembled, a well wrapped, filled filo pastry can be refrigerated for up to several days. And baked pastries freeze very well and reheat beautifully — no defrosting necessary! So if you come home tired and grumpy some bleak night, you can just pull out some ready-made pastries from the freezer, heat them in a 350°F oven for about 35 minutes, and VOILÀ! Instant contentment!

VEGETABLE STRUDEL

Preparation time:
1 hour to assemble;
30 to 35 minutes
to bake.

Yield:
6 to 8
servings

1 Tbs. butter
2 cups minced onion
1 large carrot, diced
3 cups shredded cabbage
2 cups chopped broccoli
½ lb. mushrooms, minced
1 tsp. salt
1 tsp. caraway seeds
4 medium cloves garlic, minced

1 to 2 Tbs. fresh lemon juice
3 Tbs. minced fresh dill
5 scallions, minced (greens & whites)
fresh black pepper to taste
1 cup crumbled goat or feta cheese
¾ cup fine bread crumbs

⅓ to ½ cup olive oil or melted
  butter —or oil spray, for the filo
1 lb. filo leaves (see pages 135-36)

1) Preheat oven to 375°F. Have ready a 9 x 13-inch baking pan.

2) To make the filling, melt the butter in a large, deep skillet or a Dutch oven. Add onion, and cook for 5 minutes over medium heat. Add the carrot, cabbage, broccoli, mushrooms, and salt, and continue to cook over medium heat, stirring intermittently, until the vegetables are just tender (about 5 minutes). Remove from heat; stir in the caraway, garlic, lemon juice, dill, scallions, black pepper, cheese, and ½ cup of the bread crumbs.

3) Brush the baking pan with a little olive oil or melted butter, or spray it with oil spray. Lay a sheet of filo in the pan, and brush or spray with oil, or brush with butter. Lay another sheet on top, and repeat the process. Continue layering the filo, oiling or buttering in between, until you have a stack of about 12 leaves.

4) Sprinkle the stack of filo with the remaining bread crumbs, then add the filling, spreading it to within ½ inch of the edges. Layer more filo over the filling, brushing or spraying each layer with olive oil, or brushing with melted butter. Use all the filo.

5) Cut the unbaked strudel into squares, and bake until crisp and brown (30 to 35 minutes). Cool at least 10 minutes before serving.

Cheese Tyropitas

40 minutes to prepare;
30 minutes to bake.
(Can be assembled in
advance and refrigerated.)

Yield:
5 or 6
servings
(10 pastries —
1 or 2 per person)

a little oil for the tray
1 Tbs. olive oil
1 cup finely minced onion
8 oz. (1 cup) cottage cheese
8 oz. (1 cup) feta cheese, crumbled
3 large cloves garlic, minced
3 Tbs. minced fresh mint
1/3 cup lightly toasted sunflower seeds
1 Tbs. fresh lemon juice
1 lb. filo leaves, defrosted (see p. 135)
1/3 to 1/2 cup olive oil or melted butter
— or oil spray — for the filo

1) Preheat oven to 375°F. Lightly oil a baking tray.

2) Heat 1 Tbs. olive oil in a small skillet. Add the onion, and
sauté over medium heat until soft (5 to 8 minutes).

3) To make the filling, simply mix together all the ingredients
(including sautéed onions), except the filo and oil (or melted butter).

4) For each individual pastry, layer 2 filo leaves with olive oil or
melted butter brushed (or sprayed, if you're using oil spray) between.
Oil or butter the top surface, then fold the double sheet into thirds
lengthwise — one side over, then the other. Place about 1/4 cup filling
near one end, then fold the nearest corner over it triangularly.
Keep folding over the filled triangle until you reach the end. Oil
or butter the top, and place the triangle on the baking tray. Repeat
until you've used up the filling.

Fold on dotted lines.

1.   2.   3.

5) Bake for 30 minutes, or until golden and crisp. (Some of the filling
might leak a little bit during the baking, but don't worry about it.)

Spinach Borek

Preparation time:
1 hour to prepare;
30 minutes to bake.
(Can be prepared in
advance and refrigerated.)

Serve these with Tahini Dip (p. 114)
and a side of yogurt.

a little oil for the tray

2 lbs. fresh spinach, or
2 10-oz. packages
frozen chopped spinach

1 Tbs. olive oil (plus more
later, for the filo)

1½ cups minced onion

½ tsp. salt

fresh black pepper, to taste

3 large cloves garlic, minced

1 cup minced walnuts, toasted

⅓ cup fine bread crumbs

¼ cup minced fresh dill

¼ cup minced fresh mint

3 Tbs. fresh lemon juice

½ tsp. grated orange rind

½ cup dried currants

a few gratings of fresh nutmeg

OPTIONAL: 1 cup crumbled feta
or goat cheese

1 lb. filo leaves, defrosted (see p. 135)
approximately ½ cup olive oil

1) Preheat oven to 375°F. Lightly oil a baking tray.

2) Wash and stem the spinach, chop it fine (or defrost the frozen
   spinach), and put it in a colander over the sink to drain.
   Press out all excess liquid.

3) Heat 1 Tbs. olive oil in a large, deep skillet. Add the onion and
   the salt, and sauté over medium heat for 8 to 10 minutes, or
   until the onion softens. Add the drained spinach and cook,
   stirring over high heat for just a few minutes, or until the spinach
   is wilted. (If using frozen spinach, cook over medium heat for
   about 8 minutes.) Remove from heat.

4) Add all remaining ingredients (including optional cheese), and mix well.

5) To assemble each individual pastry, follow the method described in
   Step 3 on the preceding page. Instead of triangles, you can make
   squares by folding the sides over the filling, then folding the filling
   over and over toward the other end, as illustrated:

Brush the tops with
a little more oil.

← Fold side edges over first
(dotted lines lengthwise)

6) Bake for 30 minutes. Cool a little before eating. the filling is hot!
   These also taste good at room temperature.

Greek Pizza

30 minutes to prepare;
30 minutes to bake.
(Can be assembled in
advance and refrigerated)

Yield:
4 to 6
servings
(easily doubled)

2 Tbs. olive oil
1 cup minced onion
¼ tsp. salt
2 tsp. dried basil
1 tsp. dried oregano
1 lb. fresh spinach, cleaned, stemmed, and minced
8 large cloves garlic, minced
freshly ground black pepper

3 Tbs. lemon juice
½ lb. filo leaves
½ cup olive oil or melted butter— or oil spray – for the filo
½ lb. mozzarella cheese, grated
2 medium-sized ripe tomatoes, thinly sliced
½ cup Kalamata (Greek) olives, pitted
¾ lb. feta cheese, crumbled

1) Preheat oven to 375°F.

2) Heat 2 Tbs. olive oil in a large, deep skillet. Add onion and salt, and cook over medium heat for about 8 minutes, or until the onion softens. Add herbs and spinach, and cook over fairly high heat, stirring, until the spinach is limp and the liquid has mostly evaporated (about 5 to 8 minutes). Remove from heat; stir in the garlic, black pepper, and lemon juice. Set aside.

3) Brush a large baking tray with olive oil, and begin layering the filo leaves, brushing or spraying with oil (or brushing with melted butter) between the layers. Continue until you have a pile of 10 leaves. Gently cut into large-ish squares. (You can choose the dimensions.) Sprinkle the top surface of each square with grated mozzarella.

4) Use a slotted spoon to transfer the spinach mixture to the top of the mozzarella layer, leaving behind whatever liquid failed to evaporate. Spread the spinach mixture evenly into place, leaving a small border of pastry around the edges.

5) Arrange the tomato slices and olives over the spinach, and sprinkle crumbled feta over the top. Bake for 30 minutes, then allow to cool for about 10 minutes before serving.

ENCHILADAS

An enchilada is a soft corn tortilla wrapped around a filling and baked in a sauce. Usually the filling is quite plain (cheese, chicken, or beef) and bland, and the sauce is the spicier element. The following three pages contain recipes for some unusual, not-so-plain enchilada fillings and for two sauces.

TO ASSEMBLE AND BAKE ENCHILADAS:

Enchiladas are easy to assemble, once the filling and sauce are prepared and the tortillas are premoistened. The procedure is as follows:

1) If you are using frozen tortillas, defrost them first — fully wrapped — to prevent their drying out.

2) Prepare the filling and sauce.

3) Moisten the tortillas (this encourages flexibility) in one of several ways:
   a) Sauté them very briefly on each side in a little oil. ("Very briefly" means approximately 10 seconds.)
   b) Dip them briefly in the sauce. ("Briefly" means a dunking, not a bath.)
   c) Dip them just as briefly in water (least desirable, however easiest).

4) Assemble the enchiladas by placing a few tablespoons of filling on one side of each tortilla and rolling it up. Pour a small amount of sauce into a shallow baking dish, add the enchiladas, and pour the remaining sauce over the top. Cover with foil, and bake for about 30 minutes in a 325°F oven. Serve hot.

Enchilada Fillings
❋ ❋ ❋ ❋ ❋ ❋ ❋ ❋ ❋ ❋ ❋ ❋ ❋ ❋

Each of these recipes fills 10 or 12 enchiladas. That's about 5 or 6 servings (2 apiece).

I. Cheese *with* Surprises:

Preparation time:
about 10 minutes

4 oz. (½ cup) cream cheese, softened
½ lb. jack cheese, grated
   (about 2 packed cups)
½ cup chopped green olives
½ cup chopped ripe olives (any kind)

1 small bell pepper (any color), minced
⅓ cup raisins
2 scallions, finely minced
   (whites and greens)
a few dashes of cayenne

Combine in a bowl and mix well.

❋ ❋ ❋ ❋ ❋ ❋ ❋ ❋ ❋ ❋ ❋ ❋ ❋ ❋ ❋ ❋ ❋ ❋ ❋ ❋

II. Avocado

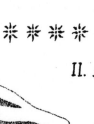

Preparation time:
about 10 minutes
(Make this shortly
before filling and
baking the enchiladas.)

½ cup fresh lemon juice
4 medium-sized avocados,
   perfectly ripe
3 medium cloves garlic, minced
6 scallions, finely minced
   (whites and greens)

¾ cup minced fresh cilantro
2 medium-sized ripe tomatoes, diced
1 tsp. salt
¾ tsp. ground cumin

1) Place the lemon juice in a medium-sized bowl. Peel and pit the avocados, cut them into small dice, and add them to the lemon juice. Toss lightly.

2) Add the remaining ingredients and mix gently.

III. Zucchini and Pepper

Preparation time:
30 minutes

Yield:
enough to fill
12 enchiladas
(6 servings)

2 Tbs. olive oil
1½ cups minced onion
6 medium cloves garlic, minced
¾ tsp. salt
1 large bell pepper (any color), minced
5 small (6-inch) zucchini, diced
1½ tsp. ground cumin
1 Tbs. dried basil
1½ tsp. dried oregano
cayenne and black pepper to taste
1⅓ cups (packed) grated jack cheese

1) Heat the oil in a large, deep skillet. Add onion, garlic, and salt, and sauté over medium heat for 8 to 10 minutes, or until the onion is quite soft.

2) Add the bell pepper, zucchini, and seasonings. Stir and cook over medium heat another 5 to 8 minutes, or until the zucchini is just tender.

3) Remove from heat and stir in the cheese. Allow to cool for a few minutes before filling the tortillas.

❊ ❊ ❊ ❊ ❊ ❊ ❊ ❊ ❊ ❊ ❊ ❊ ❊ ❊ ❊ ❊ ❊ ❊ ❊ ❊

Enchilada Sauces

1. Salsa Verde :

5 large green tomatoes, diced
1 cup minced onion
3 large cloves garlic, minced
1 tsp. salt
1 medium Anaheim or poblano chile,
    minced (or ½ cup canned diced
    green chiles)

¼ to ½ tsp. cayenne
¼ cup each:
    minced fresh parsley
    minced fresh basil
    minced fresh cilantro
    minced scallions (whites
        and greens)

1) Place tomatoes, onion, garlic, salt, chiles, and cayenne in a saucepan.
   Bring to a boil, lower heat, and partially cover. Simmer for 15 minutes.
2) Cool to room temperature before stirring in the herbs. You can leave it
   chunky or purée in a blender or food processor.

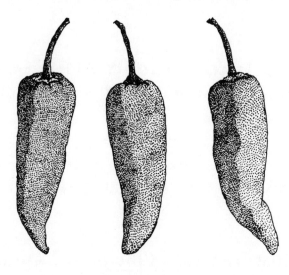

2. Red Sauce:

5 medium-sized ripe tomatoes, diced
1 large red bell pepper, minced
1 tsp. salt

5 large cloves garlic, minced
½ tsp. crushed red pepper
½ tsp. ground cumin

1) Place all ingredients in a saucepan and bring to a boil. Lower heat,
   partially cover, and simmer for about 15 minutes.
2) You can leave it chunky or purée in a food processor or blender. For
   extra smooth sauce, pass the purée through a fine strainer or a sieve.
3) That's all.

AND

Most cultures seem to have some version of a savory filled pastry in their cuisine. In many cases the dough is identical, the method of preparing and cooking very similar, and the distinguishing factor is the filling. One example of such a pastry is that which is known as ravioli (if you're Italian), kreplach (if you're Jewish), and wonton (if you're Chinese). They all use a similar noodle dough and are shaped in a similar fashion, but their fillings are all different, and their origins are worlds apart. (Realizations of this sort can lead us to philosophical reveries about the connectedness of us all. Or they can simply lead us to conclude that a resounding majority of human beings just happen to love this kind of food.)

Another example of a pastry-without-borders is the type known to Russians as piroshki and to Italians as a calzone. Whereas ravioli, kreplach, and wontons all use a noodle dough, piroshki and calzones are made with an easy-to-make <u>yeasted</u> dough. Essentially, they are filled breads: a soft, hot, and savory filling enclosed in a crisp, chewy pastry.

On the following page you'll find a recipe for the dough that can be used for either piroshki or calzones. After the dough recipe and basic method are recipes for several fillings for each.

❊Dough ❧ Method❊
...for Piroshki ᴬⁿᵈ Calzone❊❊❊

Yield: 6 to 8 Piroshki or Calzones
(about 4 to 6 servings)

This is a yeasted dough requiring only one rising period. The preparation time, including rising (but not including baking) is about 2 hours. The baking takes only 20 minutes.

1½ tsp. (half an envelope) dry yeast
1 cup lukewarm water
2 tsp. honey or sugar
1½ tsp. salt
2 cups unbleached white flour,
plus extra for kneading

1 cup whole wheat bread flour
¼ cup cornmeal
3 Tbs. olive oil or melted butter
(plus extra, for the baking tray)
1 batch of the filling of your
choice (recipes follow)

1) Combine the yeast, water, and honey or sugar in a large bowl. Stir, and let it stand for 5 minutes.

2) Beat in salt, flours, and cornmeal with a wooden spoon until too thick to mix, then turn it out onto a floured surface and knead for about 5 minutes. (See kneading diagram, p.63.)

3) Use olive oil for calzones and melted butter for piroshki, and generously grease the mixing bowl. Return the dough to the bowl, brush its top surface with oil or butter, and let it rise in a warm place until doubled in bulk (about 1 hour).

∿ PREPARE THE FILLING WHILE THE DOUGH RISES.∿

4) Preheat oven to 425°F. Butter or oil a baking tray.

5) Punch the dough to deflate it, and turn it out onto the floured surface again. Divide the dough into 6 or 8 equal parts, and knead each part into a ball. Roll each ball into a circle or oval about ¼ inch thick. Place about ¼ cup filling onto one side, and carefully stretch the other side of the dough over the filling. Crimp the edges firmly with the flat side of a fork. (The resulting shape will bear some resemblance to a U.F.O.) Prick it with the fork in a few choice spots and deposit the pastry on the prepared tray.

6) Bake 15 minutes. Cool for 10 minutes before eating — the filling is hot!

PIROSHKI

Each of the following Piroshki fillings is enough for about 8 pastries. Figure on about 1 or 2 Piroshki per person as a main course. (Try making two different fillings, so your guests can have one of each.)

Make the dough first (opposite page). Prepare the filling(s) while it rises.

DILLED CHEESE

Preparation time: 10 minutes

1 lb. (2 cups) firm cottage cheese
8 oz. (1 cup) crumbled feta cheese
1 to 2 Tbs. fresh lemon juice
6 scallions, finely minced
  (whites and greens)

¼ cup minced fresh parsley
3 Tbs. minced fresh mint (1 Tbs. dried)
1 Tbs. minced fresh dill (1 tsp. dried)
salt and pepper to taste

Make the dough first (preceding page). As it rises, combine all of the above ingredients and mix well. Proceed as described on opposite page, steps 5 and 6.

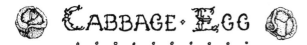 CABBAGE · EGG

Preparation time: 20 minutes

1 Tbs. butter or canola oil
1½ cups minced onion
1 tsp. salt
3 cups shredded cabbage
  (or minced Brussels sprouts)
½ tsp. caraway seeds

fresh black pepper to taste
1 large carrot, grated
2 tsp. prepared horseradish
2 Tbs. minced fresh dill
  (2 tsp. dried)
6 hard-boiled eggs, chopped
  (ok to delete some or all yolks)

(Make dough first — recipe on preceding page.)

1) Melt the butter or heat the oil in a large, deep skillet. Add onion and salt, and sauté over medium heat for about 5 minutes.

2) Add cabbage or Brussels sprouts, caraway, and black pepper. Cook over medium heat, stirring often, for 10 minutes. Stir in carrot and horseradish and cook for 5 minutes more. Remove from heat.

3) Stir in dill and chopped eggs. Proceed to fill the dough and bake the piroshki as described on the opposite page, steps 5 and 6.

MUSHROOM

Dough and Method, page 146.

Preparation time: 30 minutes

1 Tbs. butter
1½ cups minced onion
1¼ tsp. salt
1 lb. mushrooms, chopped
1 to 2 Tbs. lemon juice
2 medium cloves garlic, minced
8 oz. (1 cup) cream cheese (lowfat ok)
½ cup fine bread crumbs
¼ cup minced fresh parsley
2 Tbs. minced fresh dill (2 tsp. dried)
2 Tbs. minced fresh chives (optional)
fresh black pepper to taste

1) Melt the butter in a large, deep skillet or Dutch oven. Add the onion and half the salt, and sauté over medium heat for about 5 minutes or until the onion begins to soften.

2) Add the mushrooms and remaining salt. Continue to sauté for about 10 minutes, or until the mushrooms have cooked down. Stir in lemon juice and garlic, and cook for just 5 minutes longer. Remove from heat and immediately cut in the cream cheese. Stir until it melts.

3) Add remaining ingredients, and taste to adjust seasonings. Proceed as described on page 146.

CALZONE

Dough and Method, page 146.   Each of these recipes fills 6 to 8 calzones.

Pesto

Method A: 5 minutes to prepare
Method B: 15 minutes to prepare

A. If you already have some pesto (recipe on p.104), this filling is very simple. All you need to do is combine:

½ to 1 cup pesto
2 cups ricotta cheese
fresh black pepper to taste
grated parmesan to taste

} Mix well, and proceed as per p.146, steps 4-6.

B. If you don't have pesto on hand, and you don't have any fresh basil with which to make some (and you don't feel like spending too much money on a miniscule container of it at your upscale deli), here is an easy substitute, which I have affectionately nicknamed "winter pesto":

6 Tbs. dried basil (the freshest dried available)
6 Tbs. olive oil
5 to 6 medium cloves garlic, minced

½ cup grated parmesan
¾ cup ground walnuts (grind them in a blender with quick spurts)

1) Place the basil and oil in a medium-sized skillet. Let stand 15 minutes.
2) Cook over low heat, stirring, for about 15 minutes. Remove from heat and stir in remaining ingredients. Use this mixture as the pesto in Part A, above.

Provolone

10 minutes to prepare.

3 Tbs. olive oil
5 medium cloves garlic, minced
½ cup fine bread crumbs

¾ lb. provolone cheese, grated
2 medium-sized ripe tomatoes, sliced
freshly ground black pepper

1) Combine the oil and garlic in a small dish. Brush each circle of dough (p.146) with this mixture. (Add a little extra oil if you run short.)
2) Sprinkle the dough with about 1 Tbs. bread crumbs, then a handful of cheese. Arrange a tomato slice or two on top; sprinkle with more crumbs, and grind on some black pepper. Proceed as per p.146, steps 5 & 6.

Zucchini

15 minutes to prepare.

NOTE: Make the dough first (page 146).

2 Tbs. olive oil
2 cups minced onion
1 tsp. salt
1 tsp. dried oregano
1½ lbs. zucchini (about 5
   medium-small ones), cut
         into small dice
8 medium cloves garlic, minced
fresh black pepper to taste
crushed red pepper to taste
a handful of minced fresh basil
      (if available)
about ½ lb. mozzarella cheese,
      grated (optional)

1) Heat the olive oil in a large, deep skillet. Add onion, salt, and oregano, and sauté over medium heat until the onion begins to soften (about 5 minutes).

2) Add zucchini and garlic, and continue to sauté another 5 to 8 minutes, or until the zucchini is just tender.

3) Remove from heat, and add black pepper and crushed red pepper to taste. Stir in the basil.

4) Following the method on p. 146, fill each calzone with about ½ cup of the zucchini mixture, followed by a handful of grated mozzarella. Fold, crimp, and bake as per instructions.

BLINTZES

There's a special quality to blintzes made at home in one's own kitchen. Somehow, those served in restaurants never quite measure up. Maybe this is just an illusion—the subjectivity of a person for whom the presence of a homemade blintz summons memories of a loving mother or grandmother cooking something delicious in the next room. But I think there's some truth to the theory that, in order for blintzes to come out good (really, _really_ good), the person making them must have great fondness for the persons eating them.

The blintz pancake is practically identical to a crêpe, except that the blintz, for some reason, is cooked on one side only. The blintz pancake recipe can be found on the following page.

Blintz fillings are usually sweet. The most common one is made from cottage cheese or pot cheese. Fruit (usually cherries or blueberries; sometimes peaches) is the next-most-common filling. Filling recipes are on the page after next.

Filled blintzes can be refrigerated or frozen before being sautéed and served. Sautéed blintzes can be frozen, then defrosted and heated in a 325°F oven.

On page 154 is a wonderful recipe that uses blintzes: Blintz Soufflé. You might not want to wait until you have leftover blintzes to try it. (It's a rare event to have leftover blintzes, anyway.)

THE BLINTZ PANCAKE

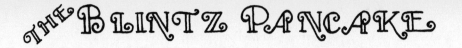

This recipe makes approximately 18 pancakes, enough to feed 6 people 3 apiece or 3 people 6 apiece — or any arrangement in between. The batter can be made in advance and stored in a covered container in the refrigerator. The cooked pancakes don't stack well, so it's best to fill them first and then wrap tightly and refrigerate. Sauté the filled blintzes just prior to serving.

3 eggs
½ tsp. salt
¾ cup unbleached white flour
1⅓ cups milk (lowfat ok)
2 Tbs. melted butter, plus
   additional melted butter
      for sautéing

TOPPINGS:
Sour cream or yogurt
fresh fruit
confectioners' sugar

1) Combine the eggs, salt, flour, milk, and 2 Tbs. melted butter. Beat well. (It's easiest to do this in a blender.)

2) Place a 6-inch crêpe or omelette pan over medium heat. If it's not a nonstick pan, brush it lightly with butter. Pour in a small amount of batter — just enough to cover the bottom surface — and tilt the pan in all directions until the bottom is coated. Cook over medium heat until the edges of the pancake begin to pull away from the sides of the pan. (This will happen quickly.) Turn out the pancake, cooked side up, onto a clean, dry towel. Repeat until you've run out of batter.

3) TO FILL: Use about 1 heaping Tbs. filling (recipes opposite) for each blintz. Place the filling on one side, fold over, fold in sides, and roll it up. Set aside on a plate or platter.

4) TO SAUTÉ: Use about 1 Tbs. butter for every 3 blintzes. Get the pan medium-hot, and sauté on both sides until golden brown and slightly crisp. Serve right away, with toppings.

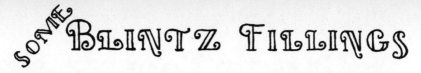

SOME BLINTZ FILLINGS

Each of these recipes should fill about 18 blintzes.

CHEESE:

Just a few minutes to prepare.

> 1 lb. cottage or pot cheese (ricotta is also OK)
> 1 egg, beaten (optional)
> 2 Tbs. sugar or honey
> 3 Tbs. unbleached white flour
> 1/4 tsp. salt

1) If you're using cottage cheese, pass it through a sieve into a medium-sized bowl. If you're using pot cheese or ricotta, just put it into the bowl - no sieve necessary.

2) Add remaining ingredients and mix well.

FRUIT:

About 20 minutes to prepare.

> 3 cups fruit (fresh or frozen, defrosted and drained):
> whole blueberries
> OR
> sliced, pitted cherries
> OR
> peeled, sliced peaches

> 1 Tbs. fresh lemon juice
> 1 Tbs. unbleached white flour
> sugar or honey to taste
> OPTIONAL: a dash of cinnamon
> a drop of almond extract

1) Place the fruit in a medium-sized saucepan all by itself. Cook it, partially covered, over medium heat for 5 minutes.

2) Stir in the lemon juice and sprinkle in the flour as you continue to stir. Cook another 5 minutes over medium heat, stirring frequently. Midway into the cooking add sugar or honey and optional seasonings. Remove from heat and cool for at least 15 minutes before filling blintzes.

BLINTZ SOUFFLÉ

The late Louis Bardenstein, who was renowned in Rochester, New York (my home town), as Bardy, the Kosher Caterer, created this inspired dish. I have personally witnessed people swooning with pleasure while eating this ethereal delicacy. So hold on to your chair while consuming Blintz Soufflé, or you may find yourself transported out of this realm and into Blintz Heaven.

♪ Two notes:

1. This is called a soufflé, but technically it is a custard, as the egg whites aren't beaten separately and folded in. So don't get confused when you read the soufflé method on pages 164-65 and wonder why it doesn't apply here.

2. This can be made with frozen, defrosted blintzes.

2 Tbs. melted butter
18 filled blintzes (any filling),
   unsautéed
2 cups sour cream or yogurt
   (or a combination)
6 eggs (ok to delete up to
   3 yolks)

3 to 4 Tbs. sugar or honey
1 tsp. vanilla extract
1 tsp. cornstarch
¼ tsp. salt (rounded measure)
fresh fruit, for the topping

1) Preheat oven to 350°F. Coat the bottom of a 9 x 13-inch baking pan with melted butter.

2) Arrange the blintzes in 2 rows in the pan — any way they'll fit.

3) Put all the other ingredients (except the fruit topping) in a mixing bowl — or a blender or food processor. Whip until smooth. Pour this custard over the blintzes, and bake for 45 minutes or until firm and lightly browned on top. Serve hot, warm, or at room temperature, with fresh fruit.

Pasta

(For other pasta sauces, see pages 104-107.)

Pasta

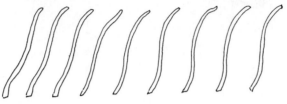

Spaghetti, linguine, macaroni, fettucine, lasagna — NOODLES!

Just about everybody loves pasta. It's inexpensive, easy, versatile, and most importantly, fun to eat. It can be dressed up to please even the most jaded, sophisticated palate. You can also dress it down, and bring contentment to the fussiest preschool-aged child.

This chapter presents a few simple pasta recipes reflecting a variety of ethnic cuisines (East European, Italian, Chinese, Jewish). You can find more ideas in the "Sauces, Dips, and Spreads" section, particularly on pages 104 through 109. Always keep one of these sauces on hand, and good, quick pasta dinners can become a regular (and delightful) part of your busy weekly routine.

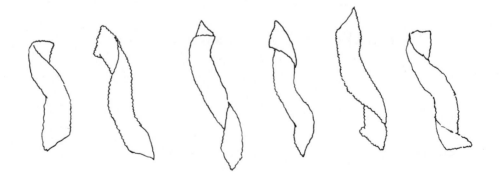

Pasta Primavera ("spring pasta") refers to the combination of pasta with delicately cooked early fresh vegetables. Together, pasta and vegetables create a wonderful blend of texture and soul. As you discover the unlimited possibilities for combining them, more and more quick and elegant ideas for dinner will enter your everyday repertoire. The recipe below is one example of a Pasta Primavera. Try it, and then experiment with different vegetables ~ ideally, what is just appearing, in slender, young form, at your produce market (or whatever is just dawning in your garden).

Confetti Spaghetti

30 minutes to prepare.   Yield: 4 or 5 servings

This version of Pasta Primavera bears the colors of the Italian flag.

3 to 4 Tbs. olive oil
2 cups sliced onion
½ tsp. salt (more, to taste)
2 cups chopped broccoli
2 cups chopped cauliflower
a handful of slender green
    beans, trimmed
a handful of sugar snap
    or snow peas, trimmed

1 medium red bell pepper, diced
6 to 8 medium cloves garlic, minced
freshly ground black pepper
1 lb. spaghetti or linguine
4 scallions, minced (whites and greens)
2 handfuls minced fresh parsley
2 handfuls minced fresh basil
grated parmesan

1) (Preliminary: Put up a large potful of water to boil for the spaghetti.) Heat the oil in a large skillet. Add onion and salt, and sauté over medium heat for about 5 minutes, or until the onion begins to soften.
2) Add broccoli and cauliflower. Stir and cook until the vegetables are just barely tender ~ about 5 more minutes. Add green beans, peas, and bell pepper, and cook for another 5 minutes or so. Stir in garlic; add black pepper to taste. Taste to adjust salt, and set aside.
3) Cook the pasta in plenty of boiling water until <u>al dente</u>. Drain, transfer to a large bowl, and add the sauté. As you toss the mixture, sprinkle in the scallions, parsley, basil, and parmesan. Serve <u>immediatamente</u>!

Hot Marinated Cauliflower
((((& Macaroni)))))

About 40 minutes to prepare.   Yield: 4 or 5 servings

¼ cup olive oil
2 cups chopped onion
dried oregano ⎫
dried basil ⎪
dried thyme ⎬ 1 tsp. each
crumbled rosemary ⎭
1½ tsp. salt
lots of fresh black pepper
3 bay leaves
½ lb. mushrooms, sliced

10 large cloves garlic, coarsely chopped
⅓ cup red wine vinegar
1 cup water
4 Tbs. tomato paste
2 medium heads of cauliflower, cut
    or broken into 1-inch florets
1 lb. elbow macaroni
grated parmesan ⎫
minced fresh parsley ⎬ for the top
minced fresh basil ⎭

1) Heat the olive oil in a very large saucepan or sauté pan—or a Dutch oven. Add onion, dried herbs, salt, pepper, bay leaves, and mushrooms, and sauté over medium heat until the onion is translucent (8 to 10 minutes).

2) Add the garlic, vinegar, water, and tomato paste, and whisk until well blended. Add the cauliflower and bring to a boil. Cover, and turn the heat way down. Cook until the cauliflower is just tender (5 to 8 minutes). Set aside until shortly before serving.

3) Soon before serving, cook the macaroni in plenty of boiling water until <u>al dente</u>. Drain well and add to the sauce. (If you made the sauce earlier, reheat it—gently—while the macaroni cooks.) Mix well and transfer to a serving bowl.

4) Serve topped with generous amounts of grated parmesan and minced fresh parsley and basil. This tastes good at any temperature—even cold!

Cauliflower Paprikash

30 minutes to prepare.   Yield: 4 or 5 servings

1 medium cauliflower
1 Tbs. plus 1 tsp. butter
2 cups chopped onion
2 cups sour cream (lowfat OK)
1 Tbs. horseradish
1 Tbs. mild paprika
3/4 tsp. salt

fresh black pepper to taste
1 lb. wide egg noodles
2 Tbs. poppy seeds
2 Tbs. minced fresh dill
2 Tbs. minced fresh chives
extra paprika for the top

1) Break or cut the cauliflower into 1-inch florets. Steam them until just tender and set aside.

2) Meanwhile, melt 1 Tbs. butter in a medium-large saucepan. Add the onion, and sauté over medium heat until it begins to soften (5 to 8 minutes). Turn the heat to very low.

3) Add the sour cream and horseradish to the onion, and beat well with a whisk. Cook and stir over very low heat for 5 minutes. Stir in paprika, salt, pepper, and the cooked cauliflower. Set aside until shortly before serving time.

4) Just before serving, cook the noodles in plenty of boiling water until just tender. (If necessary, gently reheat the sauce while the noodles cook. Don't let it boil!) Drain the noodles, and transfer them to a large serving bowl. Toss immediately with 1 tsp. butter and the poppy seeds. Spoon the sauce over the noodles. Sprinkle the top with dill, chives, and a little extra paprika. Serve right away.

Lasagna al Pesto

Yield: 6 to 8 servings

... all green.

a little oil for the pan
about 16 green lasagna noodles
1 lb. fresh spinach (or 2 10-oz. packages frozen, chopped spinach – defrosted)
2 lbs. (4 cups) ricotta cheese
1 cup pesto (p.104)

4 large cloves garlic, minced
1/2 tsp. salt
fresh black pepper to taste
3/4 cup grated parmesan
1/3 cup toasted pine nuts or minced walnuts
1 lb. mozzarella cheese, grated

1) Preheat oven to 350°F. Lightly oil a 9 x 13-inch baking pan.

2) Bring a large potful of water to a boil. Add the noodles, and cook them for 4 or 5 minutes. (They will be undercooked.) Drain them, and lay them flat and straight on a table, counter, or tray.

3) Meanwhile, thoroughly wash and dry the spinach. Remove and discard the stems; finely mince the leaves. (If using frozen, defrosted spinach, thoroughly drain and squeeze out all extra water.)

4) Place the ricotta in a large bowl. Stir in the spinach, pesto, garlic, salt, black pepper, 1/2 cup of the parmesan, and nuts. Mix well.

5) Place a layer of noodles in the bottom of the prepared pan. Spread about 1/3 of the filling over the noodles (OK if uneven), and sprinkle about 1/3 of the mozzarella on top. Follow with another layer of noodles, another 1/3 of the filling, and another 1/3 of the mozzarella. Repeat this pattern one more time with a third layer of everything. Top with one final noodle layer and the remaining 1/4 cup of parmesan on the very top.

6) Bake for 50 minutes. If the top browns too quickly during baking, cover loosely with foil.

PEANUT AND SESAME NOODLES

15 minutes
to prepare.

Yield:
4 to 6
servings

1 cup high-quality peanut butter
1½ cups boiling water
4 to 5 Tbs. vinegar (rice or cider)
1¼ tsp. salt (to taste)
2 medium cloves garlic, minced
2 Tbs. honey or sugar
1 Tbs. soy sauce
½ tsp. crushed red pepper (to taste)
4 Tbs. Chinese sesame oil

optional: ½ lb. firm tofu, cut
  into small dice
1 lb. vermicelli noodles
1 medium cucumber, peeled, seeded,
  and cut into thin strips
4 scallions, finely minced (whites
  and greens)
¾ cup minced cashews and/or
  peanuts, lightly toasted
optional: minced fresh cilantro

1) Place the peanut butter in a medium-sized bowl. Add boiling water, and mix patiently with a spoon until uniformly blended.

2) Stir in vinegar, salt, garlic, honey or sugar, soy sauce, crushed red pepper, sesame oil, and optional tofu. Taste to adjust seasonings; set aside.

3) Cook the vermicelli in plenty of boiling water until just tender. Drain, and immediately transfer to a serving bowl. Pour the sauce over the top, and toss with two forks. As you toss, add the cucumber strips and minced scallions.

4) Serve immediately, topped with toasted nuts and a sprinkling of cilantro.

Lukshen Kugel

30 minutes to prepare;
20 minutes to bake.
(Do Step 3 while waiting
for the water to boil.)

Yield:
5 or 6
servings

"Lukshen" means "noodles" in Yiddish. This unusual kugel, provocatively sweet and tart, contains no dairy products. (For more about Kugels, see p. 195.)

a little oil for the pan
1 lb. fine egg noodles
1 Tbs. canola oil
1 cup minced almonds
3/4 tsp. cinnamon
3/4 cup minced prunes
3/4 cup minced dried apricots

2 Tbs. fresh lemon juice
2 Tbs. honey or brown sugar
4 eggs (OK to delete up to 2 yolks)
1 tsp. salt
1 20-oz. can crushed pineapple
    (packed in unsweetened juice)
extra cinnamon for the top

1) Preheat oven to 375°F. Lightly oil a 9 x 13-inch baking pan.

2) Put up a large pot of water to boil. When it boils, add the noodles, and cook them until they are about 2/3 done (i.e., softened, but still pronouncedly al dente). Drain and transfer to a bowl.

3) Meanwhile, heat 1 Tbs. oil in a medium-sized pan. Add 3/4 cup of the almonds and the 3/4 tsp. cinnamon, and sauté over medium-low heat for several minutes, stirring frequently, until the almonds are nicely toasted. Stir in the dried fruit, lemon juice, and honey or sugar, and cook just a minute or two more. Add this to the bowlful of noodles and mix well.

4) Beat the eggs in a small, separate bowl. Stir these into the mixture, along with the salt and the entire can of pineapple, liquid included. Spread into the prepared pan. Sprinkle the top with the remaining 1/4 cup almonds and a little cinnamon.

5) Bake uncovered for 20 minutes.

Serve hot, warm, or at room temperature.

EGG STRAVA-GANZA

Soufflés

Soufflés, elegant and elusive — and deceptively filling — have long been a source of intimidation for novice cooks. The accumulation of mystique surrounding this baked egg puff (which is basically what a soufflé is) has led many people to believe that only official gourmets are qualified to create one. I would like to deflate this notion and to encourage cooks of all levels of experience to give soufflés a try. THIS IS NOT COMPLICATED! If you can separate eggs, beat the whites until stiff, and fold (all described in more detail below), you're most of the way there.

HERE ARE THE THINGS YOU NEED TO KNOW:
... how, in some cases, to make a basic white sauce, which involves melting some butter, whisking some flour into it to make a smooth paste (called a "roux"), and slowly pouring in some hot milk as you whisk it to keep it smooth;

... how to separate eggs, remembering to put the whites in a large enough bowl, because when you beat them they will greatly (7 to 8 times!) increase their volume;

... how to beat egg whites, using a whisk or an electric mixer, until they are stiff. The little peak of egg white on the tip of the beater should be stiff enough to point upward unassisted;

AND

... how to fold beaten egg whites into a thick batter, using a rubber spatula with a firm-but-gentle cutting, lifting, and side-of-bowl scraping motion, which will incorporate air into the mixture.

You'll also need to be able to refrain from opening the oven while the soufflé is baking. Most important of all, you need punctual guests, who will be seated and ready before the soufflé emerges from the oven. The average puff span of a soufflé is approximately 1½ minutes, after which it will partially collapse. (It will still taste great, but we're going for the dramatic aesthetic moment.) So don't plan to serve a soufflé when inviting chronically late people to dinner. (Or you can invite these people and plan to serve a soufflé, but tell them the wrong time to arrive, like an hour early.)

OTHER POINTERS:

• Use a 2-quart soufflé dish or an equivalent straight-sided casserole.

• Don't forget to butter the baking dish.

• Make sure your oven is accurate and heats evenly.

• Separate the eggs earlier in the day. Cover the bowls, and allow the eggs to come to room temperature. (It's easier to separate cold eggs than room temperature eggs, but room temperature eggs yield maximum volume.)

ABOUT THESE RECIPES:

• The yield is low—only about 4 servings apiece. You can double the recipes without too much trouble, and bake the doubled amounts in two soufflé dishes side by side, on the same oven level.

• ALL THE YOLKS ARE OPTIONAL IN ALL THESE RECIPES! I've tested them with all, some, and none of the yolks. They've all puffed up beautifully and tasted wonderful each way.

Tempus Fugit.

Ricotta & Pesto Soufflé

Preparation time:
15 minutes to assemble;
45 minutes to bake.
(This assumes the pesto
is already on hand.)

Yield
about 4
servings

♪ NOTE: This recipe calls for
pesto. There is a recipe
on p.104, or you can
use a good commercially
prepared brand.

a little melted butter and
grated parmesan for the
soufflé dish

1 lb. (2 cups) ricotta cheese
6 eggs, separated and at
room temperature

2 Tbs. unbleached white flour
½ tsp. salt
lots of fresh black pepper
⅓ cup grated parmesan
1 cup pesto (recipe
on p. 104)

1) Preheat oven to 375°F. Lightly brush a 2-quart soufflé dish with melted butter, and sprinkle it with grated parmesan.

2) Place the ricotta in a large mixing bowl. Add all, some, or none of the egg yolks, the flour, salt, pepper, ⅓ cup parmesan, and the pesto. Beat with a whisk until well combined.

3) Place the egg whites in a separate large bowl, and beat until they form stiff peaks. Gently but persuasively fold the beaten whites into the ricotta mixture. Use a firm rubber spatula, and turn the bowl as you fold. Transfer the batter into the prepared soufflé dish.

4) Without a moment's hesitation, place the soufflé into the oven, and reduce the temperature to 350°F. Let it bake undisturbed for 45 minutes. Serve immediately.

Apple & Cheddar Soufflé

Preparation time:
1¼ hours, including
baking.

NOTE: Use the food processor
to grate both cheese and
apple in seconds flat.

This makes a perfect
brunch served with
orange juice and
freshly baked muffins
(recipes pp. 92 to 97).
Bake the muffins first,
and then the soufflé.

Yield
about 4
servings

a little melted butter
  for the soufflé dish

2 cups milk (lowfat ok)
3 Tbs. butter
6 Tbs. unbleached white flour
6 eggs, separated and at room
  temperature (yolks optional)

1 packed cup grated cheddar
2 cups peeled, grated tart apple
½ tsp. cinnamon
a grating or two of nutmeg
¾ tsp. salt
½ cup finely minced walnuts

1) Preheat oven to 375°F. Lightly brush a 2-quart soufflé dish with
   melted butter.

2) Heat the milk slowly in a small saucepan. Remove from heat just
   before it boils, and set aside.

3) Melt 3 Tbs. butter in a medium-sized saucepan. Whisk it as you
   gradually sprinkle in 3 Tbs. of the flour. Cook over low heat,
   whisking constantly, for about 1 minute.

4) Keep whisking as you drizzle in the hot milk. Cook over low heat,
   stirring steadily, until the sauce thickens (5 to 8 minutes). Remove
   from heat and transfer to a large bowl. (If you choose to add the
   egg yolks, beat them well and drizzle them into the sauce, whisking
   constantly.)

5) In a medium-sized bowl, toss together the cheese, grated apple, and
   remaining 3 Tbs. flour with the spices and the salt. Fold this
   into the sauce.

6) Place the egg whites in a large bowl and beat until stiff. Fold them
   gently-but-quickly into the sauce. Turn the mixture into its prepared
   pan, and sprinkle the top with walnuts.

7) Bake undisturbed for 40 minutes. Serve immediately.

Cauliflower & Sour Cream Soufflé

40 minutes to prepare;
40 minutes to bake.

Yield:
about 4
servings

a little melted butter for the
   soufflé dish
1 medium head cauliflower
2 Tbs. butter
1½ cups minced onion
¾ tsp. salt
fresh black pepper to taste

1 tsp. caraway seeds
2 Tbs. fresh lemon juice
4 Tbs. unbleached white flour
5 eggs, separated and at room
   temperature (yolks optional)
1 cup sour cream, at room
   temperature (lowfat ok)
2 tsp. horseradish

1) Preheat oven to 375°F. Lightly brush a 2-quart soufflé dish with melted butter.

2) Break or chop the cauliflower into small (½-inch) pieces. Steam these until tender, then set aside.

3) Melt 2 Tbs. butter in a medium-sized saucepan. Add onion and salt, and cook over medium heat, stirring, for 5 minutes. Add black pepper, caraway, and lemon juice. Keep cooking and stirring for about 10 more minutes.

4) When the onions appear to have wilted considerably, turn the heat to low, and gradually sprinkle in the flour, whisking steadily. Cook, stirring frequently, for 5 minutes more.

5) If you are using any of the egg yolks, beat them together with the sour cream and horseradish. Stir this into the onion mixture, turn the heat way down, and cook with great subtlety for 5 more minutes, stirring often. (If you are deleting the yolks, just stir the sour cream and horseradish into the onions and remove from heat.) Transfer to a large bowl, and stir in the steamed cauliflower.

6) In a separate large bowl, beat the egg whites until stiff. Fold these into the first mixture. Transfer to the soufflé dish, and pop it right into the oven. Let it bake in privacy for 40 minutes. Serve right away.

Dilled Asparagus Soufflé

40 minutes to prepare; 40 minutes to bake.	Delicious! And very pretty when it comes out of the oven.	Yield: about 4 servings

a little melted butter for the soufflé dish
1½ lbs. asparagus
3 Tbs. butter
½ cup minced onion
½ tsp. salt
fresh black pepper to taste
1 tsp. dry mustard

½ tsp. dried tarragon
4 Tbs. unbleached white flour
1½ cups hot milk (lowfat ok)
5 eggs, separated and at room temperature (yolks optional)
3 Tbs. minced fresh dill
½ packed cup grated mild cheddar (optional)

1) Preheat oven to 375°F. Lightly brush a 2-quart soufflé dish with melted butter.

2) Break off and discard the bottom inch-or-so of each asparagus spear. Cut the spears into ½-inch pieces, on the diagonal and steam them until just barely tender. Rinse under cold water; drain well and set aside.

3) Melt the butter in a medium-sized saucepan. Add onion, salt, pepper, mustard, and tarragon, and cook, stirring, over medium heat for about 8 minutes, or until the onion is soft and translucent. Turn the heat way down, and stir constantly as you sprinkle in the flour. The resulting roux will be very thick. Keep cooking it another 2 to 3 minutes anyway, stirring frequently with a wooden spoon.

4) Drizzle in the hot milk, whisking constantly. Continue to cook and stir over very low heat 5 minutes longer – until you have a thick, smooth sauce. Transfer to a large bowl.

5) [OPTIONAL: Beat the egg yolks in a small separate bowl, then drizzle them into the sauce, beating well.] Stir in dill, cheese, and asparagus.

6) Place the egg whites in a separate large bowl and beat until stiff. Fold them into the first mixture, and transfer to the prepared pan. Bake undisturbed for 40 minutes, then serve _tout de suite_!

Cheddar Spoonbread

30 minutes to prepare;
35 minutes to bake.

Spoonbread, a traditional dish from southern U.S.A., is a soufflé made with cornmeal. It is often served for lunch, brunch, or a light supper, with a sweet accompaniment, such as fruit preserves, honey, or maple syrup. The following version is augmented by whole corn and cheddar cheese, making it a more substantial main dish than the traditional recipe. Serve it with cinnamon applesauce, freshly baked bread, and a green salad.

a little melted butter
   for the soufflé dish

2 cups milk (lowfat ok)
1 Tbs. butter
3 cups corn (fresh or frozen)

3/4 tsp. salt
1 1/2 cups yellow cornmeal
1 1/2 packed cups grated cheddar
   (sharp or medium)
6 eggs, separated and at room
   temperature (yolks optional)

1) Preheat oven to 400°F. Lightly brush a 2-quart soufflé dish with melted butter.

2) Heat the milk in a small saucepan until it just reaches the boiling point. Remove from heat and set aside.

3) Melt 1 Tbs. butter in a medium-sized saucepan. Add corn and salt, and sauté over medium heat for about 3 minutes. Stir in the cornmeal.

4) Drizzle the hot milk into the sautéed corn mixture, whisking steadily. Transfer into a large bowl and stir in the cheese. If using the egg yolks, beat them in a small bowl first, then drizzle them into the mixture, beating well with a wooden spoon.

5) Place the egg whites in a separate large bowl, and beat until stiff. Fold them into the corn mixture with a rubber spatula, combining the two as well as possible without deflating the whites. Transfer to the soufflé dish, pop it into the preheated oven, and reduce the temperature to 315°F. Bake 35 minutes and serve, pronto!

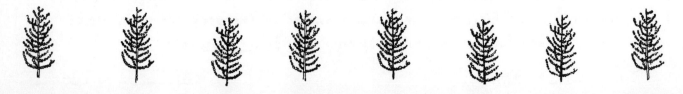

Pesto-Polenta Spoonbread

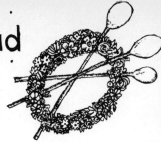

Polenta is a cornmeal mush, traditionally served as a pasta course in Northern Italian cuisine.

20 minutes to prepare;
35 minutes to bake.
(This assumes the Pesto
is already on hand.)

This soufflé goes beautifully with a crusty bread and Chilled Marinated Cauliflower (p. 41).

Yield:
about 4
servings

a little melted butter and grated parmesan
   for the soufflé dish
1 cup yellow cornmeal
2½ cups water
¾ tsp. salt
½ cup pesto (p. 104 ~ or you can use a good
               storebought brand)
5 eggs, separated and at room temperature
          (yolks optional)
extra grated parmesan for the top

1) Preheat oven to 400°F. Lightly brush a 2-quart soufflé dish with melted butter, and sprinkle in some grated parmesan.

2) Place cornmeal and water in a medium-sized saucepan. Mix with a wooden spoon until well blended. Stir in the salt. Heat until it comes to a boil; lower heat and simmer for about 5 minutes, stirring frequently. It will be very thick. Remove from heat.

3) Stir in the parmesan and pesto. If desired, vigorously beat in all or some of the egg yolks (or leave them out). Transfer to a large bowl.

4) Place the egg whites in a separate large bowl and beat until stiff. Fold them quickly but carefully into the first mixture as best you can. (It doesn't have to be uniform.) Transfer to the soufflé dish, and sprinkle the top with a little extra parmesan. Place the dish in the oven, and turn the heat down to 375°F. Bake for 35 minutes, then serve without further ado.

Cheese Soufflé

30 minutes
 to prepare;

40 minutes
 to bake.

Yield:
4 servings

a little melted butter for
 the soufflé dish
3 Tbs. butter
3 Tbs. unbleached white flour
2 tsp. dry mustard
1¼ cups hot milk (lowfat ok)

6 eggs, separated and at room
 temperature (yolks optional)
1½ packed cups grated sharp
 cheddar (about ½ lb.)
½ tsp. salt
fresh black pepper } to taste
cayenne

1) Preheat oven to 375°F. Lightly brush a soufflé dish with melted butter.

2) Melt 3 Tbs. butter in a medium-sized saucepan. Sprinkle in the flour and dry mustard, whisking constantly. Cook this roux all by itself over low heat, still whisking, for a minute or two.

3) Drizzle in the hot milk, whisking steadily. Cook over low heat, stirring often with a wooden spoon, for 5 minutes, or until nicely thickened. Remove from heat and transfer to a large bowl.

4) [OPTIONAL: Beat the egg yolks in a small bowl, then drizzle them into the sauce, beating vigorously.] Stir in the cheese, and season to taste with salt, black pepper, and cayenne.

5) Place the egg whites in a separate large bowl, and beat them until stiff. Fold them swiftly and adeptly into the first mixture, then transfer the whole thing to the soufflé dish. Bake 40 minutes undisturbed, and serve it fresh from the oven to your eager guests.

Omelettes

Everyone seems to have a personal method for making omelettes, and few of these methods would be considered "correct" according to classic methodology. But unless you intend to cook professionally, you don't need to struggle with learning <u>the</u> method. If you are comfortable with the way you make omelettes, all you need to take into account is the personal taste of whoever will be eating the result. But if you are NOT comfortable with your omelette making, here are some pointers to help improve things for you:

1) Always let the eggs come to room temperature first (as illustrated).

2) Invest in a good, heavy omelette pan — nonstick, if possible, 6 to 7 inches in diameter, with sides that angle outward slightly.

3) If it is not nonstick, keep the pan seasoned. Scrub it with water and salt (no soap!) after use. Dry it by heating it; brush it with oil while it is still hot. Keep it oiled until its next use.

HOW TO MAKE AN OMELETTE:

• Have the filling ready (and heated, if necessary) before you start.

• Have the plate(s) ready.

• Have your guest(s) ready. (If the omelette has to sit and wait, it will take insult and toughen.)

Make sure the pan is very hot before adding the beaten eggs. Melt 1 to 2 tsp. butter for each 2-egg omelette. The butter will sizzle, then quiet down. This is the right moment to add the eggs. Keep the heat constant, and work quickly, lifting the edges of the omelette and tilting the pan to let the uncooked egg flow into contact with the hot surface. As soon as the eggs are set, add some filling, fold the omelette in half, and slip it onto a plate. Serve A.S.A.P.!

❀ Some Omelette Fillings ❀

Spanish Omelette:

15 to 20 minutes to prepare.

Yield: 2 servings
(easily multiplied)

1 Tbs. olive oil
½ cup minced onion
1 medium clove garlic, minced
¼ tsp. salt
½ tsp. dried oregano
1 tsp. dried basil

1 small bell pepper, in very thin strips
1 medium-sized ripe tomato, diced
4 to 6 green olives, sliced off the pit
freshly ground black pepper
cayenne

1) Heat the oil in a medium-sized skillet. Add onion, garlic, salt, and herbs, and sauté over medium heat for about 5 minutes, or until the onion begins to soften.

2) Stir in the bell pepper, and cook over medium heat another 5 to 8 minutes, until the pepper is tender. Add tomato and olives; season to taste with black pepper and cayenne.

Sherried Mushroom Omelette:
Very sherry-y!

20 minutes to prepare.

Yield: 2 servings
(easily multiplied)

1 to 2 tsp. butter
12 large mushrooms, minced
a scant ½ tsp. salt
a pinch of dried thyme
2 tsp. unbleached white flour

¼ cup dry sherry
1 scallion, minced (include the green)
1 Tbs. minced fresh dill
2 Tbs. sour cream (optional)

1) Melt the butter in a medium-sized skillet. Add mushrooms, salt, and thyme, and cook over moderate heat, stirring often, for about 5 to 8 minutes — or until the mushrooms have cooked down. Sprinkle in the flour, and cook for about 2 minutes longer, stirring constantly.

2) Add the sherry. Cook over low heat, stirring often, for 5 minutes more. Remove from heat; stir in scallion and dill, and, if desired, the optional sour cream.

OTHER OMELETTE IDEAS:

ANY COMBINATION OF THINGS YOU LOVE: Small touches of your favorite savory, pungent, mild, or smoked cheese; salsa; other fresh herbs; fruit. This is a great place to practice innovating!

Gourmet Quickies:

MINCED FRESH CHILES (Anaheim or poblano), lightly sautéed with garlic. Possibly add some grated jack cheese, a sprinkling of minced fresh cilantro, and/or a few slices of ripe avocado. Add a little ground cumin to the eggs; serve with your favorite salsa.

MARINATED ARTICHOKE HEARTS, sliced into small pieces. If you so desire, add some grated Swiss cheese, and beat some prepared horseradish and dry mustard into the eggs.

SPINACH, quickly sautéed in a little olive oil. Add garlic, a diced tomato, and some crumbled feta cheese. Grind in lots of black pepper.

HERBS: Minced fresh basil, dill, and chives with tomato slices and goat cheese.

Leftovers:

LEFTOVER GRILLED OR ROASTED VEGETABLES: Eggplant, peppers, zucchini, and onions are especially good in omelettes.

OTHER LEFTOVERS: The enchilada fillings (pages 142-43) taste great in omelettes as well. Try making a double batch to be sure to have some left over. Also, many of the casseroles in this book would make fascinating omelette fillings. Experiment boldly (especially if you only have a little bit of something left over and you're eating alone). You might discover something great.

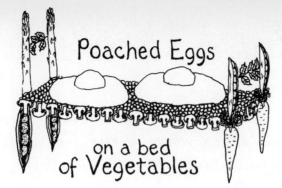

Poached Eggs
on a bed of Vegetables

Preparation time:
about 20 minutes.

Yield:
2 servings
(easily multiplied)

First, you sauté a panful of vegetables, then you poach the eggs directly on top.

This is a colorful, easy stovetop supper-for-two, perfect with a tossed salad and some cooked grains. If you have two frying pans, you can easily double the amounts to serve four.

NOTE: The vegetables are flexible — make substitutions as desired.

1 Tbs. butter or olive oil
1 cup minced onion
10 large mushrooms, sliced
2 cups chopped broccoli
½ tsp. salt
1 small red or green bell
    pepper, diced
2 medium cloves garlic, minced

3 handfuls minced fresh greens
    (spinach, escarole, collards, etc.)
a few dashes of cayenne
1 heaping Tbs. minced fresh basil } or 1 tsp.
1 heaping Tbs. minced fresh dill   }   dried
1 medium-sized ripe tomato, diced
4 to 5 Tbs. fine bread crumbs
4 eggs
freshly ground black pepper

1) Melt the butter or heat the oil in a large (9- or 10-inch) skillet. Add the onion, and cook for 5 minutes over medium heat. Add mushrooms, broccoli, and salt, and cook for about 5 minutes more, or until the broccoli is bright green and just tender.

2) Add bell pepper, garlic, and greens. Cook and stir for just a few minutes, or until the peppers are just tender, and the greens are wilted. Season to taste with cayenne and herbs. Stir in the tomato and bread crumbs.

3) Use the back of a soup spoon to indent four little beds for the eggs. Break the eggs into their nests, cover, and poach for about 5 minutes over medium heat — until the eggs are set to your taste. Grind some black pepper on top, and bring the whole pan to the table.

Eggs Florentine

40 minutes to prepare.

Yield: 2 servings
(easily multiplied)

3 Tbs. butter, plus a little for
   the baking dishes
2 Tbs. unbleached white flour
1¼ cups hot milk
2 tsp. Dijon mustard (optional)
¾ cup minced onion
about 8 mushrooms, sliced

2 medium cloves garlic, minced
½ tsp. salt
about 4 handfuls chopped
   fresh spinach
freshly ground black pepper
freshly grated nutmeg
4 eggs

1) If you are going to fry the eggs, preheat the broiler. If you plan to bake them, preheat the oven to 350°F. Lightly butter two au gratin dishes or rimmed ovenproof single-serving plates.

2) Melt 2 Tbs. butter in a small saucepan over medium-low heat. Whisk in the flour, and continue to cook and whisk for about a minute. Drizzle in the hot milk, still whisking. Cook for about 5 minutes, whisking frequently and vigorously, until nicely thickened. Stir in the mustard, if desired, and set aside.

3) Melt the remaining 1 Tbs. butter in a medium-sized skillet. Add onion, mushrooms, garlic, and salt, and sauté over medium heat for 8 to 10 minutes, or until the onion is quite soft. Add the spinach, turn the heat up, and cook for just a minute or two until the spinach is wilted and bright green. Use a slotted spoon to remove this mixture from the pan and divide it between the two baking dishes.

4) (A) If you are frying the eggs, do that now—to your liking. Transfer the cooked eggs to the beds of spinach, two to a dish.
(B) If you are baking the eggs, make two little indentations on each bed of spinach, and break an egg into each. Bake uncovered for 10 minutes, or until the eggs are set to your preference. Remove from the oven, and turn up the dial to broiling temperature.

5) Spoon as much sauce over the top as will fit. Grind on some pepper, grate on some nutmeg, and broil for just a minute or so until bubbly. Serve right away. (Place the baking dish on another, larger plate, and remind the eaters that the egg dish is hot.)

Frittata

15 minutes to prepare;
10 to 15 minutes to bake.

Yield: 4 servings

1 Tbs. olive oil
½ cup minced onion
¾ tsp. salt
dried oregano ⎱ a pinch
dried thyme ⎰ of each
8 to 10 mushrooms, sliced
about 1 cup diced zucchini
   and/or summer squash

½ cup minced bell pepper
1 small clove garlic, minced
2 handfuls chopped spinach and/or arugula
   (or any other leafy green)
freshly ground black pepper
a few leaves of fresh basil (if available)
4 or 5 eggs (ok to delete a yolk or two)
¼ lb. fontina cheese, grated or sliced
   (optional)

1) Preheat oven to 375°F.

2) Heat the oil on the stovetop in a 9- or 10-inch cast-iron skillet. Add the onion and half the salt, and sauté over medium heat for about 5 minutes.

3) Add dried herbs, mushrooms, zucchini or squash, bell pepper, and garlic, and cook, stirring, over medium-high heat for another 5 minutes — or until the vegetables are just tender.

4) Turn the heat up, and add the spinach and/or other greens with remaining salt and black pepper to taste. Stir and cook for just a minute or two — until some of the liquid evaporates. Stir in the basil.

5) Beat the eggs in a separate bowl, then pour them into the vegetables. Sprinkle in some cheese, if desired. Place the pan in the preheated oven for about 10 to 15 minutes, or until the frittata is solid when you shake the pan. (If you so desire, you can add some extra cheese to the top midway through the baking.)

6) Serve cut into wedges — hot, warm, or at room temperature. This will even taste good cold in a sandwich on lightly toasted bread, with a little mayonnaise, and sliced, very ripe tomatoes.

Vegetable Upside-Down Cake (page 192)

Carrot-Cashew Curry (page 199) with Indian Pulao (page 224), Raita (page 118), and Apricot-Lime Chutney (page 117)

From back to front: Russian Beet Salad (page 42), Chilled Marinated Cauliflower (page 41), and Swiss Green Beans (page 43)

Clockwise from front left: Whole Wheat Poppy Seed Cookies (page 263), Cashew Shortbread (page 264), and Rugelach (page 265)

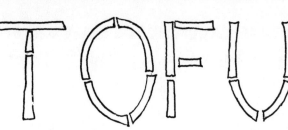

TOFU

SO WHAT IS THIS STUFF CALLED TOFU? Are you afraid to ask, because it seems that everyone else knows, and they'll think you're a dope?

I am happy to offer a few words on behalf of tofu, having been completely won over by the charms of this humble and versatile food. Tofu is a curd —like cheese—made from soy milk, a nondairy substance made from soy-beans. It is commonly used in East Asian cuisines. Soft and bland in its basic form, tofu's primary talent is its chameleon-like ability to absorb seasonings. In addition, it's a wonderful, inexpensive way to slip some nonanimal protein into one's diet. (It is also a good source of calcium and vitamin E, and has no cholesterol.) Look for plain tofu (you get to choose between "soft" and "firm") in natural foods stores, Chinese or Japanese groceries, and in the produce sections of many supermarkets. It is usually sold in one-pound units, packed in water in sealed plastic tubs. Store it immersed in water in the refrigerator, and tofu will keep as long as a week. There are other types of tofu available as well. Very firm tofu that has been baked and variously seasoned can be found, vacuum-packed in plastic and refrigerated, in natural foods stores. Silken tofu (available in 10-oz. vacuum-packed boxes—unrefrigerated—in natural foods stores, Asian groceries, and many supermarkets) is an ultrasmooth variety that whips up like a dream in the blender, acquiring the exact consistency of fresh mayonnaise (see pages 40 and 55).

Tofu has many applications. You can choose to feature it (as in the following recipes), to marinate it (p. 183) for use in salads, grains, and cooked vegetables, or to use it more anonymously as a protein and texture booster for salad dressings, casseroles, soups, purées, etc. Tofu also makes wonderful baby food. It is soft and digestible and has magical healing and comforting powers. (See "Tofu for Children", p. 188.)

For further ideas and a wealth of information, read The Book of Tofu, by William Shurtleff and Akiko Aoyagi (Ten Speed Press, 1975).

Sweet & Sour Tofu with Cashews

45 minutes to prepare.

(Put up some rice to cook before you begin.)

Yield: 4 to 5 servings

3/4 lb. firm tofu
1 20-oz. can pineapple chunks
 (packed in unsweetened juice)
about 1½ cups orange juice
1 tsp. grated orange rind
2 large cloves garlic, minced
1 Tbs. grated fresh ginger
2 Tbs. soy sauce
½ tsp. salt (plus a little more)
1 to 2 Tbs. honey or sugar

2 Tbs. vinegar (rice or cider)
crushed red pepper to taste
2 Tbs. Chinese sesame oil
1 medium onion, chopped
1 small carrot, thinly sliced
1 small bell pepper, chopped
1 medium-sized ripe tomato, chopped
4 Tbs. cornstarch
3 scallions, cut into thin strips
1 cup cashews, lightly toasted

1) (Do this ahead): Cut the tofu into 1-inch cubes. Place them in a medium-sized saucepan and cover with water. Bring to a boil, lower heat to a simmer, and cook for about 10 or 15 minutes. Drain and set aside.

2) Drain all the liquid from the can of pineapple into a 4-cup capacity liquid measuring cup. Add enough orange juice to make 2½ cups of liquid. Set aside the pineapple chunks.

3) Add the orange rind, garlic, ginger, soy sauce, ½ tsp. salt, honey or sugar, vinegar, and crushed red pepper to the pineapple juice and whisk. Transfer to a saucepan and heat until hot, but not boiling. Cover and set aside, keeping the whisk handy.

4) Heat a large wok. Add the sesame oil and the onion. Salt lightly and stir-fry over high heat for about a minute. Add the carrot, and sauté about 3 minutes more. Add tofu and bell pepper, salt lightly again, and cook about 2 minutes longer, keeping the heat steadily high. Stir in the tomato. (Turn the heat down temporarily during the next step.)

5) Place the cornstarch in a small bowl. Whisk in a little of the heated sauce from Step 3, then whisk the dissolved cornstarch back into the sauce. Turn the heat back up as you add this to the stir-fry.

6) Cook for another few minutes, stirring constantly, until the sauce has thickened and everything is coated and glossy. Stir in the scallions at the very end. Serve hot, over rice, topped generously with toasted cashews.

Szechwan Tofu Triangles
in Triple Pepper Sauce

45 minutes to prepare.
(Put up some rice to
cook as you begin.)

Yield:
6 servings

1½ lbs. very firm tofu
about 5 Tbs. peanut oil
½ cup dry sherry
¼ cup soy sauce
1¾ cups water
¼ cup plus 1 tsp. vinegar
　　(cider or rice)
3 Tbs. honey or sugar
8 large cloves garlic, minced

1 Tbs. dry mustard
4 Tbs. cornstarch
3 cups chopped onion (1-inch chunks)
1 medium yellow bell pepper, in strips
1 medium red bell pepper, in strips
1½ tsp. salt
crushed red pepper ⎫
freshly ground black pepper ⎭ to taste
6 scallions, minced (whites + greens)

1) Cut the tofu into triangles, as illustrated: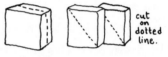
cut on dotted line.

2) Heat 4 Tbs. oil in a wok or skillet until it is hot enough to bounce a drop of water. Fry the tofu triangles for a few minutes on each side, until their outer surfaces crispen. Drain on paper towels.

3) In a medium-sized saucepan, combine sherry, soy sauce, water, vinegar, honey or sugar, garlic, and dry mustard. Heat it until it almost boils; remove from heat. Place the cornstarch in a small bowl, and pour in some hot liquid, whisking until it dissolves. Whisk this back into the saucepan. Keep the whisk in there— you'll need it.

4) Heat the wok or skillet again. Add the remaining oil, and cook the onion over high heat for about 2 minutes. Add bell peppers, salt, and red and black pepper, and cook for about 2 minutes longer. Gently stir in the tofu triangles.

5) Whisk the sauce (from Step 3) to reintegrate the cornstarch, and pour all of it into the wok. Stir and cook over high heat for about 8 minutes, adding the scallions at the very end. When the sauce is thick and everything is coated, serve hot over rice.

Tofu Marinades

Tofu is an excellent absorber of marinades, especially when it is sautéed or boiled ahead of time. With the discovery of tofu's special marination talent, the world of simple tofu meals takes on a new dimension: FLAVOR! (Add this to the list of tofu's more obvious attributes: softness, substance, innocence...)

Once you get into the habit of marinating tofu, you will be able to design more satisfying simple meals around brown rice, green salads, and steamed or sautéed vegetables. You will find that good food has never been so delicious and accessible.

How To MARINATE Tofu:

Begin with the firmest plain tofu you can find. Cut it into cubes or rectangles of any size, and either sauté it in a little oil or boil it in water—for about 10 minutes. Drain and proceed. (You don't need to cool it first.) This precooking process expels some of the tofu's water, firming it up considerably, and enhancing its ability to absorb strong flavors without diluting them.

FOR SALADS:

Simply add small cubes of precooked tofu to a jarful of your favorite salad dressing (see pages 39 and 40). Let it marinate for a minimum of an hour or two—and up to a week or longer. Toss the tofu-au-jus into green salads immediately before serving.

FOR ADDING TOFU TO COOKED RICE OR VEGETABLES:

3 to 4 Tbs. soy sauce
2 medium cloves garlic, minced
2 tsp. grated fresh ginger
1 Tbs. Chinese sesame oil
1 Tbs. vinegar (rice or cider)
1 to 2 tsp. honey or sugar
    (optional)

Combine all ingredients in a medium-sized bowl. Add ½ lb. tofu, diced and precooked. Stir, cover, and let sit at least an hour. Stir gently into freshly cooked rice or vegetables just before serving.

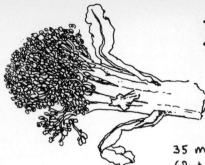

Broccoli & Tofu
... in spicy peanut sauce

35 minutes to prepare.
(Put up some rice to
cook before you begin.)

Yield:
serves 4 or 5

1 lb. firm tofu
1 lb. broccoli
1 to 2 Tbs. peanut or canola oil
2 cups chopped onion
1 Tbs. grated fresh ginger
4 medium cloves garlic, minced

¾ tsp. salt
2 scallions, minced (greens and whites)
Spicy Peanut Sauce (recipe follows)
1 cup coarsely chopped
   peanuts, lightly toasted (optional)

1) Cut the tofu into 1-inch cubes and place them in a medium-sized sauce-pan. Cover the tofu with water. Bring to a boil, lower the heat, and simmer for about 10 minutes. Drain and set aside. (NOTE: Precooking the tofu in this way helps it hold its shape in the stir-fry.)

2) Trim and discard the tough ends of the broccoli stems. Shave off the tough skins of the stalks with a sharp paring knife or a vegetable peeler. Cut the stalks diagonally into thin slices. Coarsely chop the florets.

3) Heat a large wok or a skillet of comparable size. After about a minute, add the oil and onion. Cook for about 2 minutes over high heat.

4) Add broccoli, ginger, garlic, and salt. Continue to stir-fry over high heat for about 5 minutes, or until the broccoli is bright green and just tender. Stir in the precooked tofu and the scallions; cook for a few minutes more.

5) Add the sauce, stirring until everything is well coated. Serve immediately over rice, topped with lightly toasted chopped peanuts, if desired.

spicy peanut sauce

¾ cup good peanut butter
¾ cup hot water
6 Tbs. vinegar (rice or cider)

3 Tbs. soy sauce
3 Tbs. blackstrap molasses
cayenne to taste

1) Place the peanut butter and hot water in a small bowl, and mash together until the mixture is uniform.

2) Whisk in remaining ingredients. Set aside until needed for the stir-fry.

40 minutes to prepare.
(very easy!)

Tofu Sukiyaki

There are a few unusual ingredients in here, so I'll explain. <u>Mirin</u> is a sake (Japanese wine) made especially for cooking. Saifun and bean thread are two types of very thin, transparent noodles. You can buy these products at Asian groceries. If you can't find them, substitute a sweet cooking wine for the mirin, and cooked vermicelli (2 oz. uncooked measure) for the saifun or bean thread.

Serve this in bowls over rice. Be sure to include lots of the broth in each serving. Put up the rice to cook well ahead of time.

NOTE: The vegetables are flexible. Make substitutions as needed.

1 lb. firm tofu
1½ cups mirin
¾ cup soy sauce
2 cups water
2 to 3 large cloves garlic, sliced
1 Tbs. minced fresh ginger
about 2 oz. uncooked saifun
   or bean thread noodles
1 cup sliced onion
6 leaves napa (savoy) cabbage,
   cut into thin strips

1 stalk celery, in thin, diagonal strips
a handful of slender green
   beans, trimmed and cut in half (optional)
about 6 mushrooms, sliced
2 handfuls mung bean sprouts
2 handfuls snow peas, trimmed
   and cut in half
5 or 6 scallions, cut into thin
   strips (whites and greens)

1) Cut the tofu into bite-sized cubes or rectangles, and boil them in a saucepanful of water for 10 minutes. Drain and set aside.

2) Combine mirin, soy sauce, water, garlic, and ginger in a very large sauce-pan or a Dutch oven. Bring to a boil, lower heat to a simmer, and add the boiled tofu. Let it simmer quietly, covered, for about 15 minutes.

3) Add the uncooked noodles and cover again. Turn off the heat, and let it sit for 5 to 10 minutes, or until the noodles are edibly tender. At this point, it can sit for up to several hours until serving time.

4) Return to the heat shortly before serving. Let it reach a boil, then turn the heat down to a simmer. Add onion, cabbage, celery, optional green beans, and mushrooms, and cover. Five minutes later, add the remaining vegetables, cover again, and remove from heat. Wait another 5 minutes, then serve.

Tofu-Nut Balls

45 minutes to cook
the rice; 10 minutes
to do everything else.

Yield:
about 36
little balls
(6 apiece for 6 people)

These are very simple to make and fun to eat. Kids love them!

SERVING SUGGESTIONS: 1) As an hors d'oeuvre on toothpicks (to your bewildered but polite – and ultimately delighted– guests)
2) With steamed or sautéed vegetables
3) On top of pasta, with tomato sauce
4) Topped with any of the delicious sauces on pages 108 and 109.

½ cup uncooked short grain
    brown rice
1 cup water
a little oil for the baking sheet
    or frying pan

2 Tbs. soy sauce
½ lb. firm tofu, mashed
½ cup (rounded measure) ground
    almonds
½ cup fine bread crumbs
salt to taste

1) Place the rice and water in a small saucepan. Bring to a boil, cover, and lower the heat to the slowest possible simmer. Cook until very soft (mushy, even) – about 35 to 45 minutes.
2) You get to choose between sautéing the balls or baking them. If you are baking them, preheat the oven to 350°F and lightly oil a baking sheet. If you are sautéing, have ready a skillet and a little oil.
3) Place the soy sauce and half the mashed tofu in a blender or food processor, and add about ¾ of the cooked rice. Blend to a thick paste.
4) Place the remaining tofu in a medium-sized bowl. Add the blended mixture, along with the almonds, bread crumbs, and remaining rice. Taste to see if it needs salt.
5) Using your hands, form the batter into 1-inch balls. To cook, you can:
    a) Sauté them in a little hot oil for about 15 minutes, –OR–
    b) Bake them on a lightly oiled tray for 30 minutes. Serve hot.

Tofu, Spinach, & Walnut Loaf

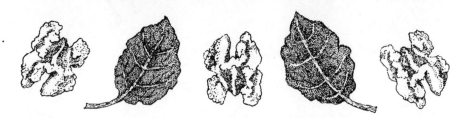

40 minutes
to prepare;
1 hour to bake.

Yield:
4 to 6
servings

NOTES: ♪ You'll need cooked brown rice for this, so plan ahead. To make rice fresh for this recipe, cook 1 cup rice in a scant 2 cups water. (This will make more than enough.)

♪ You can use fresh spinach or frozen. If using frozen, be sure it is thoroughly defrosted and drained beforehand. Squeeze out all excess water.

a little oil for the pan
1 Tbs. peanut or canola oil
2 cups minced onion
1/2 lb. mushrooms, minced
6 large cloves garlic, minced
1 cup ground walnuts
2 lbs. fresh spinach, minced – or
   2 10-oz. packages frozen
   chopped spinach, defrosted,
   and thoroughly drained

OPTIONAL: 1/3 cup dry sherry
1/4 cup Worcestershire sauce
1 tsp. salt
1 Tbs. soy sauce
1/2 lb. firm tofu, mashed
1 1/2 cups cooked brown rice
fresh black pepper to taste
1/4 tsp. nutmeg
Dilled Horseradish Sauce (p. 108)
paprika for the top

1) Preheat oven to 350°F. Lightly oil a medium-sized loaf pan.

2) Heat 1 Tbs. peanut or canola oil in a deep skillet or Dutch oven. Add the onion, mushrooms, and garlic, and sauté over medium heat for about 8 to 10 minutes.

3) Add walnuts, spinach, optional sherry, Worcestershire sauce, and salt. Stir and cook over medium heat another 5 to 8 minutes, or until the spinach is wilted and everything is well mingled. Remove from heat.

4) Stir in the soy sauce, tofu, rice, black pepper, and nutmeg. When it is thoroughly combined, taste to adjust seasonings.

5) Spread into the prepared loaf pan, and bake uncovered for 1 hour. Let sit for about 10 minutes before serving. Serve hot, with Dilled Horseradish Sauce (which you can prepare while the loaf bakes) and a sprinkling of paprika.

TOFU FOR CHILDREN

Many parents wish they could somehow cause their young children to become more readily attracted to tofu, especially since it is so nutritious and inexpensive. The truth is, children often have an innate appreciation of tofu:

* They enjoy the sensation of picking it up with their bare hands and squeezing it until it oozes out between their fingers.
* They like to chase it around on their plate with a spoon.
* They derive pleasure from throwing it on the floor and stepping on it.
* They also like to eat it.

Here are a few child-tested approaches: (good luck!)

1) Heat a little canola or peanut oil in a small skillet. Cut firm tofu into ½-inch cubes and dust them lightly with cornstarch. When the oil is very hot, fry the tofu cubes until crisp. Drain on paper towels and sprinkle with a little salt or soy sauce. This makes a delightful snack.

2) Mash some soft tofu with a ripe banana. Decorate with raisins; eat with fingers or a spoon. (NOTE: Even the youngest child can participate in making this one.)

3) Add some cottage cheese and diced firm tofu to freshly cooked noodles. Salt lightly and serve at any temperature.

4) Sneak some mashed soft tofu into mashed potatoes.

5) Make Tofu-Nut Balls (p. 186), and serve them with lots of ketchup.

Casseroles, Mélanges,
...and other groupings

Shepherd's Pie

A deep-dish casserole: vegetable hash on the bottom, and garlicky mashed potatoes on top.

45 minutes to prepare;
25 to 30 minutes to bake.

Yield: 4 to 6 servings

MASHED POTATO TOPPING
(Make this first):

2 large potatoes
1 Tbs. butter (optional)
½ cup milk (lowfat or soy ok)
3 large cloves garlic, minced
salt ⎫
fresh black pepper ⎬ to taste
½ cup minced fresh parsley

VEGETABLE HASH:

1 Tbs. canola or olive oil
1 ½ cups minced onion
4 large cloves garlic, minced
1 tsp. salt
fresh black pepper to taste
1 stalk celery, finely minced
1 lb. mushrooms, chopped
1 1-lb. eggplant, diced
1 medium bell pepper, minced

2 tsp. dried basil
½ tsp. dried thyme
½ tsp. dried oregano
1 cup peas (fresh or frozen)
¾ cup grated cheddar (optional)
¼ cup fine bread crumbs
3 Tbs. cider vinegar
cayenne to taste
paprika

OPTIONAL: Spiked Mushroom Sauce ⎫ both recipes
or Dilled Horseradish Sauce ⎬ on page 108

I. THE MASHED POTATO TOPPING:

Peel or scrub the potatoes, and cut them into 1-inch chunks. Cook in plenty of boiling water until soft. Drain and transfer to a medium-large bowl. Add optional butter, garlic, and milk, and mash well. Add salt and black pepper to taste, and stir in the parsley. Set aside.

II. THE VEGETABLE HASH (AND ASSEMBLY):

1) Preheat oven to 350°F. Have ready a 2-quart casserole or its equivalent. (A 9 x 13-inch baking pan will work fine.)

2) Heat the oil in a large, deep skillet or a Dutch oven. Add the onion, and sauté over medium heat for about 5 minutes, or until it begins to soften.

3) Add garlic, salt, pepper, celery, mushrooms, eggplant, and bell pepper. Stir until well combined, cover, and cook over medium heat for about 10 minutes, stirring frequently. Add the herbs, stir, and cover again. Cook for about 5 more minutes, or until the eggplant is perfectly tender. Remove from heat.

4) Stir in the peas, ½ cup of the optional cheddar, the bread crumbs, and the vinegar. Add cayenne to taste. Transfer this mixture to the casserole or baking pan, and spread it out.

5) Spoon and/or spread the mashed potatoes over the vegetables. If desired, sprinkle the remaining cheddar over the top. Dust generously with paprika.

6) Bake uncovered for 25 or 30 minutes, or until lightly browned on top and bubbly around the edges. Make the sauce of your choice while the Shepherd's Pie bakes. To serve, spoon a little sauce onto each plate. Add a chunk of pie, potato side up, and spoon extra sauce over the top. Serve hot.

Vegetable Upside~Down Cake

40 minutes to prepare;
40 to 45 minutes to bake

Yield:
4 to 6
servings

First you put a savory medley of sautéed vegetables in the pan, then an herbed quick-bread batter gets poured on top. Bake it and invert onto a tray, and you end up with a handsome two-layered dish — savory cake on the bottom and vegetables on top. Impressive and easy; any beginner can make this!

PART I: "THE VEGETABLES"

3 Tbs. butter
1 heaping cup chopped onion
2 cups small broccoli florets
1 medium-sized carrot, diced
1½ cups small cauliflower florets
1 cup minced red bell pepper

1 cup corn (fresh or frozen)
5 medium cloves garlic, minced
5 scallions, minced (whites and greens)
salt, pepper, and cayenne to taste
1 packed cup grated sharp cheddar

1) Preheat oven to 350°F. Grease an 8-inch baking pan with 2 tablespoons of the butter. Put up a medium-sized saucepan of water to boil. Have ready a strainer and a bowl of ice water.

2) Melt the remaining tablespoon of butter in a small skillet over medium heat. Add the onion, and sauté until translucent and soft (8 minutes).

3) Meanwhile, when the water comes to a boil, drop in the broccoli, carrot, and cauliflower, and blanch for just 30 seconds. Drain in the strainer over a sink, the immediately drop into the ice water. After a few minutes, drain again, dry with paper towels, and transfer to a bowl.

4) Add the sautéed onion and the remaining uncooked vegetables. Mix well, and season to taste with salt, pepper, and cayenne. Spread the vegetables into the buttered pan, and sprinkle the cheese over the top. (Wipe out the bowl so you can use it again for Part 2.)

PART II: "THE CAKE"

1 cup unbleached white flour
½ cup whole wheat pastry flour
1 tsp. baking powder
½ tsp. baking soda
½ tsp. salt
1 to 2 Tbs. sugar
½ tsp. each: dried oregano and thyme
2 Tbs. minced fresh dill
1 egg
1 cup buttermilk or yogurt
2 Tbs. melted butter

1) Sift together flours, baking powder, soda, and salt into a large bowl. Stir in sugar and herbs. Mix well, and make an indentation in the center.

2) In a separate medium-sized bowl, beat together the eggs, buttermilk or yogurt, and melted butter.

3) Pour the liquid mixture into the well in the center of the dry ingredients. Mix by hand — minimally but thoroughly — until well combined, being sure to scrape the bottom and sides of the bowl.

4) Carefully spread the batter over the vegetables in the pan ("PART I"). Use a blunt knife and/or rubber spatula to distribute it as evenly as possible.

5) Bake for 40 to 45 minutes — until a toothpick inserted into the center comes out clean. Have ready a clean serving tray slightly larger than the baking pan. Let the cake cool in the pan for about 10 minutes, then invert the cake firmly and carefully onto the tray. Bring the whole thing to the table to delight your dinner guests. Cut into squares; serve hot, warm, or at room temperature.

 *Tsimmes*

15 minutes to assemble;
1½ to 2 hours to bake.

Yield: 4 to 6 servings

Tsimmes is a festive Jewish dish that combines vegetables and fruit; savory with tart and sweet. There is no official recipe – each family seems to have its own traditional version, handed down by word-of-mouth, generation to generation. One thing all versions have in common is the technique: just throw everything together and bake it for a long time.

Serve Tsimmes with Spinach Kugel (opposite page) and a freshly baked challah (p.73) for a warming winter supper.

> 3½ lbs. sweet potatoes or yams (or a combination)
> 2 large carrots, sliced
> 1 large (3- to 4-inch diameter) apple, sliced
>   (peeling optional)
> 1 heaping cup chopped onion
> 2 cups chopped dried apricots
> 3 to 4 Tbs. fresh lemon juice
> 1 tsp. salt
> ½ tsp. cinnamon
> 2/3 cup orange juice
> 1 cup apple juice
> ¼ cup fine bread crumbs or matzo meal

1) Preheat oven to 350°F.

2) Peel the sweet potatoes and/or yams, and cut them into 1-inch pieces. Place them in a large bowl, add all remaining ingredients except bread crumbs or matzo meal, and toss until nicely combined. Don't worry if it's not perfectly uniform.

3) Transfer to a 2-quart casserole or equivalent baking pan, sprinkle with crumbs or matzo meal, and cover with foil. Bake for 1½ to 2 hours, or until everything is very tender and indistinguishable from everything else.

Vegetable Kugels

Kugel (which, in loose translation from the Yiddish, means "pudding") is a basic item in Eastern European Jewish cuisine. Generally, a kugel is a baked rectangular casserole consisting of small units of food (noodles or a finely chopped or grated combination of vegetables) held together with beaten eggs.

The classic vegetable kugel is Potato (page 197), and here, in addition, are two others: one made with spinach (below), and another with a combination of grated carrot and zucchini (page 196). NOTE: There is also a recipe for a noodle kugel on page 162.

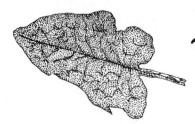

Spinach Kugel

10 minutes to prepare;
45 minutes to bake.

Yield: 4 to 6 servings

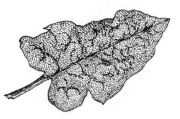

Fresh spinach is delicious in this recipe, but frozen works just fine as well. This reheats beautifully in a microwave oven—it makes a great hot lunch on a cold day. It also makes a great cold lunch on a hot day: a kugel for all seasons.

a little oil for the pan
2 lbs. fresh spinach (or 2 10-oz. packages frozen chopped spinach, defrosted)
1 lb. (2 cups) cottage cheese
4 eggs, beaten (yolks optional)
1 tsp. salt

¼ tsp. nutmeg
1½ Tbs. fresh lemon juice
fresh black pepper to taste
1 cup fine bread crumbs or matzo meal (¼ cup reserved for the top)
paprika

1) Preheat oven to 375°F. Lightly oil a 9 x 13-inch baking pan.

2) Clean and finely mince the spinach. (If using frozen, make sure it is thoroughly defrosted first.) Place the spinach in a colander over the sink and press out all excess water. Transfer to a medium-sized bowl.

3) Add remaining ingredients, except for ¼ cup of the bread crumbs or matzo meal and the paprika. Mix well; transfer to the prepared pan.

4) Sprinkle the top with the reserved bread crumbs or matzo meal and paprika. Cover the pan tightly with foil and bake for 35 minutes, then uncover and let it bake 10 minutes more. Serve hot, warm, at room temperature, or even cold, cut into squares.

Carrot~Zucchini Kugel

30 minutes to prepare;
1¼ hours to bake.

(Use a food processor
to grate things.)

a little oil for the pan
6 cups coarsely grated zucchini
　(approximately 7 medium zukes)
1 tsp. salt
2 Tbs. butter or canola oil
3 cups finely minced onion
3 large cloves garlic, minced

3 cups grated carrot (about
　5 medium carrots)
3 eggs, beaten (ok to delete yolks)
1¼ cups fine bread crumbs
　or matzo meal
fresh black pepper to taste
a little extra oil for the top (optional)

1) Preheat oven to 375°F. Lightly oil a 9 x 13-inch baking pan.

2) Place the grated zucchini in a colander over the sink. Sprinkle
with ½ tsp. of the salt and let it stand 15 minutes. Squeeze out
all excess moisture and set aside.

3) Melt the butter or heat the oil in a medium-sized skillet. Add
onion and remaining salt, and sauté over medium heat for
about 10 minutes, or until the onion is very soft. Add the garlic
and sauté about 2 minutes longer. Remove from heat.

4) In a medium-large bowl mix together the zucchini, sautéed onion,
and grated carrot. Beat in the eggs and bread crumbs or matzo
meal. Grind in some black pepper and mix well.

5) Spread the batter into the prepared pan. Bake for 1½ hours. (For
a crisper top surface, brush lightly with oil about halfway
through the baking.) Serve hot, warm, or at room temperature,
cut into squares.

Tante Malka's Potato Kugel Deluxe

25 minutes to prepare;
1¼ hours to bake.

Yield: about 6 servings

Simple and wholesome: a crispy potato pudding.

a little oil for the pan
4 medium-sized potatoes
3 Tbs. butter or canola oil
3 cups minced onion
½ lb. mushrooms, minced
2 tsp. salt
3 large cloves garlic, minced
fresh black pepper to taste

2 Tbs. minced fresh dill
4 eggs, beaten (OK to delete yolks)
1 cup sour cream (optional)
½ cup bread crumbs or matzo meal

for the top { paprika (optional)
a little extra oil

1) Preheat oven to 375°F. Lightly oil a 9 x 13-inch baking pan.

2) Scrub and coarsely grate the potatoes. (A food processor with the grating attachment works beautifully.) Set aside.

3) Melt the butter or heat the oil in a large, deep skillet. Add the onion, and sauté over medium heat for about 5 minutes. Add the potatoes, mushrooms, and salt, and sauté for about 10 minutes more. Stir in the garlic during the last minute or so. Remove from heat, and transfer to a large bowl.

4) Add remaining ingredients and mix well. Spread evenly into the prepared pan, and dust the top with paprika. Bake for 1 to 1¼ hours until crisp on top. For an extra crisp top, brush with a little extra oil halfway through the baking. Cut into squares, and serve hot or warm.

Humble Vegetable Casserole

30 minutes to prepare;
30 minutes to bake.

... an easy, soothing, delicious one-dish meal. Good in any season.

a little oil for the pan
4 medium-sized potatoes, thinly
   sliced (peeling optional)
1 or 2 Tbs. butter or canola oil
1½ cups sliced onion
1 tsp. caraway seeds
1 lb. mushrooms, sliced
4 cups chopped broccoli
1½ tsp. salt

2 medium cloves garlic, minced
black pepper to taste
1 Tbs. minced fresh dill (1 tsp. dried)
2 hard-boiled eggs, chopped (ok
   to delete yolks)
½ cup minced pickles (dill or sweet-
   your choice)
1½ cups grated cheddar (optional)
¾ cup milk (lowfat or soy ok)
paprika

1) Preheat oven to 350°F. Lightly oil a 9 x 13-inch baking pan.

2) Put the potatoes in a saucepan, and cover them with water. Boil until just tender. Drain well and set aside.

3) Melt the butter or heat the oil in a large, deep skillet or a Dutch oven. Add onion and caraway seeds and sauté over medium heat for about 5 minutes or until the onion begins to soften. Add mushrooms, broccoli, and salt. Cook for about 5 minutes longer – until the broccoli is bright green and barely tender. Remove from heat, and gently stir in the potatoes, garlic, black pepper, and dill. Spread into the baking pan.

4) Sprinkle with chopped egg, minced pickles, and, if desired, grated cheese. Pour the milk over the top, and dust lightly with paprika.

5) Bake uncovered for 30 minutes. Serve hot or warm, cut into squares.

Carrot~Cashew Curry

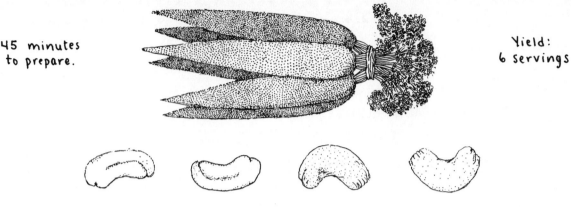

45 minutes
to prepare.

Yield:
6 servings

PRELIMINARY: Put up some rice to cook before you begin. Use 3 cups water to 2 cups rice. Bring to a boil together, cover, and turn heat to very low. White rice (plain or basmati) will be done 20 minutes later. Brown rice (plain or basmati) will be done 40 to 45 minutes later.

1 Tbs. canola or peanut oil
1 Tbs. grated fresh ginger
1 tsp. mustard seeds
1 tsp. dill seeds
1 tsp. ground cumin
1 tsp. ground coriander
1 tsp. turmeric
2 cups sliced red onion
4 large cloves garlic, minced
2 tsp. salt

2 medium-sized potatoes,
    thinly sliced
5 large carrots,
    thinly sliced
2 cups orange juice
1/4 tsp. cayenne (to taste)
1 medium red bell pepper,
    thinly sliced
1 cup yogurt
1 1/2 cups toasted cashews
Chutney (pp. 116-17)
Raita (p. 118)

1) Heat a large, deep skillet or Dutch oven. Add oil, ginger, mustard seeds, and dill seeds, and sauté over medium heat for 3 to 5 minutes, or until the seeds begin to pop.

2) Add the remaining spices, and the onion, garlic, salt, potatoes, and carrots. Sauté for another 5 minutes, then add the orange juice. Cover, turn the heat to medium-low, and simmer until the potatoes are tender (15 minutes).

3) Add cayenne and bell pepper. Cover and let it stew another few minutes, until the peppers are just barely cooked. (At this point it can be set aside until shortly before serving time.)

4) Heat the curry just before serving, stirring in the yogurt at the very last minute. Serve over rice, topped with cashews, with Chutney and Raita.

✴ Potato, Panir, & Pea Curry ✴

30 minutes to prepare.

Yield: 4 servings

"Panir" refers to a mild curd cheese. You can use cottage cheese or crumbled firm tofu — either will achieve the desired textural effect. Before you begin cooking the curry, put up 2 cups white or brown rice (plain or basmati) to cook in 3 cups water. Bring to a boil, cover, and lower heat to the gentlest simmer possible. Let cook undisturbed for 15 to 20 minutes (white) or 35 to 45 minutes (brown). Fluff with a fork and serve.

2 large potatoes, thinly sliced (peeling is optional)	a pinch of thyme
	1¼ tsp. salt
2 Tbs. peanut or canola oil	5 medium cloves garlic, minced
1 Tbs. mustard seeds	3 Tbs. fresh lemon juice
½ tsp. caraway seeds	2 cups firm yogurt
3 Tbs. sesame seeds	cayenne to taste
2 tsp. cumin seeds	2 cups peas (fresh or frozen)
½ tsp. ground coriander	1 cup large curd cottage cheese
½ tsp. turmeric	(or ½ lb. firm tofu, crumbled)
½ tsp. ground cloves	Chutney (pp. 116–17)
	Raita (p. 118)

1) Place the potato slices in a large enough saucepan, and fill it with plenty of water to cover them. Bring to a boil, lower the heat to a simmer, and cook until just tender. Drain and set aside.

2) Meanwhile, heat the oil in a large, deep skillet or Dutch oven. Stir in the seeds and spices, and cook over low heat for several minutes, or until the seeds begin to pop.

3) Add the cooked potatoes along with the salt and garlic. Keep the heat medium-low, and gently stir the potatoes until they are thoroughly coated with all the seasonings.

4) Add the lemon juice and yogurt, and cover. Let it cook, disturbing it every now and then to stir it, for about 5 to 10 minutes. (Be careful not to let the potatoes get mushy.) Add cayenne to taste.

5) Stir in the peas and cottage cheese or tofu. Cook for just a few minutes longer. Serve hot, over rice, with Chutney and Raita.

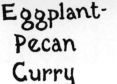

Eggplant-Pecan Curry

45 minutes to prepare.

Begin cooking rice ahead of time. (See instructions on opposite page.)

Yield: 4 servings

2 Tbs. peanut or canola oil
1 Tbs. grated fresh ginger
1½ cups minced onion
1½ tsp. salt
2 tsp. dry mustard
1½ tsp. turmeric
½ tsp. cayenne
2 tsp. ground cumin
½ tsp. allspice

about 1½ cups water
1 1½-lb. eggplant, cut into 1-inch cubes (peeling is optional)
5 medium cloves garlic, minced
1 small red bell pepper, thinly sliced
1 medium-sized ripe tomato, peeled, seeded, and minced*
1 cup chopped, toasted pecans
Chutney (pp. 116-17)
Raita (p. 118)

1) Heat the oil in a large, deep skillet or Dutch oven. Add ginger, onion, and salt, and sauté over medium heat for 5 minutes. Add all the spices, and sauté another 5 minutes or so, adding the water a little at a time.

2) Stir in the eggplant and garlic. Cover, lower the heat, and cook for about 10 to 15 minutes. Interrupt it every so often for a stir, and to see if perhaps it needs a little more water to keep it from sticking.

3) When the eggplant is tender, add the bell pepper and tomato. Cook and stir over medium heat for another 10 minutes. Serve hot, over rice, topped with pecans, with Chutney and Raita.

*NOTE: To peel and seed a tomato, core it first, then lower it into a saucepan of simmering water for 20 seconds or so. Take it out and pull off the skin. Cut it open; squeeze out and discard the seeds. That's it!

Savory Vegetable Cheesecake

DDDDDDDDDDDDDDDD

30 minutes to prepare;
60 minutes to bake
(plus time to rest
before serving).

Yield:
6 or more
servings

3 packed cups coarsely grated
   zucchini (about 3 or 4
     small zucchini)
a little salt

a little oil for the pan
1 Tbs. olive oil
1 cup minced onion
½ tsp. salt
1 cup grated carrot
2 Tbs. unbleached white flour
2 tsp. dried basil
½ tsp. dried oregano

½ tsp. dried thyme
5 medium cloves garlic, minced
¼ cup minced fresh parsley
1 Tbs. fresh lemon juice
3 cups (1½ lbs.) ricotta cheese
1 packed cup grated mozzarella
½ cup grated parmesan
3 beaten eggs
black pepper to taste
2 medium-sized tomatoes, sliced into
   rounds, with each round sliced
     in half (into "Ds")
3 to 4 Tbs. fine bread crumbs

1) Place the grated zucchini in a colander over a sink. Salt lightly and let stand 15 minutes. Squeeze out all excess moisture.

2) Meanwhile, preheat the oven to 375°F. Lightly oil the bottom of a 9-inch springform pan.

3) Heat 1 Tbs. olive oil in a large, deep skillet or a Dutch oven. Add the onion and ½ tsp. salt, and sauté over medium heat for about 5 minutes. Add zucchini, carrot, flour, and dried herbs, and cook, stirring, over medium heat for about 5 more minutes. Remove from heat; stir in garlic, parsley, and lemon juice.

4) Place the cheeses and eggs in a large bowl, and beat vigorously for a minute or two. Add the vegetable mixture, and mix well. Season to taste with black pepper, and adjust salt, if necessary.

5) Transfer the mixture to the prepared pan. Arrange the tomato "Ds" in a lovely pattern on the top, and sprinkle with bread crumbs.

6) Bake in the center of the oven for 50 minutes. Cool for at least 20 minutes before removing the sides of the pan. Serve at any temperature.

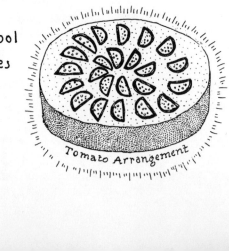

Tomato Arrangement

SAVORY APPLE CASSEROLE

20 minutes to prepare;
45 minutes to bake.

Please don't be deterred by the seemingly strange presence of sauerkraut in this recipe. It blends in beautifully, conferring tartness and texture. Let your guests try to guess what this mystery ingredient is. They will probably be stumped.

Serve this simple, unusual dish with holiday meals, or as a main dish for a cold winter supper, with soup, bread, and salad.

NOTE: Use the slicing attachment of the food processor to cut the apples in seconds flat. (Just core them and feed into the machine.) Without cleaning the processor in between, switch to the grating attachment for the cheese.

1 Tbs. butter or canola oil
1 cup minced onion
2 tsp. dry mustard
1 32-oz. jar sauerkraut, rinsed
   and thoroughly drained
6 medium-sized tart apples,
   thinly sliced (peeling optional)
2 Tbs. unbleached white flour

1 tsp. cinnamon
salt
cloves   } a dash of each
nutmeg
2 Tbs. honey or brown sugar
1/3 lb. medium-sharp cheddar,
      grated (optional)
1/2 cup fine bread crumbs
3/4 cup minced walnuts

1) Preheat oven to 375°F. Have ready a 2-quart-capacity casserole or an equivalent pan (9 x 13-inch).

2) Melt the butter or heat the oil in a medium-sized skillet. Add the onion and mustard, and sauté over medium heat for about 5 minutes, or until the onion softens. Add the sauerkraut, and cook for about 5 more minutes. Set aside.

3) Toss together the apples, flour, and spices in a large bowl. Add honey or sugar and mix well.

4) Now for the fun part. Make the following pattern in the casserole or baking pan: a layer consisting of half the apples, then half the onion-sauerkraut, then half the optional cheese (or not). Repeat this pattern, using the other half of everything. Sprinkle the very top with bread crumbs and walnuts. Cover and bake for 30 minutes, then uncover and bake 15 minutes more. Serve hot, warm, or at room temperature.

influenced vegetable stew

... similar to a Greek "stifado", but with Mexican-style seasonings.

♪NOTE 1: This recipe calls for 2 cups cooked kidney beans. You can soak and cook ½ cup dried beans, or use a 15-oz. can, rinsed and drained.

♪NOTE 2: If you choose fresh tomatoes over purée, here's how to peel and seed them: Drop them into simmering water for about 10-20 seconds. Retrieve and pull off the peel. Cut in half and squeeze out the seeds. Mince the remaining pulp.

♪NOTE 3: Put up some rice to cook before you begin.

3 cups sliced potatoes
   (peeling optional)
1 Tbs. olive oil
2 cups sliced onion
2 tsp. salt
2 tsp. cinnamon
1 Tbs. ground cumin
3 Tbs. fresh lemon or lime juice
1 large cauliflower, cut into
   1-inch florets
2 large carrots, thinly sliced

8 to 10 medium cloves garlic, minced
1 ½ cups water
1 Tbs. honey
1 ½ cups tomato purée — OR— 4 medium-
   sized tomatoes, peeled, seeded,
      and minced
2 cups cooked kidney beans (1 15-oz.
   can, rinsed and drained)
freshly ground black pepper
cayenne to taste
minced fresh parsley

squeezable wedges of lemon or lime

1) Place the potatoes in a saucepan and cover them with water. Boil until tender. Drain well and set aside. (You can save the water to use in step 3.)

2) Heat the oil in a Dutch oven or a very large wok with a cover. Add the onion and 1 tsp. salt, and sauté over medium heat for 5 minutes. Add the cinnamon and cumin, and sauté for a few minutes longer.

3) Stir in the lemon juice, cauliflower, carrots, and remaining salt. Cover and cook over medium heat for about 5 minutes. Add the potatoes, half the garlic, and the water. Stir, cover, and cook until the vegetables are just tender (8 to 10 minutes).

4) Stir in remaining garlic, honey, and tomatoes (or purée). Cover and cook about 5 minutes more. Stir in the beans; season to taste with black pepper and cayenne. Serve hot over rice, topped with minced parsley, and garnished with wedges of lemon or lime.

Mushroom Mystery Casserole

...Fashioned after one of my mother's specialties, which she fondly calls "Mush-mosh."

30 minutes to prepare;
35 to 40 minutes to bake.

Yield: 4 or 5 servings

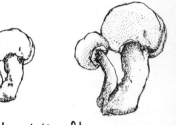

a little oil for the pan

1 Tbs. butter or canola oil
2 cups chopped onion
2 stalks celery, minced
2 lbs. mushrooms, chopped
1 ½ tsp. salt
2 tsp. dry mustard
½ tsp. dried thyme
3 large cloves garlic, minced
fresh black pepper to taste

3 Tbs. unbleached white flour
4 to 6 Tbs. dry sherry
½ cup (packed) grated sharp
   cheddar or Swiss cheese
4 healthy slices whole-grain
   toast, cut into cubes
1 cup milk (lowfat or soy OK)
4 eggs (OK to delete 2 yolks)
paprika

1) Preheat oven to 350°F. Lightly oil a 2-quart casserole or 9 x 13-inch baking pan.

2) Melt the butter or heat the oil in a large, deep skillet or a Dutch oven. Add onion and celery, and sauté over medium heat for about 5 minutes, or until the onion begins to soften.

3) Add mushrooms, salt, dry mustard, and thyme. Continue to sauté over medium heat, stirring frequently, for about 10 minutes more. Stir in the garlic and some freshly ground black pepper during the last few minutes.

4) Gradually sprinkle in the flour, mixing constantly. Cook for a minute or two, stirring, over low heat. Add sherry, stir, and cook for 5 minutes more.

5) Spread into the prepared casserole or baking pan. Sprinkle with grated cheese and cubes of toast.

6) Beat together the milk and eggs, and pour this over the top. Dust with paprika, and bake for 35 to 40 minutes, or until firm on top and bubbly around the edges. Serve hot or warm.

Persian Eggplant

40 minutes to prepare;
40 minutes to bake.

Yield: 4 to 6 servings

2 Tbs. olive oil
2 cups chopped onion
½ lb. chopped mushrooms
2 tsp. ground cumin
6 medium cloves garlic, minced
1 1½-lb. eggplant, cut into
    1-inch cubes
2 tsp. salt
3 Tbs. fresh lemon juice
½ cup (packed) dried currants

½ cup uncooked bulgur
3 Tbs. minced fresh dill (1 Tbs. dried)
freshly ground black pepper
cayenne
2 Tbs. butter
2 Tbs. unbleached white flour
1¾ cups hot milk (lowfat or soy OK)
2 hard-boiled eggs, grated (optional)
paprika for the top

1) Preheat oven to 350°F. Have ready an ungreased 9 x 13-inch baking pan.
2) Heat the olive oil in a large, deep skillet or Dutch oven. Add the onion, and
   sauté over moderate heat for 5 minutes. Stir in mushrooms, cumin, garlic,
   eggplant, and salt, cover, and cook for 10 minutes over moderate heat.
3) Stir in lemon juice, currants, and bulgur. Cover, and simmer over low
   heat for about 10 to 15 minutes, stirring intermittently. When the eggplant
   is edibly tender, remove from heat. Stir in the dill, and add black pepper
   and cayenne to taste. Spread into the ungreased baking pan.
4) Melt the butter in a small saucepan. Sprinkle in the flour, whisking constantly
   over low heat. Continue to cook and whisk for about 2 more minutes.
   Whisk in the hot milk, then cook and stir for about 5 minutes longer –
   until smooth and slightly thickened. Remove from heat, and stir in the
   grated hard-boiled eggs, if desired.
5) Pour the sauce over the eggplant mixture in the pan. Dust the top with
   paprika, and bake uncovered for 40 minutes. Serve hot or warm.

BEANS & GRAINS

(For bean and grain cooking charts, see pages 276-81.)

Beans and Grains

In the original edition of this book, the Beans and Grains section consisted of a few recipes plus a list of "Plain Grains" that included only three: brown rice, millet, and bulgur. In the more than ten years that have passed since that time, I've become acquainted with many more types of beans and grains than I'd ever dreamed existed. I've discovered a fantastic assortment of textures, flavors, and colors in these simple, nutritious foods, and I've had a wonderful time eating them, both separately and mixed together. I strongly encourage you to cook a variety of beans and grains on a regular basis, and to experiment boldly with different combinations.

A dinner of plain cooked beans and/or grains — delicious, warming, and peaceful — can provide a refreshing change from more complicated fare. If desired, you can add extra depth with minimal touches, like a sauce (pages 104-109), some tofu — plain or marinated (page 183), or a handful of toasted nuts or seeds. Add some cooked greens and/or squash — or a green salad. You'll be amazed at how complete and satisfied you'll feel.

The following pages provide descriptions of many types of beans and grains currently available. In-depth cooking instructions for all of these appear at the back of the book, beginning on page 276.

NOTE: One of the reasons why our knowledge about the existing varieties of beans and grains has been so limited is that many of them haven't been very widely available until recently. Many types have been "lost" over the years, including certain ancestral grains grown by the Mayas, Aztecs, Incas, and Native Americans. Heirloom beans (old-fashioned varieties that have been grown for years on small family farms) are making a comeback, although in limited quantities. It is my pleasure to acquaint you with many of these in the hope that you will fall in love with them, as I have. Increasing the demand will help ensure the availability of these ancient, wonderful foods.

Beans

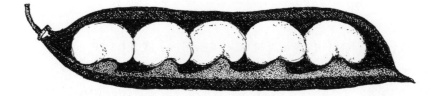

All varieties of beans are rich in protein and fiber. In addition, they contain lysine, an essential amino acid missing from most grains (which is why the combination of beans and grain often makes a complete protein). Many beans also contain folacin and minerals, as well.

To briefly acquaint you with a wide assortment of beans, here are some descriptions and mini-histories. (Cooking charts for beans and grains begin on p. 276.)

❁ ADUKI (AZUKI; ADZUKI) BEANS:
Small (¼-inch) ovals with a deep red-brown color and a white line. Nutty, delicious, and quick-cooking. Thousands of years old (from China and Japan).

❁ BLACK BEANS:
Medium-sized; black with a white stripe. Deep, earthy flavor—very pretty when cooked. Originally from Latin America (Central and South) and the Caribbean. Easy to find in all kinds of stores.

❁ BLACK-EYED PEAS:
Available fresh, dried, canned, or frozen. Relatively quick-cooking. Medium-sized; cream-colored with a dark blotch. Related to the mung bean—originally from Asia. Introduced to this continent with the African slave trade, and has become closely associated with the cooking of the American South. Black-eyed peas have a vegetable-like, slightly bitter flavor.

❁ CHESTNUT BEANS (an heirloom variety):
Very large, plump, shiny, and dark reddish-brown when cooked, these beans are absolutely delicious and delightful to eat. (My own personal favorite.)

✵ FAVA BEANS (aka COW BEANS or FUL):

Large and tan; easy to grow in cool or temperate climates. These beans are creamy and good-flavored – they taste especially good fresh. Prevalent in Middle Eastern, Egyptian, Italian, Spanish, and Portuguese cuisines.

✵ GARBANZO BEANS (aka CHICK-PEAS or CECI):

Medium-small and round with a little beak. Nutty, rich flavor. Ancient origins (dating back, at least, to Mesopotamia 5000 B.C.); travelled to India via the Mediterranean. Very common and easy to find, both canned and dried.

✵ KIDNEY BEANS (including SMALL RED BEANS and CANNELLINI):

First cultivated in Mexico thousands of years ago. The white version is called cannellini (popular in Europe). All kidney beans have a rich flavor, meaty and slightly sweet. Very satisfying-tasting. Common and easy to find, both canned and dried.

✵ LENTILS (Red, green, brown, French):

Dating back to prebiblical times, with origins unknown. Extremely popular and basic in India and the Middle East. Economical and nutritious (containing iron, in addition to protein and fiber). Great for soups and salads. Quick-cooking (presoaking unnecessary).

✵ LIMA BEANS (including BABY LIMAS or BUTTER BEANS and CHRISTMAS LIMAS):

Native to Peru, they spread all through the Americas, and were later introduced to the African continent. Baby limas are buttery and tender. Christmas limas, an heirloom variety, are larger. With their fun shape, and rich, meaty flavor, they feel good in the mouth.

✵ MUNG BEANS:

Originally from India, these small, dark beans are commonly used in Indian cuisine to make a purée called moong dal. They are also famous as the "bean" in bean sprouts and bean thread noodles.

✵ PEAS, DRIED (whole and split; green and yellow):

Dried peas are easy to cook and have a deep, earthy flavor. They originated thousands of years ago in Egypt, then travelled through the Mediterranean and onward to Asia (most notably India) and Europe. Dried peas become mushy when cooked, and are most famous in the form of a thick, comforting soup.

✴ PINK BEANS (an heirloom variety):
    Very similar to pintos and also to small red beans.

✴ PINTO BEANS (including the new hybrids, RATTLESNAKE and
APPALOOSA BEANS):
    Pinto beans are closely related to kidney beans, although they are
slightly smaller and tan instead of red. They have a down-to-earth
flavor, and are most famous for their role as <u>refritos</u> (refried beans)
in Mexican cooking. Rattlesnake beans are very similar to regular
pintos. Appaloosa beans are larger and thinner — a little more
elegant.

✴ RUNNER BEANS (SCARLET, WHITE, BLACK):
    Large and beautiful, with a distinctive flavor, runner beans were
originally cultivated in the Americas for ornamental uses. Easy to
grow, but not that easy to find commercially.

✴ SOYBEANS:
    Did you know that there are over a thousand varieties of soybeans
in existence, and that they come in various colors as well? Soybeans
were originally grown in China thousands of years ago. Nowadays,
most of the world's soybean crop is grown in the Western Hemisphere,
where it is used largely to feed livestock and for export. Yet plain, cooked
soybeans are nutty and crunchy, and make good food for humans, too.
Now that Asian cuisines are becoming more popular, soybean products
are gaining status and appreciation in the U.S. These products include
soy sauce, tofu, tempeh, miso, soy flour, and soy milk (an excellent
substitute for cow's milk).

✴ WHITE BEAN FAMILY (including NAVY, PEA, GREAT NORTHERN,
FLAGEOLET, ANASAZI, CALYPSO):
    These all hail from the Western Hemisphere, and were "discovered"
by European explorers, who sent the seeds back home. White beans
have a slightly bitter flavor. The smaller ones (navy and pea beans)
are round and very pretty when cooked. White beans are the perfect
choice for traditional baked bean-type casseroles, and also go very
well in soups and salads.

Grains

RICE:

Forty thousand kinds of rice exist in the world today, but fewer than twenty are grown in the United States. That's still quite a few, when you consider that most people are familiar with only two or three types. Here is a list of the most common and/or interesting types available:

BROWN RICE:

Brown rice is the whole grain, with only the inedible hulls removed. It is coated with bran, which gives it texture and flavor. Long-grain is more separate and fluffier when cooked than short-grain, which is softer, stickier, and chewier. High in complex carbohydrates, vitamin E, magnesium, protein, and fiber, brown rice has more natural nutritional value than white rice, which is artificially enriched.

WHITE RICE:

Plain white rice cooks in about half the time of brown rice. As with brown rice, the long-grain variety is fluffier and the short-grain is stickier (used in Japanese cuisine to make sushi). Almost all the nutrients are stripped from white rice during milling, but most American brands are enriched with thiamine, niacin, and iron (and occasionally riboflavin, vitamin D, and calcium).

AROMATIC RICES (including BASMATI):

These rices produce a noticeable nutty aroma when cooked. The most well-known aromatic rice is basmati, which originated in India and Pakistan, but is now grown in the U.S. as well. Basmati (which means "queen of fragrance") rice, brown or white, has a long, slender shape when cooked. Other aromatic rices include Wehani (an earthy red rice developed by the Lundberg Family Farms in California), Texmati, white jasmine (originally from Thailand), Thai basmati, and Indonesian basmati.

THAI BLACK (JAPONICA) RICE:

A medium-grain rice with a black bran coating, grown at Lundberg Family Farms. Tiny and red when cooked, it has a delicious, deep, slightly sweet flavor.

⚞ WILD RICE:

Not really a rice, but an aquatic grass, wild rice is the only grain native to North America. It was once a staple for the Native American tribes in Minnesota and parts of Canada, and still grows there. Black on the outside and tan on the inside, wild rice is chewy and has a slightly bitter flavor. It's also rich in magnesium, B vitamins, potassium, and zinc. Manitok wild rice is an especially delicious variety. It is lighter in color and sweeter-tasting than other types of wild rice.

⚞ ITALIAN (ARBORIO) RICE:

Arborio, vialone nano, and padano— these starchy, short- or medium-grain rices are grown in the Piedmont and Lombardy regions of Italy. They are most commonly used to make a popular dish called risotto.

⚞ GLUTINOUS (SWEET) RICE:

Also known as sticky rice, this is the ideal choice for rice puddings and other desserts. It is especially popular in East Asian cuisines.

AND IN ADDITION TO RICE:

Many of the following grains, while largely unheard-of until only a short time ago, are widely available today—and well worth discovering. Here are some brief descriptions, including some nutritional information. For cooking instructions, consult the charts beginning on page 276.

⚞ AMARANTH:

This "lost" Aztec grain (largely destroyed by the Spaniards in the 16th century) is enjoying a late 20th century comeback. Although tiny, amaranth is a nutritional powerhouse, high in protein and fiber, brimming with vitamins, and containing lysine, an essential amino acid absent from most other grains. Amaranth is porridgelike when cooked, with each granule remaining crunchy within the gelatinous, chewy cereal. Its flavor is slightly sweet and really good—try it for breakfast. (NOTE: Amaranth can also be popped like popcorn.)

⚞ BARLEY (HULLED AND PEARL):

Hulled (outer husk removed; everything else still there) barley is chewier and needs to cook longer. Pearl barley is more refined (husk gone, and bran largely gone as well), but still good. Barley contains lots of minerals and fiber and mixes well with other grains.

⚞ BUCKWHEAT and KASHA:

Quick-cooking and strong flavored. The roasted variety is called "kasha". It's not really wheat (it's technically a grass—in the same family as rhubarb) so it can be eaten by people with wheat allergies. Buckwheat is very nutritious (protein, B vitamins, calcium).

✺ BULGUR and CRACKED WHEAT:

Both are forms of cracked wheat, but bulgur is processed and precooked, so all it needs is to soak and/or cook slightly. Cracked wheat is uncooked, so it takes longer to prepare and comes out more like cereal. Various forms of bulgur may look different from one another, as they could be milled with varying granulations from different types of wheat.

✺ CORN:

Corn (all 300 varieties of it) is the most famous grain native to the Americas, North and South. The easiest and most common cornmeal preparation is polenta, which is simply a cornmeal mush. Polenta is very easy to make and versatile, and can be seasoned with sharp cheeses or other strong flavors, like Pesto (p. 104).

✺ COUSCOUS:

Light, light, light! And very mild tasting. Made from semolina flour which, in turn, is milled from the endosperm of hard durum wheat, couscous is presteamed, so all it needs is soaking. Whole wheat couscous, made from the whole grain, is also becoming increasingly available. It is delicious and has a deeper flavor than light-colored couscous.

✺ KAMUT:

Yellow, fat, chewy, and sweet, kamut feels good in the mouth and is fun to eat. This large grain (three times the size of wheat berries) tastes great all by itself, and also combines beautifully with cooked beans for a textural experience. Kamut is high in protein and minerals, especially magnesium and zinc. It also comes in flakes, which make great cereal.

✺ MILLET:

Very nutritious—rich in protein, phosphorus, iron, magnesium, potassium, and B vitamins. Alkaline, and therefore a stomach soother. Delicious, nutty flavor. Inexpensive, easy-to-find, and quick-cooking. In short, millet is an all-around winner.

✺ OATS:

Groats or berries, steel-cut (Irish or Scottish), rolled (flattened and presteamed), bran, or flour. Oats are a sturdy grain containing protein, B vitamins, calcium, and fiber. Whole oat groats or steel-cut oats make the best oatmeal; they have more nutritive value than the more common rolled oats, as the latter are more processed.

QUINOA (pronounced "keen-wah"):

The nutritional supergrain! Not only is it highest in protein of all the grains, but quinoa's protein is complete, which means it contains all eight of the essential amino acids. It also has calcium and iron, so you can see why the Incas named it the "mother grain." Uncooked quinoa is similar in size and shape to uncooked millet, but when it is cooked, quinoa expands to five times its original volume (as opposed to rice and most other grains, which expand to three times), and pretty little circles form around it, like halos. It tastes especially good mixed with rice.

RYE BERRIES:

Whole grain rye. High in protein, rich in flavor – pleasant and slightly tart. Very chewy. Slender and distinct when cooked.

SPELT:

This precursor to modern strains of wheat is similar to both kamut and wheat berries (and is somewhere between the two in size) but has a different biological composition, so it can often be enjoyed by people with wheat allergies. Another advantage that spelt has over wheat berries is that it takes only about half as long to cook.

TEFF:

Teff is new to the West, having been brought here from Ethiopia in the 1980s by a biologist named Wayne Carlson. It is a tasty, nutritious, red, white, or brown cereal grain, minute in size and big in nutrients, especially iron and calcium. When cooked, these tiny particles form a thick porridge that solidifies when it cools down, much like polenta. Teff flour is used to make <u>injera</u>, the famous spongy Ethiopian sourdough flatbread.

TRITICALE:

This is a hybrid of whole wheat (<u>Triticum</u> in Latin) and rye (<u>Secale</u> in Latin), but with a balance of amino acids that is better than either. These large, brown grains have a flavor sweeter than wheat and more subtle than rye. Triticale is also available as a flour (low in gluten, so combine it with wheat flour if using for yeasted bread) or flakes (good for breakfast).

WHEAT BERRIES:

Whole grain wheat, with only the outermost hull removed. Very chewy, these take a long time to cook. Cooked wheat berries are a nice addition to breads (see page 72) and mix well in pilafs with other cooked grains. Soft (white) wheat berries are very round, glutinous, sweet, nutty, and mild. Hard (red) wheat berries cook up to be more distinct and chewy, with an earthy flavor.

Frijoles, Etc. Casserole

40 minutes to prepare;
40 to 45 minutes to bake.

Yield:
4 to 6
servings

Think of this delicious two-layer casserole as a savory cobbler — with spicy, cheesy beans and vegetables on the bottom and a crusty corn bread baked right on top. It's exotic and impressive, but at the same time straightforward and down-to-earth. A real crowd-pleaser!

NOTE: This calls for 6 cups cooked pinto beans. That's 3 15-oz. cans, or, if you're using dried beans, start with 2 cups. Soak and thoroughly cook them well ahead of time. (4 hours to soak; 1½ hours to cook.)

a little oil for the pan
2 Tbs. olive oil
3 cups minced onion
1 tsp. salt (possibly more)
10 large cloves garlic, minced
2 tsp. ground cumin
1 Tbs. dried basil
1 tsp. dried oregano
1 Tbs. chile powder
4 medium (7-inch) zucchini,
    cut into ½-inch chunks

2 medium bell peppers or mild
    chiles, cut into small strips
6 cups cooked pinto beans
    (3 15-oz. cans)
freshly ground black pepper
cayenne to taste
1 packed cup grated mild white
    cheese (optional)
1 batch Corn Bread Batter (recipe follows)
salsa (optional condiment)

1) Preheat oven to 350°F. Lightly oil a 9 x 13-inch baking pan.

2) Heat the olive oil in a large, deep skillet or a Dutch oven. Add the onion and half the salt, and sauté for about 8 to 10 minutes over medium heat — until the onion begins to soften.

3) Add half the garlic plus the cumin, basil, oregano, chile powder, zucchini, bell peppers and/or chiles, and remaining salt. Stir, cover, and cook over medium heat for 5 minutes longer.

Continued on next page → → →

4) Remove from heat; stir in the remaining garlic and the beans. Season to taste with black pepper and cayenne, and stir in the cheese, if desired. Transfer to the prepared pan, and spread it out. Add the corn bread batter, distributing it as evenly as possible over the top.

5) Bake for 40 to 45 minutes, or until the top is very firm to the touch and a toothpick inserted all the way through the corn bread topping comes out clean. Serve hot, with salsa or plain.

ᴑ ᴑ

Corn Bread Batter
ᴑ ᴑ ᴑ ᴑ ᴑ ᴑ ᴑ

1 cup unbleached white flour

½ tsp. salt

2 tsp. baking powder

1 tsp. baking soda

1 cup yellow cornmeal

1 cup buttermilk or yogurt

1 egg

2 Tbs. olive oil or melted butter

1) Sift together the flour, salt, baking powder, and baking soda into a medium-sized mixing bowl. Stir in the cornmeal, and make a well in the center.

2) In a separate container, beat together the buttermilk or yogurt, egg, and oil or melted butter. Pour this mixture into the dry ingredients, and stir just enough to thoroughly blend.

ᴑ ᴑ

SPICED LENTILS
with SPINACH and APPLES

45 minutes to prepare
(most of it lentil-cooking time).

Yield: 4 to 6 servings

Serve this easy stew with Indian Pulao (p.224), Raita (p.118), and Chappatis (p.99), for a simple and lovely Indian dinner.

1 Tbs. canola or peanut oil	1 tsp. ground coriander
1 Tbs. butter	½ tsp. turmeric
2 cups minced onion	3 Tbs. fresh lemon juice
2 cups dried lentils	3 large cloves garlic, minced
5 cups water	1 tsp. salt (or more, to taste)
2 stalks celery, minced	black pepper to taste
1 tsp. ground cumin	cayenne to taste
2 tsp. dry mustard	½ lb. fresh spinach, chopped
1 Tbs. minced fresh ginger	2 medium-sized tart apples, peeled and chopped

1) Heat the oil in a medium-sized skillet, and melt in the butter. Add the onion, and cook over medium heat for about 15 minutes, stirring occasionally, until the onion is soft and turning golden.

2) Meanwhile, place the lentils and water in a large saucepan or Dutch oven, and bring to a boil. Lower the heat, partially cover, and let simmer for 15 minutes.

3) Add to the onion: celery, cumin, mustard, ginger, coriander, and turmeric. Cook together over medium-low heat for 10 minutes, or until the celery is tender. Scrape all of this into the lentils, add the lemon juice and garlic, and stir. Simmer, partially covered, for 10 more minutes — until the lentils are tender.

4) Stir in the salt, black pepper, cayenne, spinach, and apples. Cook for just a few minutes longer — until the spinach is wilted and the apples begin to soften. Serve hot.

Spicy Baked Beans with Molasses

20 minutes to assemble;
1½ hours to bake.

Yield:
6 servings
or more

NOTE: This recipe calls for 6 cups cooked navy or pea beans, which is 3 15-oz. cans. If using dried beans, start with 2 cups, and cook in plenty of water until tender (1½ hours).

TO PEEL AND SEED A TOMATO: Drop it into simmering water for 10 to 20 seconds. Retrieve it and pull off the skin. Cut it open and squeeze out the seeds.

These delicious baked beans go beautifully with Green Chile and Cheese Corn Bread (p. 89).

1 Tbs. canola oil
2 cups chopped onion
2 Tbs. grated fresh ginger
2 tsp. salt
10 large cloves garlic, minced
2 Tbs. chile powder
2 tsp. ground cumin
2 tsp. dried dill
1 tsp. allspice
freshly ground black pepper
2 medium carrots, diced
2 medium stalks celery, minced
1 medium bell pepper, diced

4 Tbs. Dijon mustard
4 Tbs. dark molasses
¾ cup rum (optional)
2 Tbs. fresh lemon juice
6 medium-sized ripe tomatoes,
 peeled, seeded, & chopped
 (or 1 cup canned tomatoes)
6 cups cooked navy or pea beans
 (3 15-oz. cans, rinsed & drained)

OPTIONAL TOPPINGS:
minced fresh cilantro and/or parsley
salsa
Chutney (pp. 116-17)
sour cream

1) Preheat oven to 300°F.

2) Heat the oil in a large, deep skillet or Dutch oven. Add the onion, ginger, and ½ tsp. of the salt, and sauté over medium heat for about 5 minutes, or until the onion begins to soften.

3) Add half the garlic, the chile powder, cumin, dill, allspice, and a few hefty grindings of fresh black pepper. Sauté for another few minutes, then stir in the carrots, celery, and remaining salt. Cover and cook over medium heat for about 5 minutes longer — until the vegetables are just beginning to get tender.

4) Stir in the bell pepper, mustard, molasses, rum, lemon juice, tomatoes, and remaining garlic. Sauté for another 5 minutes, then remove from heat and stir in the beans.

5) Transfer to a 9 x 13-inch baking pan and cover tightly with foil. Bake undisturbed for 1½ hours. Serve hot, either plain, or topped with any combination of cilantro, parsley, salsa, chutney, or sour cream.

Fried Rice

Preparation time: about 20 minutes to assemble ingredients; less than 10 minutes to stir-fry. (Cook rice ahead.)

Yield: 4 to 6 servings

PRELIMININARY: Cook 2 cups brown or white rice in 3 cups boiling water until tender. (This will take 15 to 20 minutes for white, and 35 to 45 minutes for brown.) Fluff the cooked rice with a fork and set aside.

A NICE TOUCH FOR THE TOFU: You can firm up the diced tofu by boiling it first for about 10 minutes, either in plain water or in dry sherry (which will infuse it with flavor). Drain the tofu well before using.

NOTE: The vegetables – and their amounts – are flexible.

2 Tbs. plus 1 tsp. peanut
　or canola oil
2 eggs, beaten (yolks optional)
1 Tbs. grated fresh ginger
2 cups minced broccoli
1 large carrot, diced
½ tsp. salt
1 small zucchini, diced
3 medium cloves garlic, minced

1 cup green peas, fresh or frozen
a few handfuls chopped greens
　(spinach, bok choy, chard, etc.)
about ⅓ lb. firm tofu, diced
4 healthy scallions, minced
½ cup minced water chestnuts
about 6 cups cooked rice
2 to 3 Tbs. soy sauce (to taste)
Chinese sesame oil (optional)
freshly ground black pepper

1) Heat a wok or a large, deep skillet. When it is hot, add 1 tsp. of the oil and the beaten eggs. Scramble until dry, then transfer to a plate. Set aside.

2) Wipe out the wok or skillet with a paper towel and heat the pan again. Add 2 Tbs. oil and the ginger, broccoli, carrot, and salt. Stir-fry over high heat for a minute or two, then add the zucchini and stir-fry for a minute more. Add the garlic, peas, greens, and tofu. After about a minute, add the scallions, water chestnuts, rice, scrambled egg (from Step 1), and soy sauce. Turn the heat down slightly, and stir-fry just about a minute longer, or until everything is well mingled.

3) Serve immediately. Drizzle the top of each serving with a little Chinese sesame oil, if desired, and top with some freshly ground black pepper.

Spanish Rice

20 minutes to prepare.
(Cook rice well ahead.)   Yield: 4 to 6 servings

For a warming dinner on a cold, rainy night, serve Spanish Rice with Galician Garbanzo Soup (p. 20) and a green salad.

NOTE: You'll need about 6 cups cooked rice for this recipe. See "PRELIMINARY" at the top of the opposite page.

TO PEEL AND SEED A TOMATO: Drop it into simmering water for 10 to 20 seconds. Retrieve it and pull off the skin. Cut it open and squeeze out the seeds.

1 to 2 Tbs. olive oil
1½ cups minced onion
¾ tsp. salt
1 large bell pepper, minced
2 large cloves garlic, minced
½ tsp. dried oregano
2 tsp. dried basil
about 6 cups cooked rice

3 medium-sized ripe tomatoes,
   peeled, seeded, and minced
   (or 1 cup canned tomatoes,
    drained and chopped)
½ cup sliced, pitted green olives
freshly ground black pepper
cayenne
minced fresh parsley, for the top

1) Heat the olive oil in a large, deep skillet or Dutch oven. Add the onion and half the salt, and sauté over medium heat for about 5 minutes, or until the onion begins to soften.

2) Add bell pepper, garlic, and herbs. Sauté over medium heat for another 5 minutes, or until the pepper is just tender.

3) Stir in the cooked rice, tomatoes, remaining salt, and olives. Season to taste with freshly ground black pepper and cayenne.

4) Serve hot, topped with minced fresh parsley.

Broccoli & Buckwheat Godunov

Buckwheat...

...and its groats.

about
30 minutes
to prepare.

Yield:
4 to 6
servings

... an easy pilaf with deep, robust flavor. Use unroasted buckwheat or roasted (kasha).

3 cups water
2 cups buckwheat groats
1 Tbs. canola oil or butter
2 cups minced onion
½ tsp. salt
½ lb. mushrooms, chopped
1 1-lb. bunch broccoli, minced
2 Tbs. minced fresh dill (2 tsp. dried)
1 Tbs. lemon juice

TOPPINGS:
3 hard-boiled eggs, grated
    (yolks optional)
minced fresh parsley
freshly ground black pepper

1) Place the water in a medium-sized saucepan and bring to a boil. Sprinkle in the buckwheat, cover, and lower the heat to a simmer. Cook for 8 minutes, then remove from heat and let stand, covered, for another 5 minutes. Uncover, fluff with a fork, and set aside.

2) Heat the oil or melt the butter in a large, deep skillet or Dutch oven. Add onion and salt, and sauté over medium heat for about 5 minutes, or until the onion begins to soften.

3) Add the mushrooms and cook for another 5 minutes, then stir in the broccoli. Cover and cook for about 5 to 8 minutes longer, or until the broccoli is bright green and just tender.

4) Stir the cooked buckwheat into the vegetables, along with the dill and lemon juice. Stir until very well combined.

5) Serve topped with grated eggs, minced parsley, and freshly ground black pepper.

20 minutes
to prepare.
(Cook rice
well ahead.)

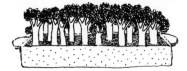

Yield:
4 to 6
servings

...Broccoli trees planted in an herbed rice pilaf. I made this up one autumn day when two artist friends of mine came to dinner.

PRELIMININARY: Cook 2 cups brown or white rice in 3 cups boiling water until tender. (This will take 15 to 20 minutes for white, and 35 to 45 minutes for brown.) Fluff the cooked rice with a fork and set aside.

1 1-lb. bunch broccoli
1 Tbs. butter or canola oil
    (plus a little for the pan)
1 cup chopped onion
3/4 tsp. salt
1 large clove garlic, minced
2 Tbs. fresh lemon juice
about 6 cups cooked rice
freshly ground black pepper

cayenne to taste
2 Tbs. minced fresh dill (2 tsp. dried)
3 Tbs. minced fresh mint (3 tsp. dried)
1/4 cup minced fresh parsley
1/2 cup toasted sunflower seeds (optional)
1 packed cup grated cheddar or Swiss
    (about 1/4 lb. cheese) – optional
a little melted butter for the top
    (optional)

1) Trim the tough bottoms from the broccoli stalks, and cut the tops into smallish spears of whatever size suits you. Cook them in a steamer over boiling water until bright green and just barely tender. Rinse under cold running water, drain well, and set aside.

2) Preheat oven to 325°F. Lightly grease a 9 x 13-inch baking pan.

3) Melt the butter or heat the oil in a large, deep skillet or a Dutch oven. Add the onion and salt, and sauté over medium heat for about 5 minutes or until the onion begins to soften. Add the garlic and lemon juice, and sauté for about 2 minutes longer. Stir in the rice, some black pepper and cayenne to taste, the herbs, and the optional sunflower seeds and/or cheese. Taste to correct salt, if necessary, and spread into the prepared pan.

4) Now for the fun part. Arrange the broccoli upright in the rice, and, if desired, drizzle with melted butter. Cover loosely with foil, and bake until just heated through (15 to 20 minutes). Serve right away.

Indian Pulao

Try serving this elegant, colorful rice dish with Spiced Lentils with Spinach and Green Apples (p. 218). They go beautifully together and take about the same amount of time to cook.

You'll need 6 cups cooked basmati rice— brown or white (see p. 212). Cook 2 cups rice in 3 cups water for 15 to 20 minutes (white rice) or 35 to 45 minutes (brown).

30 minutes to prepare
(after rice is cooked).

Yield: 4 to 5
servings

1 to 2 Tbs. butter or canola oil	3 to 4 Tbs. water (as needed)
1 cup chopped onion	2 medium-sized carrots, diced
1 Tbs. minced fresh ginger	2 large cloves garlic, minced
3/4 tsp. salt	1 medium bell pepper, diced
1 tsp. mustard seeds	1/2 cup raisins
1 tsp. turmeric	about 6 cups cooked basmati rice
2 tsp. ground coriander	1 cup chopped, toasted nuts
1 tsp. ground fennel seed	1 cup unsweetened coconut,
(optional)	lightly toasted
	Raita (p. 118) - optional

1) Melt the butter or heat the oil in a large, deep skillet or a Dutch oven. Add onion, ginger, salt, and spices, and sauté over medium-low heat for about 5 to 8 minutes, adding small amounts of water, as needed, to prevent sticking.

2) Add the carrots and garlic; stir and cover. Cook for about 5 minutes, or until the carrots begin to get tender. Stir in the bell pepper, cover again, and cook for 5 minutes longer.

3) Add the raisins and the cooked rice, and mix well. Cook and stir over very low heat for just a few minutes longer, then serve hot, topped with toasted nuts and coconut. If desired, pass a bowl of Raita to serve on the side.

Featuring:

VEGETABLES AS THEMSELVES

BRAZILIAN STUFFED PEPPERS

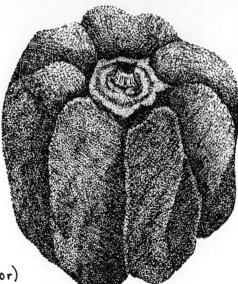

30 minutes to prepare;
30 minutes to bake.

Yield: 4 servings

4 large able-to-stand
  bell peppers (any color)

1 Tbs. olive oil
1 cup minced onion
½ tsp. salt
¾ cup each:
  minced green olives
  minced black olives

½ cup uncooked Cream of Wheat cereal
¼ cup water
3 hard-boiled eggs, minced
    (yolks optional)
½ cup raisins or currants
freshly ground black pepper

3 cups stewed tomatoes, fresh or canned

PRELIMINARY: Bring a large potful of water to a boil; lower heat to a simmer.

1) Slice across the tops of the peppers, about ½-inch from the tips. Discard the tops and remove the membranes and seeds.

2) Gently drop the peppers into the simmering water for 1 to 2 minutes. Retrieve them as soon as they're slightly tender (but still feisty), and rinse immediately in cold water. Drain well, then pat dry with paper towels and set aside.

3) Heat the olive oil in a medium-sized skillet. Add onion and salt, and sauté over medium heat for about 2 minutes, or until the onion begins to soften. Add olives and Cream of Wheat, and continue to sauté for another minute or two.

4) Stir in the water, and cook over medium heat for about 3 minutes, stirring frequently. Remove from heat; add eggs, raisins, and black pepper to taste. Stuff the peppers with this mixture.

5) Preheat oven to 350°F. Spread the stewed tomatoes in a shallow baking pan. Arrange the peppers so that they are standing in the tomatoes. Cover loosely with foil, and bake for 30 minutes. Serve hot.

REBAKED POTATOES

Preparation time:
initial bake   45 minutes
preparation   10 minutes
final bake   35 minutes

TOTAL = 1½ hours (most of it
         baking time).

Yield: 2 to 3 servings
(easily multiplied)

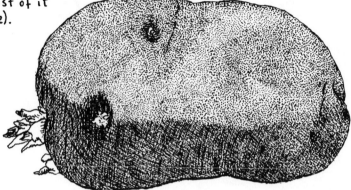

Serve these potato boats with freshly steamed broccoli for a substantial and satisfying meal. Figure on one medium-sized potato per person.

2 fist-sized baking potatoes
1 to 2 Tbs. mayonnaise (optional)
1 cup cottage cheese
1 hard-boiled egg, minced (yolk
        optional)
½ tsp. salt
1 Tbs. Dijon mustard

1 Tbs. minced fresh dill (1½ tsp. dried)
¾ cup packed grated cheddar
        (optional)
cayenne
freshly ground black pepper
1 medium-sized ripe tomato
paprika for the top

DO AHEAD: Bake the potatoes as you normally would (about 45 minutes at 375°F). Turn the oven down to 325°F when you take them out. When they are cool enough to handle, slice the potatoes in half laterally, and scoop out the insides, leaving the skins intact.

1) Place the potato innards in a medium-sized bowl, and mash them with the mayonnaise (or not) and the cottage cheese. Add the egg, salt, mustard, dill, ½ cup of the cheddar, if desired (save the rest for the top), and cayenne and black pepper to taste. Mix well.

2) Divide the filling evenly among the potato skins. Slice the tomato into rounds, and place these decoratively on top. Sprinkle the extra cheese over the tomatoes, if you like, and dust on some paprika. Place the filled potatoes in a shallow baking pan, and bake uncovered for 35 minutes at 325°F. Serve hot, warm, or at room temperature.

STUFFED ARTICHOKES

- 45 minutes to cook and prepare artichokes (do this well ahead);
- 20 minutes to make stuffing and fill;
- 30 minutes to bake.

Yield:
6 servings

1st Preliminary:

Cook 6 artichokes as you normally would, for normal consumption.
(Usually this involves boiling or steaming them for about 35 minutes, or until leaves come out easily.)
Drain the artichokes (turn upside down in a colander) and cool until handle-able.

2nd Preliminary:

To hollow out the artichokes for stuffing:
(1) Grab hold of the central leaf cluster (at the tip), and yank it out.
(2) Reach into the cavity with a regular spoon, and with a few masterful strokes, scrape out the choke (inedible fuzz) and discard it.

6 large artichokes, cooked and hollowed out
(see 1st and 2nd Preliminaries, above)

1 to 2 Tbs. olive oil
1½ cups minced onion
½ tsp. salt
¼ cup white wine (optional)
1 large clove garlic, minced
½ cup fine bread crumbs
½ tsp. dried thyme

½ tsp. paprika
2 tsp. dry mustard
2 Tbs. fresh lemon juice
freshly ground black pepper
¼ cup freshly minced parsley
1 cup minced walnuts, lightly toasted

1) Preheat oven to 325°F.
2) Heat the olive oil in a medium-sized skillet. Add the onion and salt, and cook over medium heat for about 5 minutes or until the onion begins to soften.
3) Add wine, if desired, and cook for another 5 minutes. Add garlic, bread crumbs, thyme, paprika, and mustard, and continue to cook for another 5 minutes, stirring frequently.
4) Remove from heat, and stir in lemon juice, black pepper to taste, parsley, and walnuts. Divide the filling evenly among the artichokes, filling each firmly. Place the stuffed artichokes in a shallow baking pan, standing them upright, if possible (you may need to trim the stem ends to stabilize their posture). Cover the pan loosely with foil, and bake for 30 minutes. Serve hot, warm, or at room temperature.

The Various Cuts of Vegetables

I think that many people are deterred from cooking with fresh vegetables as frequently as they might like, because it seems too inconvenient, and also because of a widespread fear of chopping. Food processors have helped to embolden many. These useful machines come with slicing and grating attachments that can render a whole soup's-worth of vegetables into uniform diminutive units in a matter of seconds. However, a food processor can't give you the variety of shapes and dimensions procurable by hand with a good sharp knife and a little know-how.

The more shapes and sizes you can carve out of a vegetable, the more possibilities you will find for preparing it. For example, the thinner a vegetable is cut, the more quickly it can be cooked on the stovetop, either in a skillet or a wok. (This even includes very hard vegetables, like potatoes, yams, or winter squash.) If cut correctly, an entire wokful of assorted vegetables can be stir-fried together, without compromising the texture or integrity of any of them (see pp. 234-36). And as you become more adept at chopping and slicing, a whole new world of raw vegetables will open for you as well, and your salads will soar.

The key to good vegetable chopping lies in one's relationship with a chosen knife or cleaver. Shop carefully for a high-quality one that feels good in your hand. Keep it sharp (the sharper, the safer), and take good care of it. Also, remember that the second key to safety is <u>attention</u>. ALWAYS KEEP YOUR EYES ON YOUR HANDS WHILE YOU CHOP! Most cuts occur during lapses of attention.

<u>A NOTE ABOUT KNIVES</u>: For most vegetables you need a straight-edged blade. Use serrated knives only for acidy fruits and vegetables (citrus, tomatoes, bell peppers, chiles).

The following 4 pages provide some cutting guidelines →

BEETS - As a rule, they should be peeled. But don't bother using a peeler. It's much easier to remove their skins if you blanch them first for about 20 minutes in boiling water. The skins will just rub off.

CARROTS - Scrub them instead of peeling if they're very fresh, but peel them if the skin is rough or otherwise unacceptable. The same goes for POTATOES, SWEET POTATOES, YAMS, TURNIPS, RUTABAGAS, CELERY ROOT, DAIKON RADISHES, and PARSNIPS.

WINTER SQUASH (acorn, butternut, etc.) - Peel if you intend to slice them for sautéing. But if you plan to bake them, leave them in their skin.

SUMMER SQUASH/ZUCCHINI - Only peel these if the skins are overly tough or ugly. (Don't forget, the insides can be perfectly fine even if the skins look bad.)

CUCUMBERS - Peel if they're waxed or if the skin is bitter.

MUSHROOMS - Peel if they are spotty or not too fresh, especially if you're serving them raw (with dips or in salads).

EGGPLANT - You don't need to peel them if the skin is smooth and tight. However, some people will not be convinced that eggplant skin is _ever_ edible. If these people are coming to dinner, peel.

BROCCOLI STALKS - Use a peeler to shave off the tough outer skin without losing too much of the tender insides.

 _DON'T PEEL_ fresh, unscathed garden vegetables, especially your own homegrown cucumbers. Get a good scrub brush and become accustomed to using it. The clean skins of fresh vegetables are full of minerals and fiber.

Cutting Each Vegetable......

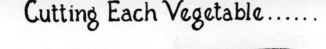

First, a ground rule for safety: Always place the vegetable in the most stable position possible. This usually means flat side down. Since most vegetables are curved, a flat surface must be introduced by an initial cut somewhere (often down the center). Thereafter, this flat surface—plus the firm hold of your free hand—will help prevent the vegetable from rolling away, causing its escape to places unknown and/or the accidental grazing of your knuckles.

A LITTLE-KNOWN FACT ABOUT GARLIC: The easiest way to peel garlic is to lay it down on its side (one or two cloves at a time), and whack it firmly with the flat side of a large knife. After this treatment, the garlic skin will magically loosen.

To Quarter Mushrooms:

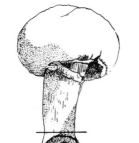

First, cut off the base,

then cut it down the center. Place each half flat side down, and cut it in half again, lengthwise.

To get thin slices out of a potato (enabling you to sauté it, as a departure from boiling...)

First, cut it in half lengthwise. Then cut each half laterally to the desired thinness.

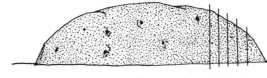

The base of an asparagus stalk will detach just where it's supposed to, if snapped off gently by hand.

An effective cut for asparagus, especially for a stir-fry, is <u>diagonal</u> — at 1½-inch intervals. Start from the base and work toward the tip, turning the asparagus ¼ turn after each slice.

This cutting method can also be used for carrots and broccoli stalks.

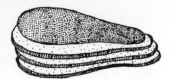
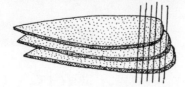
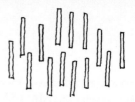

To cut matchsticks ("julienne") from zucchini, eggplant, or carrots, first cut the vegetable into thin slices lengthwise. The easiest way to do this is to cut one slice first,

making one flat surface. Lay the vegetable down on this surface while you continue, and the whole cutting process will be more stable.

After the lengthwise slices are cut, pile them up, and begin cutting widthwise strips, as illustrated. (Do this in several batches.)

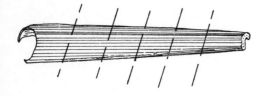

For celery matchsticks, cut each stalk at approximately 2-inch intervals. Then slice each piece thinly into lengthwise strips.

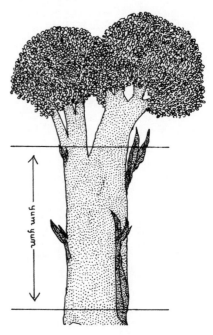

The stalk is actually the most succulent part of the broccoli plant. It is crisp, sweet, and juicy, but unfortunately these traits are obscured by its tough outer skin and limp-looking leaves. Shave these off with a paring knife or vegetable peeler, and slice the stalk thinly for use in salads, as a dipping vegetable, or in a stir-fry.

Cauliflower can be sliced into thin "trees". In this form, it sautés very quickly and is lovely in salads. Also, you can break cauliflower into chunkier "florets" by hand.

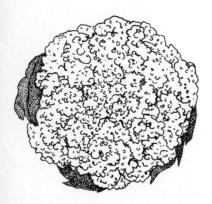

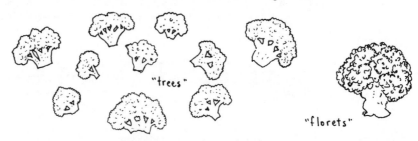

"trees"

"florets"

Zucchini Half-Moons

This is the easiest way to cut zucchini. It is also the easiest shape-of-zucchini to handle for steaming or sautéing.

First, cut 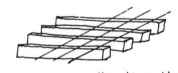 off the ends of the zuke, then cut it in half lengthwise.

Then, place each half flatside-down, and slice across at whatever interval you choose for more or less thickness.

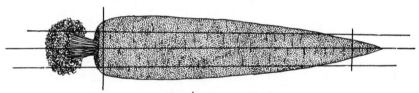

To dice a carrot:

First, make some nice, uniform carrot sticks,

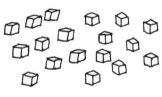

then line them up, and cut across to make little cubes.

There are no clever tricks (at least that I know of) for carving elaborate shapes from a bell pepper. Just cut it into strips or mince it as best you can.

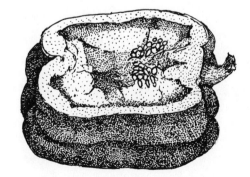

A Dinner of
Sautéed Vegetables

People who love to cook tend to search for increasingly exotic and complex ideas with which to experiment. Very few enthusiastic gourmets will probe in the opposite direction, toward simplicity. Yet the search for the simple can be engaging and challenging, and the results can be inspiring.

You can quickly, easily, inexpensively, and pleasurably prepare a meal of stir-fried vegetables, and if you follow only a few certain guidelines your creation can be surprisingly elegant and satisfying. I would like to dispel the common notion that a meal consisting primarily of cooked vegetables is necessarily (a) underseasoned and mushy; (b) inadequate, both nutritionally and quantitatively; (c) depressing; and (d) just generally low class. How you cook a vegetable, how fresh and lovely it is in its raw state, and how you cut the vegetable prior to cooking it — attention to these variables makes all the difference.

Here is the brief list of Essential Efforts which, if heeded, will readily separate the ho-hum vegetable dinner from the sensually thrilling one:

Effort #1: Become the proud owner of a real Chinese wok.

Effort #2: Practice your vegetable chopping to the point where you are able to cut any vegetable to exactly the size and shape you want it to be. (See pp. 229-33.)

Effort #3: Find a local produce merchant who sells the finest, freshest vegetables possible at all times, and adopt this merchant as your very own. Take the slight, extra trouble of shopping carefully and frequently, buying vegetables closest to the prime of their season.

Effort #4: Follow the cooking method described on the following 2 pages. There is no particular skill or talent required here — just pay careful attention to what you are doing.

Basic Trick: To group the vegetables, after they are cut, according to their respective cooking times, so that none will over- or under-cook. You accomplish this by adding the slower-cooking vegetables to the wok earlier than the quicker-cooking ones.

Heat the wok alone first — for up to a minute. Then add a little oil (canola or peanut), and if you are using onions, add them now, and sauté them alone first. Then add whatever "Group 1" vegetables you are using, and sauté until partially done. Next, add "Group 2" items and cook until everything is <u>almost</u> done. Selections from "Group 3" come in at the very end, as these vegetables cook practically on contact with the other ingredients.

Group 1

Plan on about ¾-1 lb. raw vegetables per serving.

potatoes, sliced thin
celery
carrots
broccoli
cauliflower
cabbage
eggplant
winter squash
asparagus (if thick)

Group 2

mushrooms
peppers
zucchini
summer squash
asparagus (if thin)

Group 3

GREENS:
(spinach
chard
escarole
etc.)
scallions
bean sprouts

You don't have to use all of these vegetables. You can use just some, or even just one. It's easier, and a good way to practice if you're new at this.

Remember: The more thinly a vegetable is sliced, the more quickly it cooks.

Basic Goal: To cook the vegetables quickly (over high heat, stirring almost constantly) so that each vegetable is done to its own individual perfection.

Good Things to Do: 1) Hover over the wok as you sauté. <u>Stir Very Much</u>.
2) Have everything all ready beforehand, and within arm's reach of the stove.
3) Keep the heat high, and keep the vegetables moving in the wok. Work quickly.

Try one or several of these in your sauté. Have all extras prepared beforehand, and add them during the last few minutes of the cooking.

Extras

chopped, toasted nuts

pieces of tofu (plain or marinated - see p. 183)

sliced water chestnuts

cooked noodles (rinsed and drizzled with sesame oil)

sesame seeds

soaked, sliced black mushrooms

SEASONINGS: wine

soy sauce

minced garlic

grated ginger

crushed red pepper flakes

Chinese sesame oil

OR, a combination,

such as:

Hal's Special Sauce

10 minutes to prepare.   Enough for 3-4 servings

½ cup orange juice*

¼ cup soy sauce

1 Tbs. grated fresh ginger

2-3 cloves garlic, minced

1-2 Tbs. honey

2 tsp. Chinese sesame oil

2 Tbs. cornstarch

1) Combine the 1st 6 ingredients.

2) Place the cornstarch in a bowl; whisk the liquid mixture into it.

3) Set aside, but keep the whisk handy, as you will need to whisk the sauce again just before you pour it into the sauté.

* optional: pineapple juice, instead of orange.

Add this sauce (don't forget to whisk it from the bottom just before, to redistribute the settled cornstarch) to the wokful of vegetables about ⅔ of the way through the cooking. Once it is in the wok, stir the sauté from the bottom constantly, so the sauce gets to coat all the vegetables evenly, and so it won't stick to the bottom.

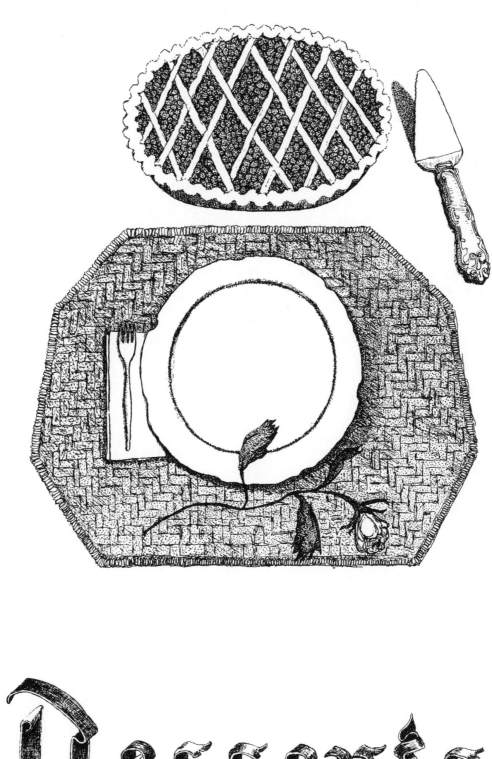

Desserts

DESSERTS
Table of Contents

It's a pleasure to present you with the following dessert recipes.

In addition to end-of-meal fare, many of these preparations are lovely additions to afternoon tea or Sunday brunch. There are several fruit pies, a rich cheesecake as well as a light one, and some traditional cookies that keep well in a tin (and are always useful to have on hand)—as well as cakes, plain and fancy, and puddings and mousses—highfat, lowfat, and in between.

I hope there is something here to please just about everyone, and that these recipes sweetly enhance and expand your repertoire.

Peach Puddingcake

20 minutes to prepare;
30 minutes to bake.

Yield: one 9x13-inch cake

a little butter or oil for the pan
2 cups unbleached white flour
2 tsp. baking powder
½ tsp. salt
1 tsp. cinnamon
½ tsp. allspice
2 eggs

1 cup (packed) light brown sugar
1 cup milk (lowfat or soy OK)
1 tsp. vanilla extract
¼ tsp. almond extract
2 Tbs. melted butter
2½ cups sliced peaches (fresh or frozen/defrosted)

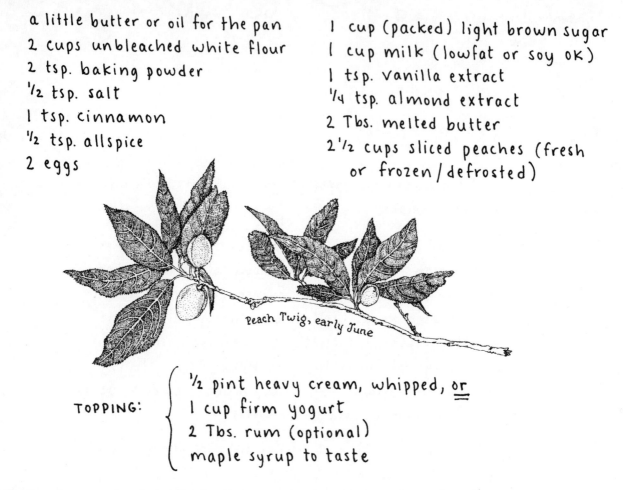

Peach Twig, early June

TOPPING: { ½ pint heavy cream, whipped, or
1 cup firm yogurt
2 Tbs. rum (optional)
maple syrup to taste

1) Preheat oven to 350°F. Lightly grease a 9 x 13-inch baking pan.

2) Sift flour, baking powder, salt, and spices into a medium-sized bowl.

3) In a separate bowl, beat together the eggs and brown sugar with an electric mixer at high speed for about 2 minutes. Stir in the milk, extracts, and melted butter.

4) Make a well in the center of the dry ingredients, and pour in the wet. Add the peaches, and stir with a wooden spoon until well combined.

5) Spread into the prepared pan and bake for about 30 minutes, or until a toothpick inserted all the way into the center comes out clean.

6) In a small bowl, fold together the whipped cream or yogurt with rum, if desired, and maple syrup to taste. Serve the puddingcake at any temperature, with a generous amount of topping.

Spicy Gingerbread

20 minutes to prepare;
30 to 35 minutes to bake.

Yield:
6 to 9 servings

a little butter or oil for the pan
6 Tbs. butter or canola oil
3 Tbs. grated fresh ginger
½ cup light-colored honey
½ cup light molasses
¾ cup firm yogurt
1 egg

2 cups unbleached white flour
1½ tsp. baking soda
¼ tsp. salt
1 tsp. dry mustard
½ tsp. ground cloves or allspice
½ tsp. cinnamon
¼ tsp. nutmeg

1) Preheat oven to 350°F. Grease an 8-inch square pan (or its equivalent).

2) Melt the butter or heat the oil in a small skillet. Add the ginger, and sauté together over medium heat for about 3 minutes, or until fragrant. Remove from heat.

3) Combine honey and molasses in a small mixing bowl, and beat at high speed with an electric mixer for 2 to 3 minutes. Add the ginger mixture, and beat for a minute more. Whisk in the yogurt and egg, then beat at high speed for an additional minute. Set aside.

4) Sift the dry ingredients together into a large mixing bowl. Make a well in the center, and pour in the wet mixture. Mix with a few decisive strokes until thoroughly combined.

5) Spread into the prepared pan. Bake 30 to 35 minutes, or until the top surface is springy to the touch. Cool at least 15 minutes before slicing.

Carob Fudge Torte

....very moist and loveable.

I. Cake

30 minutes to prepare;
30 minutes to bake
(plus time to cool
and assemble).

Yield:
a big layer cake
(enough to serve
10 to 12)

a little butter or oil for the pans
½ cup butter (1 stick), softened
¾ cup light-colored honey
2 eggs
½ cup carob powder
½ cup hot water or coffee

2 cups unbleached white flour
1 tsp. baking soda
½ tsp. salt
1 cup firm yogurt
1 ½ tsp. vanilla extract

1) Preheat oven to 350°F. Grease 2 8-inch round cake pans.

2) Place the butter and honey in a large mixing bowl. Cream together, using an electric mixer at high speed, for 3 minutes.

3) Add the eggs one at a time, beating well after each.

4) Combine the carob powder and hot water or coffee in a small bowl. Mix until it becomes a smooth paste, then beat this into the butter mixture until uniformly blended.

5) Sift together the dry ingredients into a separate medium-sized bowl. Stir this mixture into the carob-butter mixture alternately with the yogurt (flour / yogurt / flour / yogurt / flour). With each addition, mix just enough to combine. (Overmixing will toughen the cake's texture.) Stir in vanilla.

6) Divide the batter evenly between the cake pans. Bake for 20 to 30 minutes, or until a toothpick inserted into the center comes out clean.

7) Cool in the pans for 10 minutes, then remove by rapping the pans sharply and inverting the cakes onto dinner plates. Cool thoroughly.

II. Orange-Cream Cheese Frosting

8 oz. (1 cup) softened cream cheese
1 tsp. vanilla extract
½ tsp. grated orange rind
3 to 4 Tbs. honey (to taste)
extra carob powder

1) Combine everything except carob powder in a small mixing bowl. Beat until fluffy and smooth.

2) Spread half the filling on one cake layer. Place the other layer on top.

3) Spread the remaining filling on top of the second layer.

4) Sift a small amount of carob powder over the top for a nicely finished surface. If the weather is hot, chill before serving.

Oatmeal-Yogurt Cake

15 minutes to prepare;
25 to 30 minutes to bake.

Yield: 1 9×13-inch
cake

a little oil or butter for the pan
1 cup light brown sugar
½ cup (1 stick) butter, melted
2 eggs
⅔ cup firm yogurt
1 tsp. vanilla extract
2 cups unbleached white flour
1 tsp. baking soda
1 tsp. baking powder
½ tsp. salt

½ tsp. cinnamon
½ tsp. allspice
¼ tsp. nutmeg
1½ cups rolled oats
½ cup orange juice
½ tsp. grated orange rind
OPTIONAL: ½ cup raisins
OPTIONAL: Orange-Cream
 Cheese Frosting (recipe
 on preceding page)

1) Preheat oven to 350°F. Lightly grease a 9 × 13-inch pan.

2) Beat together the brown sugar and butter in a large bowl.

3) Add eggs one at a time, beating well after each.

4) Beat in the yogurt and vanilla until well blended.

5) Sift the flour, baking soda and powder, salt, and spices into a separate bowl.

6) Add half the flour mixture and all the oats to the wet mixture, stirring until well blended. Stir in the orange juice.

7) Add remaining flour mixture, along with the orange rind and raisins, if used. Mix just enough to thoroughly blend.

8) Spread into the prepared pan, and bake 25 to 30 minutes, or until a toothpick inserted all the way in comes out clean. Cool thoroughly before frosting.

Fresh Strawberry Mousse

Preparation time:
20 minutes
of doing things,
plus time to cool
and chill.

Yield:
4 to 6
servings

NEW! NO EGGS!
DELICIOUS
NONFAT OPTION!

4 cups sliced strawberries
6 Tbs. cornstarch
⅔ cup sugar
½ cup fresh lemon juice
1 tsp. grated lemon rind

½ pint heavy cream, whipped
OR
1 cup firm yogurt (nonfat OK),
stirred until smooth

1) Place the strawberries in a medium-sized saucepan. Cover and cook over medium heat for 5 to 8 minutes, until it looks like soup. Transfer to a medium-sized bowl and set aside.

2) Without washing it first, use the same saucepan for this step. Combine the cornstarch, sugar, and lemon juice in the pan, and whisk until uniform.

3) Pour the still-hot strawberry soup back into the cornstarch mixture, whisking constantly. Return the pan to the stove, and cook over medium heat, stirring constantly until thick. (This should take about 5 minutes.) Remove from heat, and stir in the lemon rind.

4) Transfer back to the same bowl the strawberries had been in, and cool to room temperature.

5) Purée until smooth in a food processor or blender, and return to the bowl. Cover tightly and chill until cold.

6) Fold in the whipped cream or yogurt and serve.

Apple-Port-Cheese Pie
with Almond Crust

Preparation time:
CRUST = 40 minutes
APPLES = 20 minutes
FILLING = 10 minutes
GLAZE + ASSEMBLY = 10 minutes

Yield:
about 6
servings

At first glance, this scrumptious cheese-filled, apple-glazed, almond-crusted pie seems like a lot of work, but it's really quite easy. I've broken down the tasks in the "preparation time" posted above, and everything but the glaze and assembly can be done in advance.

So go ahead and try this. You'll love it so much, you'll want to make it again tomorrow.

I. THE CRUST:

½ cup (1 stick) cold butter
1 cup unbleached white flour (plus extra for rolling out)
¼ cup ground almonds
3 to 4 Tbs. cold water
(foil and 2 cups dry beans for the baking)

1) Preheat oven to 375°F.

2) Use a pastry cutter or food processor to cut together the butter and flour until the mixture has the texture of coarse cornmeal. Stir in the almonds.

3) Sprinkle in the water as needed, mixing quickly with a fork or a few additional spurts of the food processor, until a firm, cohesive dough is formed.

4) Flour a rolling pin and a clean, dry surface, and roll the dough into a circle large enough to fit a 9-inch pie or tart pan. Ease the dough into the pan, pat it into place, and use your hands to form a nice edge.

5) Pierce the crust all over with a fork. Cut a piece of foil approximately to fit, and place this on top of the crust. Sprinkle about 2 cups dry beans over the foil (this keeps it flat during baking) and bake 15 minutes. Remove the foil and beans, and bake 15 minutes more. Cool before filling. (You can turn off the oven — the rest of the pie is unbaked.)

II. THE APPLES & PORT:

1½ cups port (or a comparable sweet dessert wine)	3 large (3-inch diameter) tart apples, peeled and sliced thin
1 stick cinnamon	⅓ cup light-colored honey
½ tsp. grated lemon rind	a dash of salt

1) Combine port, cinnamon stick, lemon rind, and apples in a medium-sized saucepan. Bring to a boil, turn heat down to low, cover, and simmer for 10 minutes — or until the apples are perfectly tender. Remove from heat and discard the cinnamon stick.

2) Strain, reserving both the apples and the liquid. Stir the honey and salt into the liquid. Set aside.

III. THE CHEESE FILLING:

6 oz. (¾ cup) cream cheese, softened
½ tsp. vanilla extract
¼ tsp. almond extract
2 Tbs. light-colored honey
¼ cup firm yogurt

1) Combine all ingredients in a small mixing bowl, and beat until smooth. Spread evenly into the baked, cooled crust.

2) Arrange the cooked apple slices on top in a lovely pattern.

IV. THE GLAZE:

2 Tbs. cornstarch
1½ cups of the apple-cooking liquid

1) Place the cornstarch in a small saucepan. Whisk in the liquid, and keep whisking as you bring the mixture to a boil. Turn the heat down, and cook, stirring frequently, until thick and glossy (approximately 5 to 8 minutes).

2) Without waiting for it to cool, pour the glaze over the lovely pattern of apples. Cool to room temperature, then chill until cold.

Cherry-Berry Pie

20 minutes to make the crust;
10 minutes to make the filling;
45 to 50 minutes to bake.

Yield:
4 to 6
servings

NOTE: You can use frozen
unsweetened fruit. Defrost
and drain before using.

I. THE CRUST:

2 cups unbleached white flour
1/4 teaspoon salt
3/4 cup (1 1/2 sticks) cold unsalted butter
4 to 6 Tbs. cold milk
Extra flour, as needed, for rolling the dough

1) Place the flour and salt in a food processor fitted with the steel blade attachment.

2) Cut the butter into slices and drop the pieces on top of the flour.

3) Pulse until the flour and butter are combined, and the mixture resembles a coarse meal. (You shouldn't see any big pieces of butter at this point.)

4) Add milk, 1 tablespoon at a time, pulsing after each addition. When the dough sticks to itself when gently squeezed, dump it out onto a clean, dry surface. Use your hands to press it into two balls, one larger and one smaller.

5) Using flour, as needed, to prevent sticking, roll the larger ball to fit a 9- or 10-inch pie pan. Roll the smaller ball of dough, as well, and cut it into about 12 1/2-inch strips. Refrigerate until ready to use.

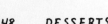

II. THE FILLING:

3 cups berries ~ any kind (Slice
    larger ones; leave smaller
       ones whole)
3 cups dark cherries, pitted
3/4 cup sugar
1 tsp. grated lemon rind
1/2 tsp. cinnamon
About 3 grates fresh nutmeg
2 Tbs. fresh lemon juice
6 Tbs. unbleached white flour
A pinch of salt
Confectioners' sugar for the top (optional)

1) Preheat oven to 375°F.

2) Gently toss together all the ingredients (except the confectioners' sugar) in a large bowl. When the filling is uniformly mixed, spoon it into the unbaked crust.

3) Decorate the top with the strips of dough, either in a woven pattern (a lattice), or just by laying the strips on top, and possibly twisting them a little. It will look beautiful, whatever you do. Press the ends of the strips to the edges of the crust.

4) Place the pie pan on a baking tray, and place the tray in the lower half of the oven. Bake for 45 to 50 minutes, or until bubbly and lightly browned. Serve warm, at room temperature, or cold, with confectioners' sugar dusted on top, if desired.

Chocolate
Crêpes

Preparation time:
Making the crêpes – 30 minutes
Filling them – 15 minutes

Yield:
8 crêpes
(4 servings)

It might sound complicated, but this recipe is actually very simple.

The pancakes can be made up to several days in advance and stored on a plate, tightly wrapped and refrigerated.

Heating and filling the crêpes – and getting them ready to serve – takes practically no time at all. The only challenge involved is to eat them slowly. It's almost impossible not to wolf them down!

I. Making the Crêpes:

1 egg
½ cup plus 2 Tbs. milk
a dash of salt
½ cup unbleached white flour
1 Tbs. unsweetened cocoa
2 Tbs. sugar
a little oil for the pan

1) Combine everything in a blender and whip until smooth.

2) Use a 6- or 7-inch crêpe or omelette pan – nonstick, if possible. Heat the pan, and brush lightly with oil.

3) Keep the heat high, and add just enough batter to coat the pan (about 2 or 3 Tbs. batter). Tilt the pan every which way until it is fairly evenly coated. Wait a few seconds for the crêpe to set.

4) Loosen the sides and flip it over. Cook on this side for about 10 seconds, then turn out the finished crêpe onto a dinner plate.

5) Continue making crêpes until you have used up the batter. (Don't forget to keep the heat high throughout the cooking.) Stack the crêpes on the dinner plate. Cover tightly with plastic wrap, and refrigerate until you're ready to fill them.

Filling and Serving the Crêpes:

> a little butter for the pan
> 1 cup orange marmalade OR
>   1 cup semisweet chocolate chips
> ½ cup heavy cream (possibly more)
> Confectioners' sugar } for the top
> unsweetened cocoa }

1) Heat a large skillet or a sauté pan over medium heat. When it is hot, add some butter, and push or swirl it all around until it melts and the pan is coated.

2) Add a crêpe, and let it heat on one side for about a minute. Then turn it over, and add about 2 Tbs. orange marmalade or chocolate chips to the center. Spread the filling around a little.

3) Fold the crêpe like so:

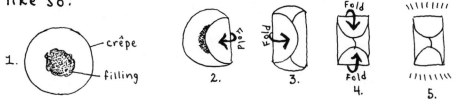

4) Push the filled, folded crêpe to the side of the pan, add a little more butter, and proceed with the next crêpe. (If the pan gets too crowded with filled crêpes, you can move some to a second warmed, buttered pan.)

5) To serve, put about a tablespoon of cream on each serving plate, and swirl it around. Place one or two warmed crêpes on top, and dust lightly with confectioners' sugar and unsweetened cocoa. Serve right away.

Stuffed Baked Apples

• • • • • • • • • • • • • • •

1 hour to prepare
(including 40
minutes of baking).

Put these in the oven as
you sit down to dinner.
They'll be ready just in
time to eat hot for dessert.

Yield:
6 servings

NOTE: If you have leftover
filling, sprinkle it on top
at serving time.

Good for breakfast or brunch, as well as dessert.

6 large, tart apples
½ cup Grape Nuts cereal
¼ cup finely minced
    walnuts or almonds
½ tsp. cinnamon
1 to 2 Tbs. brown sugar

2 cups apple juice
a few strips of fresh lemon peel
1 cinnamon stick

TOPPING { yogurt, sweetened to taste
with a little maple syrup

1) Preheat oven to 375°F.

2) Carefully remove the cores from the apples, using an apple corer
(highly specialized gadget), a vegetable peeler, an agile paring knife,
and/or a teaspoon handle. Try to get all the seeds out of there, as
well as anything else you'd prefer not to bite into.

3) Combine cereal, nuts, cinnamon, and sugar in a small bowl.

4) Place the apples in a glass baking pan, and stuff their cavities
with the filling. Pour the apple juice around them; float the
lemon peel and cinnamon stick in the juice. Cover loosely with
foil, and bake for about 40 minutes, or until the apples can be
pierced easily with a knife.

5) Serve hot, warm, at room temperature, or cold. Spoon some of the
juice over the top, and spoon on some lightly sweetened yogurt.

Apple Pie

with

Oatmeal Cookie Crust

30 minutes to prepare;
45 to 50 minutes
to bake.

Yield:
4 to 6
servings

CRUST:

1½ cups rolled oats
½ cup unbleached white flour
¼ tsp. salt (rounded measure)
¾ tsp. cinnamon
3 Tbs. brown sugar
¼ cup finely minced nuts (optional)
½ tsp. vanilla extract
½ cup (1 stick) butter, melted

1) Combine all crust ingredients in a medium-sized bowl, and mix well.

2) Press firmly and evenly into the bottom and sides of a 9- or 10-inch pie pan, forming a thick crust. Reserve a handful of crust mix for the topping.

FILLING:

6 cups peeled, sliced tart apple
3 Tbs. fresh lemon juice
1½ tsp. cinnamon
¼ tsp. allspice or ground cloves
¼ tsp. nutmeg

½ tsp. grated lemon rind
3 Tbs. unbleached white flour
¼ cup brown sugar or honey
½ cup sour cream (optional)
a handful of chopped nuts (optional)

1) Preheat oven to 375°F.

2) Place the sliced apples in a large bowl. Drizzle with lemon juice, and sprinkle with spices; toss until well coated. Add the lemon rind, sprinkle in the flour, and mix again. Gradually add the sugar or honey (and optional sour cream) as you mix. Don't worry if the apple slices break a little while being mixed and tossed.

3) Distribute the filling into the unbaked crust. Sprinkle the handful of reserved crust mix over the top, with or without the optional extra handful of nuts, and pat neatly into place.

4) Bake for 45 to 50 minutes, or until the apples are soft and the crust is nicely browned on the edges. (NOTE: If the top appears to be browning too quickly during baking, cover loosely with foil.) Serve hot, warm, or at room temperature.

⁎ Chocolate ⁎ Apple ⁎ Nut Torte ⁎

25 minutes to prepare;
45 minutes to bake,
plus time to cool.

Yield:
6 to 8
servings

NOTES:
1) Separate the eggs ahead
   of time.
2) Grind almonds & chocolate
   in a blender or food processor.
3) Use a food processor to grate
   the apple.

8 eggs (OK to delete half the yolks)
a little butter or oil for the pan
¾ cup sugar
1 cup almonds, finely ground
1 cup (packed) grated tart apple
¾ cup semisweet chocolate chips,
   ground to a coarse meal
½ cup unbleached white flour *

½ tsp. baking powder (optional)
dash of cinnamon
½ tsp. salt
½ tsp. vanilla extract
OPTIONAL TOPPING:
whipped cream laced with
   a little Amaretto liqueur

1) (Do this ahead): Separate the eggs, placing both whites and yolks in large
   mixing bowls. Cover each bowl, and let the eggs come to room temperature.
2) Preheat the oven to 350°F. Grease the bottom only of a 9- or 10-inch springform pan.
3) Beat the egg whites until they form stiff peaks. Set aside.
4) Without cleaning the beaters, beat together the egg yolks and sugar for
   about 2 minutes. Stir in the almonds, apple, and chocolate.
5) Sift the flour, baking powder, cinnamon, and salt directly into the yolk
   mixture. Add the vanilla, and stir until well combined.
6) Gently fold in the beaten egg whites, using a rubber spatula to scrape the
   heavier mixture from the bottom of the bowl. Try to incorporate the whites
   as well as possible without deflating them too much. (This is an imperfect
   process, so don't worry if the folded batter isn't uniform.) Turn into the
   prepared pan.
7) Bake for about 45 minutes, or until a toothpick inserted into the center comes
   out clean. Cool thoroughly before removing the sides of the pan and slicing.

* Fine bread crumbs or matzo cake meal can replace the flour.

Ricotta-Cherry Mousse

Preparation time:
15 minutes
(less, if using
frozen, pitted
cherries).

Yield:
4 to 6
servings

Ricotta cheese becomes ethereal and smooth when whipped. This mousse, made without eggs or cream, is a stunning – and light – dessert, and very easy to whip up.

You can make this any time of year, using frozen, unsweetened cherries (defrosted and drained), when fresh are unavailable.

Make this shortly before serving – it doesn't keep well.

1 lb. (2 cups) ricotta cheese (skim or part-skim ok)
3 Tbs. sifted confectioners' sugar
1/4 tsp. almond extract
1 tsp. vanilla extract
2 cups dark cherries, pitted and sliced
1/2 cup semisweet chocolate chips,
    ground to a coarse meal in a blender
1/3 cup lightly toasted almonds, slivered or minced

1) Place the ricotta in a medium-sized mixing bowl, and beat with an electric mixer at high speed for about 3 minutes, gradually adding the sugar.

2) Stir in the extracts. Cover and chill until shortly before serving time.

3) Within about 15 minutes of serving, fold in the cherries.

4) Serve in small bowls, topped with chocolate and almonds.

Chocolate ✿ Pudding

15 minutes to prepare,
plus about 2 hours
to chill.

Yield:
4 servings

Real! Genuine! The mother of all comfort foods!

GOOD NEWS FOR VEGANS: This tastes absolutely
wonderful made with plain or vanilla soy milk.

3/4 to 1 cup semisweet chocolate chips

2 to 3 Tbs. light brown sugar

2 cups milk (lowfat or soy OK)

a pinch of salt

3 Tbs. Cornstarch

1/2 tsp. vanilla extract

1) Combine the chocolate, sugar, and milk in a medium-sized heavy saucepan. Heat gently, whisking constantly, until all the chocolate is melted
and the mixture is uniform. Remove from heat.

2) Place the salt and cornstarch in a medium-small bowl. Pour in about
half the hot mixture, whisking vigorously until all the cornstarch
is dissolved, then whisk this solution back into the saucepan.

3) Keep stirring as you cook the pudding over very low heat for about
8 to 10 minutes more, or until thick and glossy. Remove from heat
and stir in the vanilla.

4) Transfer the hot pudding to a serving bowl or to individual cups. To
avoid a skin forming on top, lay a sheet of waxed paper over the surface. Chill completely before serving.

Coconut & Almond Macaroon Torte

PREPARATION TIME:
20 minutes to prepare;
35 minutes to bake
(plus time to cool
and a few minutes
to finish)

Yield:
about 6
servings

6 eggs
a little oil or butter for the pan
1 1/3 cups almonds, lightly toasted
1/2 cup sugar
1 cup shredded unsweetened coconut,
   lightly toasted

1/2 tsp. salt
2 tsp. grated orange rind

1/2 cup raspberry preserves
3/4 cup chocolate chips
fresh raspberries, if available,
   for garnish

1) ABOUT 1 HOUR AHEAD: Separate the eggs, placing the whites in a large bowl and the yolks in a smaller bowl. Cover and let come to room temperature.

2) Lightly grease the bottom of a 9-inch springform pan. Preheat oven to 375°F.

3) Place the almonds in a food processor with 1 tablespoon of the sugar. Use a series of long pulses to grind the almonds to a powder. Transfer to a medium-sized bowl; stir in the coconut, salt, and orange rind, and set aside.

4) Measure out another tablespoon of the sugar, add it to the egg whites, and beat until they form stiff peaks.

5) Add the remaining sugar to the egg yolks, and beat with a fork or a small whisk until the sugar is incorporated. Fold this mixture into the beaten whites.

6) Sprinkle the dry mixture over the beaten, folded eggs, and finish folding. Transfer to the prepared pan, and bake in the center of the oven for about 35 minutes, or until a sharp knife inserted all the way into the center comes out clean. Remove from the oven, and cool completely.

7) When the cake is cool, release the springform sides, and transfer the cake to a plate. Spread the raspberry preserves over the top.

8) Melt the chocolate, and spread it over the preserves. Decorate with fresh raspberries, if available.

Chocolate Honeycake

25 minutes to prepare;
25 minutes to bake
(square pan);
35 to 40 minutes to bake
(loaf pan).

Yield:
6 to 8 servings

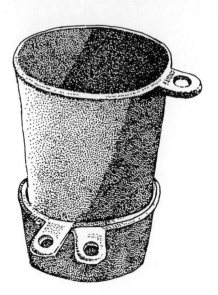

a little butter or oil for the pan
½ cup butter (1 stick) or canola oil
1 oz. (1 square) unsweetened chocolate
¾ cup light-colored honey
2 eggs
1 tsp. vanilla extract

¼ cup unsweetened cocoa
1 cup unbleached white flour
½ tsp. salt
1½ tsp. baking powder
1 cup chocolate chips
½ cup chopped nuts
(optional)

1) Preheat oven to 350°F. Grease an 8-inch square pan or a medium-sized loaf pan.

2) Melt the butter and chocolate together over low heat. If using oil, melt the chocolate alone, then remove from heat and stir in the oil.

3) Place the honey in a medium-sized bowl, and beat at high speed with an electric mixer for about 2 minutes. Add the eggs one at a time, beating well after each. Stir in the vanilla.

4) Sift together the dry ingredients into a separate medium-small bowl.

5) Beat the melted chocolate mixture into the honey-egg mixture. Fold in the dry ingredients and chocolate chips (and optional nuts), and stir until well combined. Spread into the prepared pan.

6) Bake about 25 minutes (square pan) or 35 to 40 minutes (loaf pan). It's done when a knife inserted all the way into the center comes out clean. Cool before slicing.

,, Jewish New Year Honeycake ,,

15 to 20 minutes
to assemble;
45 minutes to bake.

(The apple topping takes
about 20 minutes.)

Yield:
6 to 8
servings

a little butter or oil for the pan
1 cup light-colored honey
1 egg
3 Tbs. canola oil or melted butter
½ cup cold black coffee — or water
2 cups unbleached white flour

a scant ½ tsp. salt
2½ tsp. baking powder
cinnamon ⎫
nutmeg ⎬ a dash or two of each
allspice ⎭
½ cup minced walnuts

1) Preheat oven to 350°F. Grease a medium-sized loaf pan.
2) Place the honey in a medium-sized bowl, and beat at high speed with an electric mixer for about 3 minutes.
3) Add the egg, oil or butter, and coffee or water. Beat for 1 more minute.
4) Sift the flour, salt, baking powder, and spices directly into the honey mixture. Add half the walnuts, and stir until well combined.
5) Spread the batter into the prepared pan, and sprinkle the remaining nuts on top.
6) Bake for about 45 minutes, or until a knife inserted all the way into the center comes out clean. Cool in the pan for about 15 minutes, then rap the pan sharply to remove the cake. Cool thoroughly before slicing.

DELICIOUS APPLE TOPPING:

4 cups peeled, sliced tart apple
1 to 2 Tbs. fresh lemon juice
¾ tsp. cinnamon
OPTIONAL: honey to taste

1) Place apples, lemon juice, and cinnamon in a medium-sized saucepan. Cover and cook over medium heat until the apples are soft (about 10 minutes).
2) Remove from heat, and stir in honey to taste, if desired.
3) Spoon it, still hot or warm, onto slices of cooled honeycake.

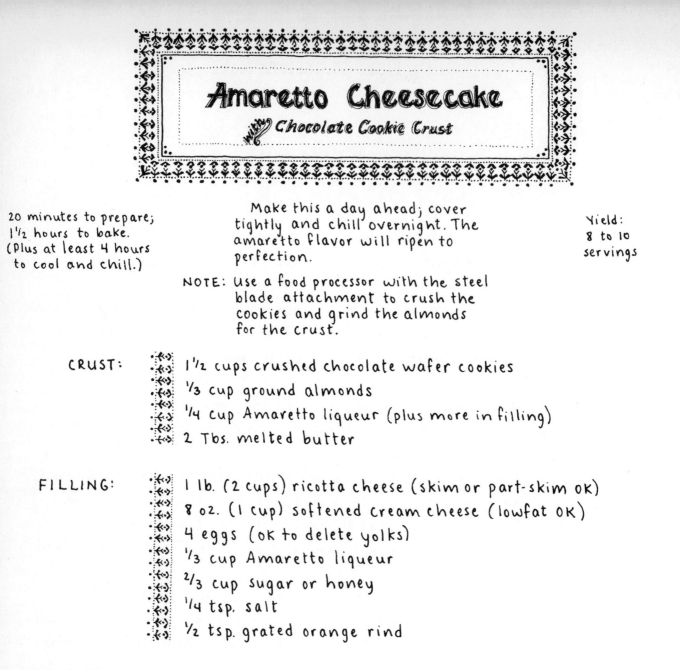

Amaretto Cheesecake
with Chocolate Cookie Crust

20 minutes to prepare;
1½ hours to bake.
(Plus at least 4 hours
to cool and chill.)

Make this a day ahead; cover tightly and chill overnight. The amaretto flavor will ripen to perfection.

NOTE: Use a food processor with the steel blade attachment to crush the cookies and grind the almonds for the crust.

Yield:
8 to 10
servings

CRUST:
- 1½ cups crushed chocolate wafer cookies
- ⅓ cup ground almonds
- ¼ cup Amaretto liqueur (plus more in filling)
- 2 Tbs. melted butter

FILLING:
- 1 lb. (2 cups) ricotta cheese (skim or part-skim ok)
- 8 oz. (1 cup) softened cream cheese (lowfat OK)
- 4 eggs (ok to delete yolks)
- ⅓ cup Amaretto liqueur
- ⅔ cup sugar or honey
- ¼ tsp. salt
- ½ tsp. grated orange rind

1) Preheat oven to 325°F.

2) Combine the crust ingredients in a medium-sized bowl, and mix until well blended. Transfer to a 9- or 10-inch springform pan; press the mixture firmly into the floor of the pan.

3) Combine all the filling ingredients in a large mixing bowl. Beat for at least 3 minutes with an electric mixer at high speed. Scrape the bottom and sides of the bowl often.

4) Pour the batter into the crust-lined pan. Bake in the center of the oven for 1 hour. Turn off the oven and leave the cake in there for another 30 minutes.

5) Remove the cake from the oven and let it cool to room temperature. Cover the pan tightly with plastic wrap, and chill for at least 4 hours before serving.

★ ★ ★ ★ ★ ★ ★ ★ ★ CHEESECAKE SOUFFLÉ ★ ★ ★ ★ ★ ★ ★ ★
w/ Strawberry~Marmalade Sauce 🍓🍓
★ ★

15 minutes to assemble;
1 hour to bake.

🍓 🍓

Yield:
about 6
servings

Like other soufflés, this is at its best fresh from the oven. All the ingredients can be prepared ahead; make the sauce while it bakes.

NOTES: ♪ Separate the eggs ahead of time- the whites should be at room temperature.
♪ It's ok to use frozen unsweetened berries. (Defrost them first.)

a little butter or oil for the pan
6 egg whites, at room temperature
1½ lbs. (3 cups) ricotta (skim or part-skim OK)
5 Tbs. unbleached white flour

a scant ½ tsp. salt
⅔ cup sifted confectioners' sugar
1 tsp. vanilla extract
½ tsp. grated lemon rind
1 tsp. grated orange rind

1) Preheat oven to 375°F. Lightly grease a 9- or 10-inch soufflé dish.
2) Place the egg whites in a large mixing bowl. Beat until they form stiff peaks. Don't bother cleaning the beaters.
3) Place the ricotta in another large bowl, and use the same beaters to whip it for about 5 minutes at high speed, gradually adding the flour, salt, sugar, and vanilla. Stir in the citrus rinds.
4) Gently fold the beaten egg whites into the ricotta mixture. Don't worry if the results are not perfectly uniform.
5) Turn into the prepared pan, and bake undisturbed for 1 hour. Serve hot, while it is still puffy, with the following sauce.

STRAWBERRY-MARMALADE SAUCE:

2½ cups strawberries
1 cup orange or lemon marmalade
optional: a few tablespoons of orange-flavored liqueur

1) Combine strawberries, marmalade, and optional liqueur in a medium-sized saucepan. Bring to a boil, then lower heat and simmer uncovered for about 10 minutes.
2) Ladle a little pool of hot or warm sauce onto each serving plate, then mound a portion of soufflé in the center. Drizzle a little extra sauce over the top. Divine!

Four Simple & Wonderful Cookie Recipes

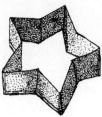

Mandelbrot

Preparation time:
1¼ hours, total.

Yield:
3½ dozen

a little butter or oil for the pan
3 eggs
½ cup light-colored honey
½ cup melted butter or canola oil
1 tsp. grated orange rind
1 tsp. vanilla extract

2¾ cups unbleached white flour
2 tsp. baking powder
½ tsp. salt
1 cup finely minced almonds
½ cup raisins or currants
½ cup minced dates (optional)

1) Preheat oven to 375°F. Lightly grease a cookie sheet.

2) In a large mixing bowl, beat together eggs, honey, and butter or oil until light and fluffy. Stir in orange rind and vanilla extract.

3) Sift the flour, baking powder, and salt into the egg mixture. Add nuts and dried fruit, and stir until well combined.

4) Divide the batter in half. Shape 2 parallel logs, each about 2 inches wide, on the cookie sheet.

5) Bake for 30 minutes. Let cool for about 15 minutes.

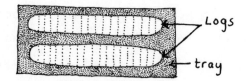

Logs

tray

6) Slice the baked logs into ½-inch pieces. Return these to the cookie sheet and bake for 15 minutes longer. Cool completely before eating.

Whole Wheat Poppy Seed Cookies

Preparation time:
45 minutes, total.

NOTE: You might need
to add dough-chilling
time, if your kitchen is hot.

Yield:
4½ dozen

a little butter or oil for the pan(s)
½ cup (1 stick) butter, softened
¾ cup (packed) light brown sugar
2 eggs
½ tsp. vanilla extract
½ tsp. grated lemon rind

⅓ cup poppy seeds
1 cup unbleached white flour
1 cup whole wheat pastry flour
2 tsp. baking powder
½ tsp. salt
extra flour for rolling the dough

1) Preheat oven to 375°F. Lightly grease 1 or 2 cookie sheets.

2) Place butter and sugar in a large mixing bowl. Beat at high speed
for about 3 minutes. Add eggs one at a time, beating well after
each. Stir in vanilla, lemon rind, and poppy seeds.

3) Sift the flours, baking powder, and salt directly into the butter mixture. Mix by hand until completely blended. If it is hot or humid in
your kitchen, wrap and refrigerate the dough for at least an hour
before proceeding.

4) Flour a clean, dry surface, and roll the dough to ¼-inch thickness.
Cut into shapes, and bake for 10 to 12 minutes, or until lightly
browned on the bottom. Cool for at least 10 minutes before eating.

Cashew Shortbread

Preparation time:
35 to 40 minutes, total.

Yield:
4 dozen

1 cup (2 sticks) butter, softened
½ cup (packed) light brown sugar
3 Tbs. granulated sugar
1 cup finely minced cashews

2 cups unbleached white flour
½ tsp. salt
½ tsp. baking powder
extra flour for rolling the dough

1) Preheat oven to 375°F.

2) Place the butter and sugars in a large mixing bowl. Beat at high speed with an electric mixer for about 3 minutes. Stir in the cashews.

3) Sift the flour, salt and baking powder directly into the bowl. Use your hands to mix the dough as quickly and efficiently as possible, until it holds together.

4) Flour a clean, dry surface, and roll the dough until it is somewhere between ¼ and ½ inch thick. Cut into simple shapes and place on an ungreased cookie sheet.

5) Bake for 10 to 12 minutes, or until lightly browned on the bottom. Cool for at least 10 minutes before eating.

Rugelach

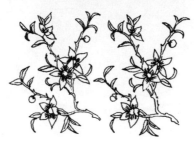

Preparation time:
  1 hour, total

NOTE: You might
need to add dough-
chilling time, if your
kitchen is hot.

Yield: 4 dozen

1 cup (2 sticks) butter, softened
1 cup cottage cheese.
2 cups unbleached white flour
½ tsp. salt
extra flour for rolling the dough

FILLING:

COMBINE
½ cup sugar
2 tsp. cinnamon
½ cup finely minced nuts
OPTIONAL: ½ cup semisweet
  chocolate chips, ground to
  a coarse meal in a blender

1) Use an electric mixer or a food processor (a few short bursts with the steel blade attachment) to mix the butter, cottage cheese, flour, and salt into a uniform dough. Divide the dough into 4 equal parts, and make each one into a ball. If your kitchen is hot or humid, wrap and refrigerate each ball of dough for at least an hour before proceeding.

2) Preheat oven to 375°F.

3) Flour a clean, dry surface. Roll each ball of dough into as perfect a circle as possible, about ¼ inch thick.

4) Sprinkle each circle with a quarter of the filling, distributing it as evenly as you can up to ½ inch of the rim.

5) Cut like so: (like a pizza), and roll each wedge from the outside edge of the circle toward the center.

6) Place the filled pastries on an ungreased cookie sheet. Bake for 20 to 25 minutes, or until nicely browned. Cool 10 minutes before eating.

Russian Coffeecake

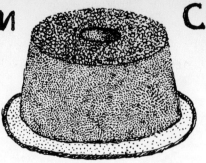

30 minutes to prepare;
up to 55 minutes to bake.

Yield:
1 large cake
(enough for 10 to 12)

a little butter or oil for the pan
1 cup (2 sticks) butter, softened
1 cup (packed) light brown sugar
4 eggs
1 tsp. vanilla extract
2 cups unbleached white flour
1 cup whole wheat pastry flour
1 Tbs. baking powder
1 tsp. baking soda
½ tsp. salt
1 cup buttermilk, at room temperature

FILLING {
½ cup semisweet chocolate chips
½ cup almonds
½ cup shredded unsweetened coconut
½ cup peach or apricot jam
½ cup dried apricots, minced

1) Preheat oven to 350°F. Generously grease a standard-size tube or bundt pan.

2) Place the butter and sugar in a large mixing bowl. Cream together with an electric mixer until light and fluffy. Add the eggs one at a time, beating well after each. Stir in the vanilla.

3) Sift together the flours, baking powder, soda, and salt into a separate medium-sized bowl.

4) Add the dry mixture and the buttermilk alternately to the butter mixture (dry/wet/dry/wet/dry). Mix just enough to thoroughly blend after each addition. Don't beat or otherwise overmix.

5) Place the chocolate chips and almonds in a blender jar. Whirl together in short spurts until ground into a coarse powder. Combine this with the coconut in a small bowl.

6) Spoon half the batter into the prepared pan, gently spreading it until even. Spoon small amounts of jam here and there onto the batter. (Don't try to spread it—just leave it in little blobs.) Sprinkle on the apricots and about 2/3 of the chocolate-nut mix.

7) Add the remaining batter, distributing it nicely. Sprinkle with the rest of the chocolate mix, and bake the cake for 45 to 55 minutes—until a probing knife inserted all the way in comes out clean. Allow to cool completely before removing from the pan.

afterword

The art of fine cooking has been revered in many cultures. Although often shrouded in mystery, its origin has always been, and will continue to be, <u>People</u>. Ironically, though, the bulk of humanity feels quite excluded from "haute cuisine". If more people can feel welcome in the world of careful, expressive and healthful (not to mention, delicious) food preparation, we won't need to turn to junk food out of lack of information about anywhere else to go. We will have someplace wonderful to go, and we can all discover ourselves as artists on the way there. Trust your own tastebuds to teach you how to create delightful food for both yourself and others. The ensuing good feelings of personal and shared pleasures will be unavoidable.

I hope this book has encouraged you to feel freer and more at home in your kitchen. I hope you gain the confidence to prepare good food the way you and your close ones love it, and to fully enjoy, appreciate, and grow with it. I hope this book gets shared with children, so more people can begin earlier to discover and delight in our human nurturing powers. Last and foremost, I hope hunger of all kinds can be brought to an end in this world, so that some day all human beings will have the opportunity to know fullest physical and spiritual strength.

Menu~ Planning Notes

Menu-planning can be a highly creative endeavor. Even if you are following recipes, it is still an act of improvisation to group different dishes together into a meal. There are no rules, but do consider these guidelines:

Try to achieve a balance of hot and cold dishes, as well as spicy and mild; sharp (as in marinated) and bland (as in soft and soothing); crispy or crunchy and creamy or smooth.

Pair off dishes that are complementary and harmonious at the same time.

Avoid redundancies, for example: a cheesy casserole with a creamily-dressed salad and a cheesecake for dessert.

Try to balance the weights of accompanying dishes. For example, if one dish is heavy, let the other ones be light. If you're planning a rich dessert, make a light meal to precede it. This way, no one will feel too stuffed afterwards.

Here are some sample menus for lunches or dinners. Try a few of these, then begin substituting other dishes. Soon you'll be creating your own menus completely. Suggestion: buy a new notebook to use as a menu diary. This will help you keep track of what you serve, and you can refer to it on uninspired days when you have to cook, but can't think of anything.

* Spicy Eggplant Purée (p. 8)
* Moroccan Orange-Walnut Salad (p. 45)
  Couscous
  Toasted Pita Bread
* Apple-Port-Cheese Pie (p. 246)

* Curried Apple Soup (p. 11)
* Potato, Panir, and Pea Curry (p. 200)
* Indian Pulao (p. 224)
* Parsley-Mint Chutney ⎫ (p. 116)
* Date & Orange Chutney ⎭
* Raita (p. 118)

....More→

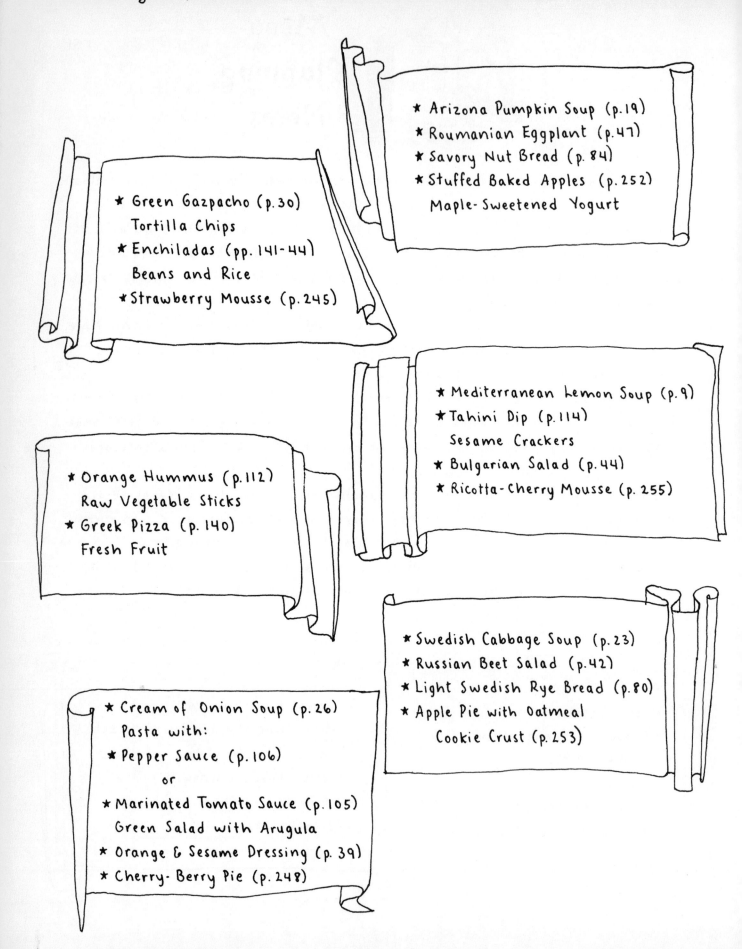

★ Arizona Pumpkin Soup (p.19)
★ Roumanian Eggplant (p.47)
★ Savory Nut Bread (p. 84)
★ Stuffed Baked Apples (p. 252)
   Maple-Sweetened Yogurt

★ Green Gazpacho (p.30)
   Tortilla Chips
★ Enchiladas (pp. 141-44)
   Beans and Rice
★ Strawberry Mousse (p. 245)

★ Mediterranean Lemon Soup (p. 9)
★ Tahini Dip (p.114)
   Sesame Crackers
★ Bulgarian Salad (p.44)
★ Ricotta-Cherry Mousse (p. 255)

★ Orange Hummus (p.112)
   Raw Vegetable Sticks
★ Greek Pizza (p. 140)
   Fresh Fruit

★ Swedish Cabbage Soup (p.23)
★ Russian Beet Salad (p.42)
★ Light Swedish Rye Bread (p.80)
★ Apple Pie with Oatmeal
   Cookie Crust (p.253)

★ Cream of Onion Soup (p.26)
   Pasta with:
★ Pepper Sauce (p.106)
     or
★ Marinated Tomato Sauce (p.105)
   Green Salad with Arugula
★ Orange & Sesame Dressing (p. 39)
★ Cherry-Berry Pie (p.248)

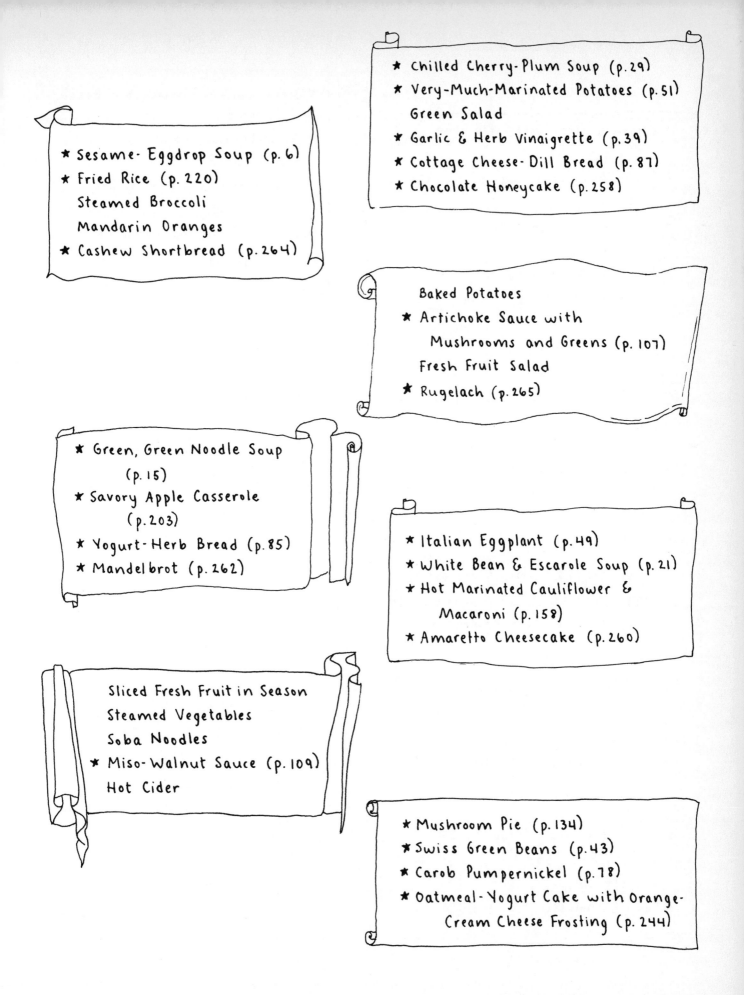

* Sesame-Eggdrop Soup (p. 6)
* Fried Rice (p. 220)
  Steamed Broccoli
  Mandarin Oranges
* Cashew Shortbread (p. 264)

* Chilled Cherry-Plum Soup (p. 29)
* Very-Much-Marinated Potatoes (p. 51)
  Green Salad
* Garlic & Herb Vinaigrette (p. 39)
* Cottage Cheese-Dill Bread (p. 87)
* Chocolate Honeycake (p. 258)

  Baked Potatoes
* Artichoke Sauce with
    Mushrooms and Greens (p. 107)
  Fresh Fruit Salad
* Rugelach (p. 265)

* Green, Green Noodle Soup
    (p. 15)
* Savory Apple Casserole
    (p. 203)
* Yogurt-Herb Bread (p. 85)
* Mandelbrot (p. 262)

* Italian Eggplant (p. 49)
* White Bean & Escarole Soup (p. 21)
* Hot Marinated Cauliflower &
    Macaroni (p. 158)
* Amaretto Cheesecake (p. 260)

  Sliced Fresh Fruit in Season
  Steamed Vegetables
  Soba Noodles
* Miso-Walnut Sauce (p. 109)
  Hot Cider

* Mushroom Pie (p. 134)
* Swiss Green Beans (p. 43)
* Carob Pumpernickel (p. 78)
* Oatmeal-Yogurt Cake with Orange-
    Cream Cheese Frosting (p. 244)

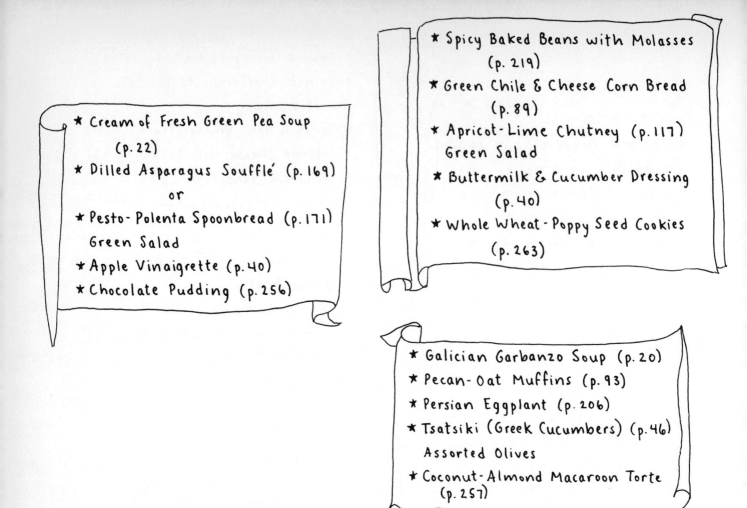

* Cream of Fresh Green Pea Soup
  (p. 22)
* Dilled Asparagus Soufflé (p. 169)
  or
* Pesto-Polenta Spoonbread (p. 171)
  Green Salad
* Apple Vinaigrette (p. 40)
* Chocolate Pudding (p. 256)

* Spicy Baked Beans with Molasses
  (p. 219)
* Green Chile & Cheese Corn Bread
  (p. 89)
* Apricot-Lime Chutney (p. 117)
  Green Salad
* Buttermilk & Cucumber Dressing
  (p. 40)
* Whole Wheat-Poppy Seed Cookies
  (p. 263)

* Galician Garbanzo Soup (p. 20)
* Pecan-Oat Muffins (p. 93)
* Persian Eggplant (p. 206)
* Tsatsiki (Greek Cucumbers) (p. 46)
  Assorted Olives
* Coconut-Almond Macaroon Torte
  (p. 257)

FOR ENTERTAINING IN WARM WEATHER,
TRY A COLD SOUP & SALAD BUFFET.
HERE ARE TWO EXAMPLES:

* Chilled Cantaloupe-Peach Soup
  (p. 28)
* Wilted Cucumbers (p. 46)
* Chilled Marinated Cauliflower (p. 41)
* Chilled Asparagus in Dilled Mustard Sauce
  (p. 53)
* Marinated Pasta Salad (p. 54)
* Tomato Fans (p. 57)
  Assorted Olives
* Corn & Molasses Muffins (p. 92)

* Chilled Marinated Mushroom
  Soup (p. 31)
* Israeli Salad (p. 44)
* Eggless Egg Salad (p. 55)
  Toasted Pita Bread
* Dill Pickle Potatoes (p. 50)
* Indian Eggplant (p. 48)
* Raita (p. 118)
  Slices of Melon with Lime

Improvisation
notes

☞ If you would love to experiment and cook without recipes, but you are insecure about it, afraid your dinner guests will throw their food on the floor (or at you);

☞ If you are tempted to alter a recipe, but you fear the heavens will punish you for deviating from the written word;

☞ If your creative spirit is inhibited by a voice from within inquiring, "With nine trillion cookbooks in print, who am I, Jo(e) Schmo, to think I have something new to offer?";

... perhaps you could use a few words of encouragement. So here they are:

Cooking is a very personal statement, whether you follow a recipe, vary it, or invent your own altogether. The same recipe made by different people on different days and in different kitchens can taste new each time. There always seems to be a personal touch — a special elusive quality — from each individual cook.

The first step toward improvisation is to find some cookbooks that appeal to you and just read them without necessarily cooking any of the recipes. This will help you to understand basic procedures and principles of cooking.

Then make a commitment to really notice and taste good food, to ask questions of other cooks, and to become deeply familiar with your own preferences. Your comfort and "vocabulary" will quickly grow, and you will find yourself more and more able to vary recipes, or even to cook without them at all.

IF YOU LOVE FOOD, YOU CAN BE A GOOD IMPROVISATIONAL COOK!

...More →

Here are some ethnic seasoning charts to help guide you through your improvisations. I have listed herbs and spices (including some vegetables and nuts used as seasonings), followed by appropriate marinating ingredients, butter and/or oil, and a general category of cheese and dairy products used for each style of cooking.

Spanish

anchovies	peppercorns
basil	saffron
bay leaves	tomatoes
bell peppers	
capers	dry wine
chiles	lemons
cinnamon	vinegar
garlic	
olives	butter
onions	olive oil
paprika	
parsley	Manchego cheese
	mild white cheeses

East European

almonds	parsley	dry wine
bell peppers	parsnips	lemons
caraway	peppercorns	sherry
celery root	poppy seeds	vinegar
cherries (sour)	tomatoes	
cinnamon	walnuts	
cucumbers		
dill	butter	
garlic		
horseradish	cottage cheese	
marjoram	cream cheese	
mushrooms	sour cream	
mustard	yogurt	
onions		
paprika		

French

almonds	rosemary
basil	sage
bay leaves	savory
bell peppers	tarragon
celery seed	thyme
chervil	tomatoes
chestnuts	walnuts
cloves	
dill	dry wine
fennel	lemons
garlic	sherry
hazelnuts	vermouth
horseradish	vinegar
marjoram	
mushrooms	Brie
mustard	Camembert
nutmeg	chèvre
olives	cream cheese
onions (leeks; shallots)	crème fraîche
paprika	Roquefort
parsley	Swiss (Gruyère, etc.)
peppercorns	

Mexican

almonds	dry wine
basil	lemons and limes
bell peppers	
chiles	olive oil
chocolate	
cilantro	cream cheese
cinnamon	mild white cheeses
corn	sour cream
cumin	
garlic	
olives	
onions	
oregano	
parsley	
peppercorns	
thyme	
tomatoes	
vanilla	

Italian

almonds
anchovies
arugula
basil
bay leaves
capers
chiles
fennel
garlic
hazelnuts
marjoram
mushrooms
olives
onions
oregano
parsley
peppercorns
pine nuts
rosemary
saffron
thyme
tomatoes

dry wine
marsala
vinegar

butter
olive oil

fontina
Gorgonzola
hard, sharp cheeses
   (parmesan, etc.)
mascarpone
mozzarella
provolone
ricotta

Mediterranean

basil
bell peppers
capers
chiles
cilantro
cinnamon
coriander seed
cucumbers
cumin
dill
garlic
mint
olives
onions
oregano
parsley
peppercorns
pine nuts
rosemary
rosewater
sesame (tahini)

tomatoes
turmeric
walnuts

dry wine
lemons
oranges
vinegar

olive oil

feta cheese
yogurt

Chinese

almonds
anise
bell peppers
cashews
chiles
cilantro
cloves
garlic
ginger

chile oil
peanut or soy oil
sesame oil

tofu

mushrooms
mustard
onions
peanuts
peppercorns
sesame

hoisin sauce
plum sauce
soy sauce
vinegar (cider or rice)
wine (plum, rice, sherry)

Indian

almonds
anise
bell peppers
cardamom
cashews
chiles
cilantro
cinnamon
cloves
coconut
coriander seed
cucumber
cumin
dill
fennel seed
fenugreek
garlic
ginger
mint
mustard seed
onions
pistachio
poppy seed
saffron

sesame seed
tamarind
tomatoes
turmeric

lemons
limes

butter
peanut oil

mild curd cheese
yogurt

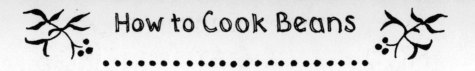

How to Cook Beans

1) SOAK THE BEANS: Presoaking dried beans allows them to cook more quickly and evenly—and to taste better. Do this with every variety except lentils and dried peas, whole or split. (These can be cooked without presoaking.)

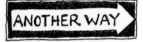 **ONE WAY** Place the beans in a large saucepan and cover them with plenty of water (the water level should exceed the beans by about 2 inches). Bring to a boil, then turn off the heat and cover. Let it sit for one hour.

ANOTHER WAY Place the beans in a bowl and cover them with water. Let them stand for 4 to 8 hours.

2) RINSE THE SOAKED BEANS. This will help get rid of the gas-inducing sugars expelled by the beans into the soaking water.

3) TO COOK: Place the soaked, rinsed beans in a pot, and fill it with enough water to cover the beans by at least 2 inches. If desired, add a few strips of <u>kombu</u>, which is a seaweed available in Japanese groceries and in most natural foods stores. Kombu aids in the digestion of beans, helps them to cook slightly faster, and enhances their flavor. (It is also high in calcium, iron, vitamins A and C, protein, and niacin.)

   Bring the water to a boil, then lower the heat to the gentlest possible simmer. (Cooking the beans with minimal agitation helps keep them whole, so they won't turn to mush.) Cook until tender—usually 1 to 2 hours. NOTE: The cooking time is somewhat arbitrary. Use the following chart as a guide, but start taste-testing toward the end of the cooking. This is not an exact science!

4) ABOUT SALT: Don't add salt until after the beans are completely cooked. Adding it sooner toughens the beans.

BEAN-COOKING CHART

(For more information and descriptions of various beans, see pp. 209-11.)

BEAN (1 cup, soaked)	TIME	YIELD
ADUKI (AZUKI; ADZUKI)	40 minutes	3½ cups
BLACK BEANS	50-60 minutes	3½ cups
BLACK-EYED PEAS	45 minutes	3 cups
CHESTNUT BEANS	1½ hours	2½ cups
FAVA BEANS	1 hour	2½ cups
GARBANZO BEANS (CHICK-PEAS)	1½ hours	3 cups
KIDNEY BEANS (INCL. CANNELLINI)	1¼ hours	3 cups
SMALL RED BEANS	1 hour	3 cups
*LENTILS (GREEN OR BROWN)	25-30 minutes	3½ cups
*LENTILS (RED)	10 minutes	3 cups
*LENTILS (FRENCH)	20 minutes	3 cups

* Don't presoak.

BEAN (1 cup, soaked)	TIME	YIELD
BABY LIMAS	40-45 minutes	3 cups
CHRISTMAS LIMAS	40-45 minutes	3 cups
MUNG BEANS	45 minutes	3 cups
*PEAS (DRIED SPLIT)	50-60 minutes	2½ cups
*PEAS (DRIED WHOLE)	1¼ hours	2½ cups
PINTO BEANS	1 hour	3 cups
RUNNER BEANS (SCARLET)	1½ - 2 hours	1½ cups
SOYBEANS	2¼ hours	3 cups
WHITE BEANS:		
NAVY	50-60 minutes	2½ cups
PEA BEANS	50-60 minutes	2½ cups
GREAT NORTHERN	50-60 minutes	3 cups
FLAGEOLET	1½ hours	3 cups
ANASAZI	50-60 minutes	3 cups

* Don't presoak.

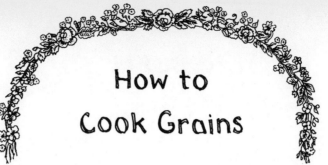

How to
Cook Grains

Most grains are cooked by adding them to boiling water, turning the heat down to a very slow simmer, and cooking them, covered, until tender. Certain grains (amaranth, cornmeal, cracked wheat, teff) become thick and porridgelike when cooked, and make excellent breakfast cereals. But for most cooked grains, the ideal consistency is tender, yet distinct. This can be accomplished by fluffing them with a fork after they are cooked, and then leaving them uncovered for about 10 minutes. This lets the steam escape and keeps the grains from becoming mushy.

Here are a couple of exceptions to the above-described method:

1) Presteamed grains, like <u>bulgur</u> and <u>couscous</u>, need only be soaked in boiling water and covered — no cooking necessary.
2) <u>Rice</u> cooks very well if it is combined with cold water in a pot and then brought to a boil. Lower heat to a simmer, cover, and cook absolutely undisturbed for the duration. Fluff with a fork when done.

ABOUT SALT: You can add some to the cooking water OR add it after the grains are cooked. This is altogether optional — you can also leave it out completely.

The following two pages contain charts showing the approximate cooking times and yields for many different grains. ⟶

(For more information and descriptions of various grains, see pp. 212-15.)

Cooking Chart for Rice and Other Grains

RICE (1 cup)	WATER	TIME	YIELD
BROWN RICE (LONG GRAIN)	1½ cups	35-45 minutes	3½ cups
BROWN RICE (SHORT GRAIN)	1½ cups	35-45 minutes	3¾ cups
BASMATI RICE (BROWN)	1½ cups	35-45 minutes	4 cups
BASMATI RICE (WHITE)	1½ cups	20 minutes	3½ cups
WHITE RICE (LONG GRAIN)	1½ cups	15-20 minutes	3½ cups
WHITE RICE (SHORT GRAIN)	1½ cups	15-20 minutes	4 cups
THAI JASMINE RICE	2 cups	20 minutes	3½ cups
BLACK JAPONICA RICE	2 cups	45 minutes	3½ cups
SWEET (GLUTINOUS OR STICKY) RICE	2 cups	45-50 minutes	3½ cups
WEHANI RICE	2 cups	45 minutes	3 cups
WILD RICE	2½ cups	1¼ hours	4 cups
MANITOK WILD RICE	2½ cups	50-60 minutes	4 cups

GRAIN (1 cup)	WATER	TIME	YIELD
AMARANTH	1½ cups	25 minutes	2 cups
BARLEY, HULLED	3 cups	1¾ hours	4 cups
BARLEY, PEARL	2 cups	1½ hours	4 cups
BUCKWHEAT / KASHA	1½ cups	10 minutes	3½ cups
BULGUR	1½ cups (soak, don't cook)	30-40 minutes	3 cups
CRACKED WHEAT	2½ cups	7-10 minutes	3½ cups
CORNMEAL (POLENTA)	2½ cups	10 minutes	3½ cups
COUSCOUS	1¼ cups (soak, don't cook)	10 minutes	2¾ cups
KAMUT	2½ cups	1¾ hours	2½ cups
MILLET	2 cups	25 minutes	3½ cups
OAT GROATS	2½ cups	35-40 minutes	2½ cups
QUINOA	2 cups (rinse first)	25-30 minutes	4 cups
RYE BERRIES	2½ cups	1¼ hours	2½ cups
SPELT	1½ cups	50-60 minutes	2 cups
TEFF	3 cups	15 minutes	3 cups
TRITICALE	2½ cups	1½ hours	3 cups
WHEAT BERRIES, HARD (RED)	2 cups	2 hours	3 cups
WHEAT BERRIES, SOFT (WHITE)	2 cups	1½ hours	3½ cups

APPENDIX

Here, at a glance, is a list of all the lowfat, nonfat, vegan (no dairy or eggs), and pareve (nondairy) recipes in this book:

Lowfat Recipes
(Containing no more than approximately 3 Tbs. butter or oil per 6 servings)

SOUPS

Zuppa alla Pavese, 5
Vegetable-Tofu, 5
Vegetable-Eggdrop (without yolks), 5
Sesame-Eggdrop, 6
Dilled Vegetable-Barley, 7
Mediterranean Lemon, 9
Fresh Corn Chowder, 10
Curried Apple, 11
Cream of Tomato, Variations I and III, 12–13
Potato & Chile (without optional
   sour cream or cheese), 16
Potato-Leek, 17
Pumpkin Tureen, 18
Arizona Pumpkin, 19
Galician Garbanzo, 20
White Bean & Escarole, 21
Cream of Fresh Green Pea, 22
Swedish Cabbage, 23
Cream of Onion, 26
Inspiration, 27
Green Gazpacho, 30
Chilled Marinated Mushroom, 31

SALADS & SALAD DRESSINGS

Tofu Dressing, 40
Buttermilk & Cucumber Dressing, 40
Israeli Eggplant, 47
Indian Eggplant, 48
Italian Eggplant, 49
Dill Pickle Potatoes, 50
Very-Much-Marinated Potatoes, 50
Eggless Egg Salad, 55
Tomato Fans, 57

ENTRÉES

Mushroom Pie with Spinach Crust, 134
Cauliflower Paprikash (with lowfat
   sour cream), 159

Lukshen Kugel, 162
Tofu Sukiyaki, 185
Carrot-Zucchini Kugel, 196
Humble Vegetable Casserole, 198
Potato, Panir, & Pea Curry, 200
Savory Apple Casserole, 203
Influenced Vegetable Stew, 204
Mushroom Mystery Casserole, 205
Spicy Baked Beans with Molasses, 219
Spiced Lentils with Spinach and Apples, 218
Fried Rice, 220
Spanish Rice, 221
Broccoli & Buckwheat Godunov, 222
The Enchanted Broccoli Forest, 223
Indian Pulao, 224
Brazilian Stuffed Peppers, 226
Sautéed Vegetable Dinner, 234

DESSERTS

Peach Puddingcake, 240
Ricotta-Cherry Mousse, 255
Chocolate Pudding, 256
Cheesecake Soufflé with Strawberry-
   Marmalade Sauce, 261

Nonfat Recipes

SOUPS

Vegetable, 4
Multi-Vegetable, 5
Alphabet, 5
Vegetable-Eggdrop (without yolks), 5
Chilled Cantaloupe-Peach, 28
Chilled Cherry-Plum (with nonfat yogurt), 29
Chilled Spicy Tomato, 32

SALADS & SALAD DRESSINGS

Apple Vinaigrette, 40
Russian Beet (with nonfat yogurt
   and no yolks), 42
Wilted Cucumbers, 46
Tsatsiki (with nonfat yogurt), 46

Vegan Recipes
(no dairy* or eggs)

*NOTE: Some of these recipes call for milk, but soy milk can substitute in all cases.

Pareve Recipes
(*no dairy**; *eggs* OK)

All the preceding vegan recipes are pareve.
Add to this list:

*NOTE: Some of these recipes call for milk, but soy milk can substitute in all cases.

INDEX

MOLLIE KATZEN

JOHN BRAIN

   With close to 4 million books in print, Mollie Katzen enjoys a coveted position on the *New York Times* list of the ten best-selling cookbook authors of all time. Selected by *Health* magazine as one of the "Five Women Who Changed the Way We Eat," Mollie is widely credited with moving healthful cooking from the fringe of American society squarely onto mainstream dinner tables.

   Born in Rochester, New York, Mollie studied at the Eastman School of Music, Cornell University, and the San Francisco Art Institute, where she received a BFA in painting. Her classic *Moosewood Cookbook*, first published in 1977, was followed by *The Enchanted Broccoli Forest* (1982), *Still Life with Menu* (1988), and *Mollie Katzen's Vegetable Heaven* (Hyperion 1997). All of Mollie's books are vibrantly illustrated with her original artwork.

   To inspire young cooks to explore the wonders of the kitchen, Mollie illustrated and authored the award-winning children's cookbooks, *Pretend Soup* (1994) and *Honest Pretzels* (1999). Mollie is now a featured writer and illustrator for Children's Television Workshop On-Line, and for *Sesame Street Parents' Magazine*.

   Since its debut in 1995, the acclaimed *Mollie Katzen's Cooking Show* has been appearing on public television stations nationwide. The new editions of *Moosewood* and *The Enchanted Broccoli Forest* are companion volumes to Mollie's third television series.

You can keep up with all of Mollie's projects by tuning in to
www.molliekatzen.com.

The End.